Whatever it is you seek—love, adventure, good health, or good fortune—Sydney Omarr has an astonishingly accurate forecast for every aspect of your life. For 18 exciting months from July 1994 to December 1995, you will learn:

- how to make your love connections strong and sexy
- how to fine-tune your life by coordinating your activities with the rhythms of the universe.
- how to use the Saturn sign to master a fear, phobia, or anxiety.
- how to use the moon and planets for prosperity
- how to relieve your stress and live a healthier life

So chart your very own star-studded course now—and make 1995 your best year ever!

SYDNEY OMARR'S DAY-BY-DAY ASTROLOGICAL GUIDE FOR AQUARIUS IN 1995

SYDNEY OMARR'S

DAY-BY-DAY ASTROLOGICAL GUIDE FOR

AQUARIUS

January 20–February 18

1995

A SIGNET BOOK

SIGNET
Published by the Penguin Group
Penguin Books USA Inc., 375 Hudson Street,
New York, New York 10014, U.S.A.
Penguin Books Ltd, 27 Wrights Lane,
London W8 5TZ, England
Penguin Books Australia Ltd, Ringwood,
Victoria, Australia
Penguin Books Canada Ltd, 10 Alcorn Avenue,
Toronto, Ontario, Canada M4V 3B2
Penguin Books (N.Z.) Ltd, 182–190 Wairau Road,
Auckland 10, New Zealand

Penguin Books Ltd, Registered Offices:
Harmondsworth, Middlesex, England

First published by Signet, an imprint of Dutton Signet,
a division of Penguin Books USA Inc.

First Printing, July, 1994
10 9 8 7 6 5 4 3 2 1

Sydney Omarr is syndicated worldwide by
Los Angeles Times Syndicate.

Printed in the United States of America

Contents

INTRODUCTION

Setting the Stage for the New Century

There's a new feeling of anticipation in the air as we go to press. There's a new century ahead and we're rushing forward to meet it! Headlines in the business news at this writing tell the story: "American Rush to Funds That Invest Abroad" and "Bell Atlantic Takes a Big Step into Mexico." Globalism is here, marking the next step in our evolution as the year 2000 approaches. There is uncharted territory ahead, full of new kinds of experiences, thanks to the mushrooming progress of high technology. There are sure to be new people in our lives, perhaps introduced over a computer screen. In this year's atmosphere, when everyone's more optimistic, more in the mood for risk taking, there are fortunes to be made as well as potential disasters for the overly optimistic.

We're here to help you chart the future and make your dreams happen. Astrology can provide you with insight into the latest trends, help you know where the action is and how to take advantage of it. This book is designed to help you ride the crest of '95 and develop ideas that take full advantage of this year's potential by moving in harmony with the cosmic cycles. We'll tell you what's "in" this year, from what you'll be wearing to where the hot jobs are. We'll help you set up your daily agenda so you'll be doing the right thing at the right time.

The most valuable knowledge of all is self-knowledge, and here astrology has much to offer you. We take you through your sun sign and beyond, into the territory of eight other planets, to help you better know yourself and how you get along with others. Remember, astrology was one of the first techniques to give psychological insights, and it's still one of the best.

We'll give you basic information, so you'll know what astrology is all about. We'll tell you everything you need to know about your sun sign. And what's more, you can look up all your planets and find out how each contributes to your total personality. If you're interested in going deeper into astrology, there's a resource list where you can find computer programs, clubs, tapes, or classes to expand your knowledge and connect with fellow astrology buffs.

Many readers are fascinated by astrology's insights into their love lives. Sometimes the one you love is not the sign you thought you were supposed to get along best with. The fact is, our hearts don't always read horoscopes. Through our "love games," you might discover the sign you're *really* attracted to—it might come as a surprise! You'll find out how a tiny planet on the edge of the solar system can change our lifestyle and how it will color the next century.

The year 1995 marks a major shift in emphasis from the materialistic, sex-and-power issues of the eighties and early nineties to a higher vision of world unity. As the groundwork is laid for the new century, we'll be reborn on a new spiritual level, brought about by the movement of Pluto from Scorpio, where it has been transiting for the last ten years, into Sagittarius. You'll be able to understand this main event of 1995 and where it will affect your life, for we've devoted two chapters to this powerhouse planet.

Your daily forecasts will guide you with wise advice, lucky numbers and moon-sign positions, so you can plan your activities in harmony with the lunar and numeric cycles.

Let this guide help you set your personal stage for the next century and make 1995 the happiest, most productive, successful year ever—in both your personal and professional lives!

CHAPTER 1

What's "In" This Year

The year 1995 is sure to be full of breakthroughs. To help you plan ahead, here are some predictions about where we're heading and what we'll be doing and wearing in '95. These ideas are based on the movement of the distant, slow-moving planets, Uranus and Pluto, into different signs. When this happens, there is a major shift in mass consciousness that shows up throughout our lives. In April, Uranus, the planet of sudden changes, electricity, and high technology, moves into Aquarius, the sign it rules, marking a big push forward in technology. Though we have covered Pluto's move into Sagittarius elsewhere in the book, we'll also be considering some more specific ways it will influence our daily lives in this chapter. Jupiter's move into Sagittarius, the sign it rules, is another powerful factor that reinforces expansive new directions in Jupiter-ruled areas.

What You'll Be Wearing

Throw out those black clothes and buy some clothes in bright colors, especially the Sagittarius-influenced colors: purple, turquoise, and orange.

Clothes will have a strong ethnic look influenced by exotic cultures, especially those with a strong religious tradition. Fashion should also have the flavors of Spain and Latin America. Clothing styles at this writing are beginning to show a more monastic, religious look. This will increase; we may all be wearing updated versions of monk's garb or ecclesiastical robes.

Outdoor hunting, fishing, and forest gear is very important this year. We should be deeply into the environmentally conscious trend, with the use of natural fabrics and with motifs that proclaim ecology consciousness. We may be buying these in ecological themed stores and washing them in environmentally conscious laundromats.

Other inspirations could be the Renaissance look, inspired by fashions of the early sixteenth century. Horse themes will abound in prints and equestrian hunt-club looks.

Clothes and clothing advertisements will trade the current sexual emphasis for a more spiritual, visionary approach.

Look for revolutionary high-tech ways of selling clothes by television, CD, or computer mail. Home shopping networks will become more sophisticated. If you want to buy an Italian suit, for instance, you might be able to view the store's merchandise on your computer screen and place an order by fax. The merchandise would then arrive the next day by high-speed mail.

What Music You'll Be Playing

Music will be more cross-culture oriented. At this writing, Paul Simon and Sting have got the right message. Blends of many cultures will influence the arts, which will become a true melting pot. At the same time, many cultures will be trying to maintain the purity of their artistic tradition.

Look for new kinds of music that is more spiritually uplifting, if not actually promoting a specific religious message. The sexual content of the early nineties Pluto-in-Scorpio period should be deemphasized as we begin to look for a higher meaning in life.

The New Games Will Serve Many Purposes

Computer games will become more sophisticated and used as a means of teaching or preaching. Learning through creative play will become more important, as will games and recreational activities that bring people and families together. In this area, there will be many new multipurpose toys, which have an extra message besides that of play.

Portability Is a Key Word

"You *can* take it with you" is the motto this year, as Pluto and Jupiter in Sagittarius have us all up and running! Everything will be on wheels. You'll be able to pack up your office in a suitcase and roll it anywhere you like, with ever-smaller personal computers, fax modems, printers, and portable phones.

Global Communication Gets Easier

Thanks to computerized communication, via E-mail and computer bulletin boards, you'll be able to talk to someone in Australia or China more easily and inexpensively than ever. Perhaps there will be a computer that instantly translates your message into any language you wish.

With so much shopping by mail, home-delivery services will be expanded and central mail-processing systems like Fedex should thrive, becoming much more sophisticated.

What You'll Be Reading and How

Publishing, which is ruled by both Sagittarius and Jupiter, is in for a rapid sea change. Books will be visualized on computers or video disks; magazines will come in CD-ROM versions. Soon we'll be able to tap into a library anywhere in the world and log in the latest magazines on our home PCs. Imagine dialing a number and having your favorite magazine appear on your TV or computer screen!

Desktop publishing will make it possible for many new players to get into the publishing field. How about writing that novel on your computer and selling it via a worldwide computer bulletin board system instead of a bookstore?

Along with a new philosophical and spiritual emphasis in the kinds of books you'll be reading, look for new interpretations of ancient manuscripts. This is also happening in astrology, as scholars are reinterpreting many ancient writings in a more astrology-friendly light.

What You'll Be Driving

The year 1995 marks the beginning of an era of incredible global mobility. While some may choose to stay home and log onto a world communication network, others may investigate the new possibilities in long-distance travel, such as high-speed trains and planes, solar-powered vehicles, and many high-tech advances in automobiles

Individual mobility also takes new leaps. Possibly, the current trend in rollerblading is only the beginning of a trend toward individual movement that is fast and fun. High-speed water transport is another way to get where you're going in record time.

What You'll Be Doing

There's a good possibility that many of us will be going back to school, either to expand our personal interests or to keep up with the new technology. Both Pluto and Jupiter in Sagittarius, which rules higher education, will make this a prime area for creative development and profitable investment. Being an intellectual, a philosopher, or a theologian will be "in" this year, as the life of the higher mind is accented.

Studying via videotape, tapping into libraries with a computer, accessing many teachers easily on electronic bulletin boards open up many educational options to a wide market. It will be easier to learn than ever.

Where You'll Be Going

The trend toward more ecologically oriented vacations and resorts designed to enhance the environment will grow. So will action-oriented vacation places, which offer either physical diversion or a chance to improve mental skills. Spiritual retreats to ashram-like resorts and vacations with a religious emphasis, such as pilgrimages to sacred places, are hot now.

Since Sagittarius is the sign of the gambler, this too, is

an area of expansion, especially in underdeveloped countries and on Native American reservations.

Sagittarius-influenced places should be where the action is: Latin America, Madagascar, Singapore, Czechoslovakia, Spain, Hungary, Moravia, Australia. Within countries, important areas are Tuscany and Naples in Italy, Provence and Narbonne in France, Toronto in Canada, Nottingham and Sheffield in England, Cologne and Stuttgart in Germany. In the United States, there's Toledo, Seattle, Pennsylvania, the Mississippi River, and New Jersey.

Your Financial Life

When Jupiter, the sign of expansion, is strong in the sign of bankers, this should be prime time for investments. There should be a much more favorable atmosphere for taking risks. The danger is in overoptimism. However, after the past few years, this time should definitely be an upswing.

Your Love Life

Interracial, cross-cultural romance could be the new trend, as long-distance communications turn to matters of love and romance. There should be many new ways to meet people, as the "personals" expand to accessing worldwide databases of eligibles. You may be able to review photos or videos of potential romances, meet and network through computer or video parties, or meet each other over a video phone.

After the telephone sex of the Pluto in Scorpio period, it's possible that lovemaking will enter the high-tech realm of virtual reality. You may find yourself falling in love with a computer-designed mate.

Hot Careers

The sky's the limit in publishing now, especially for those with high-tech knowledge. Higher education, as well as all areas of the travel business, publicity, and advertising, should present new options.

Religion will be redefined, as more people seek out the spiritual life in new ways. Churches could be revitalized as forces in the community and as educational and recreational institutions. This should open up many new kinds of careers within the context of church or spiritual life.

The sign of the Centaur, Sagittarius has always been associated with hunting, hunters, and archery. It's anyone's guess how these might provide career opportunities now.

Banks and banking, the legal and judicial profession, and any professions involving foreign trade, such as the import–export business, should present many new kinds of opportunities. Look for new high-tech areas of these businesses for the best way to get in on the ground floor.

Sagittarius Personalities in the News

New Sagittarius stars will be coming to center stage, and some old favorites should be still in the news:

On TV, there's Phil Donahue, William F. Buckley, Lesley Stahl, Don Johnson, Susan Dey, Donna Mills, Robin Givens, Charlene Tilton, Richard Pryor, Morgan Brittany.

In film, there's Steven Speilberg, Woody Allen, Kim Basinger, Jeff and Beau Bridges, Liv Ullman, Jennifer Beals, Teri Garr, Tim Conway.

In music, there's Bette Midler, Tina Turner, Frank Sinatra, Sinead O'Connor, Dionne Warwick, Beethoven.

In sports, there's Chris Evert, Cathy Rigby, Suzy Chaffee, Katarina Witt.

In fashion, there's Gianni Versace and Thierry Mugler.

Mega-celebrities: J.F.K. Jr., Darryl Hannah, Caroline Kennedy Schlossberg, Jane Fonda, Tom Hayden, Strom Thurmond.

CHAPTER 2

The Big Switch—Pluto, the Power Planet, Enters Sagittarius

1995 is sure to be a year of changes, from Teenage Mutant Ninja Turtles to religious cartoons, from dirt bikes to the World Car, from movies about Dracula to those about angelic visitations. These are only a few possible manifestations of a powerful shift in energy that marks a turning point in the decade and points us toward the coming millenium.

We're talking about the power of Pluto. This tiny planet orbiting on the farthest reaches of our solar system moves into Sagittarius on January 17 until April 21, then retrogrades back into Scorpio to tie up loose ends and take care of unfinished business before it finally moves onward to Sagittarius for good on November 10. Those who are new to astrology may well wonder how a planet so far away that it has never been accurately mapped can affect our daily lives. Pluto is the mystery planet of the zodiac, one that can't be seen, but makes a powerful impact on mass consciousness.

We'll sense Pluto power in a subtle shift in the atmosphere. Things may seem to be looking up, after the chaos and confusion of the early nineties. Now we may feel it's safe to take more risks, as if a heavy cloud has lifted. Will the second half of this decade be the "Gay Nineties" of the twentieth century? Perhaps. There will definitely be a more optimistic feeling in the air.

Yet Pluto power is as shrouded in mystery as the planet itself. We're never quite sure what is in store. This is the planet of extremes, discovered at the same time as atomic energy, as the growth of extreme political movements and the rise of mass media. Astrologers associate Pluto with intense forces that lie dormant within collective systems and burst forth, like the invisible power of the atom—or like the planet's namesake, the legendary god of the underworld, who opened the earth and kidnapped the innocent maiden Persephone, precipitating a drama that resulted in the creation of the seasons. With Pluto, our lives are forced to evolve in important ways.

Discovered in 1930, Pluto has never been explored by a satellite like other planets. Scientists guess that it is about four thousand miles in diameter. We do know that Pluto has a large moon, almost a twin planet, and a very eccentric elliptical orbit, which means it spends a varying amount of time in each sign, as little as eleven years or as long as thirty-one years. It takes about 248 years to travel through the entire zodiac. Astrologers decided that Pluto had certain qualities, based on observation of its effects in horoscopes and on what was happening at the time of the planet's discovery. Therefore, some of the most important characteristics of Pluto are power, elimination, mass movements, collective phenomena, the media, mob psychology, atomic energy, sexuality, healing, recycling, the occult, and needs for control.

We've been feeling Pluto power throughout our lives on a personal and collective level, especially during the past eleven years, when Pluto has been traveling through Scorpio, the sign it rules. Like the underworld of the mythical god Pluto, this planet inspires fear of the unknown. Perhaps that is why, during this time, there was so much fascination with vampires (*Dracula*), the more sinister side of the occult (*Kiss of the Beast*), violent aberrations (*Silence of the Lambs*), or underworld organizations like the Mafia. But the purpose of Pluto is to transform in order to transcend. Just as in the transcendance of death there is immortality, Pluto forces one to evolve to the next stage by confronting the lessons of the sign it is passing through.

As Pluto slowly moves through a single zodiac sign, important transformational changes take place that impact the whole generation born during that time. Since 1984, Scorpio-type influences were all over our mass consciousness. In order to understand how Pluto works, let's look at the past dozen years.

In Scorpio, we see Pluto at its most potent. Scorpio is

the sign of sex, and nobody can deny that our lives were saturated with a hypersexual charge—from blatant sexuality in advertisements, to suggestive clothing (in the Scorpio noncolor, black), to S&M themes in fashion, to telephone sex, to readily available adults-only videos, to the proliferation of sexually oriented adult-entertainment clubs.

At the same time, there was the Plutonian emphasis on life or death—abortion issues, suicide, mercy killing, AIDS, and new strains of sexually transmitted diseases. The irony is that, at the same time as we were bombarded with all kinds of sexual titillation, we were also told that sex is dangerous—we must have "safe sex." Sexual issues were hot topics politically, as abortion attitudes and candidates' sex lives made headlines. Rape, sexual harassment, child sexual abuse, and incest made the rounds of media talk shows and tabloids, as deep secrets were exposed and publicly analyzed.

On another note, Pluto in Scorpio brought Scorpio media celebrities to prominence: Roseanne Arnold, Demi Moore, Whoopi Goldberg, Julia Roberts, Goldie Hawn, Jodie Foster, Dan Rather, and Kevin Kline, to name a few. These people transformed our ideas about what is acceptable in our mass media—whether it's a pregnant nude, a fat bluntly sexual comedienne, the first black woman to receive an Academy Award, or the female producer–star who calls the shots with studio honchos. Other stars with strong Pluto influences in their horoscope, such as Madonna and Michael Jackson, pushed the limits of what is acceptable behavior on and off screen.

In retrospect, it might be useful to examine what some of the events of this Pluto in Scorpio transit accomplished. For better or for worse, we're freer than we were at the beginning of the eighties. The AIDS epidemic forced us to confront our attitudes toward death and toward those with different sexual orientation, resulting in a new tolerance and understanding. When many prominent personalities, such as Arthur Ashe, Rudolf Nureyev, Rock Hudson, and Halston, died, everyone was touched. Transvestite trends like "voguing" and exposure in plays like *M. Butterfly* or in films like *The Crying Game* opened up more formerly hidden areas and moved American culture to new levels of acceptance.

We also had our own personal life-or-death issues

aroused with the transformation of the insurance and health-care industries. Many of us were involved in self-transformation via the New Age and human potential movements. Plastic surgery became more prevalent as celebrities resculpted bodies with liposuction, inflated lips, and lifted faces. Body building became another way to take control of our looks and transform them, as muscle-bound heroes in life-or-death action dramas like *The Terminator* and *Die Hard* became male ideals.

Power became a key word at this time, becoming an adjective to describe meals, as in "power lunches" or exercise, as in "power aerobics," computers, such as the Macintosh PowerBook or in the titles of omnipresent self-help books. The news stories headlined those who manipulated others to get power, such as David Koresh and the Branch Davidian cult or, more positively, corporate takeovers and leveraged buyouts that transformed or eliminated entire industries.

On the other hand, there were many teachers who were dedicated to empowering others, helping people free themselves from their own limitations so they can progress in their own development. And there were endless talk shows, where people who had experienced different forms of abuse or limitation shared their experiences with the public.

At this writing, as Pluto is winding up its stay in Scorpio, we are already seeing harbingers of change. The focus is gradually shifting to Sagittarius-ruled topics and trends in the mass culture. A fire sign, Sagittarius is ruled by Jupiter, the planet of expansion and optimism, which sounds like very good news. After a decade of black clothes and sexual allusions everywhere, we can expect the happier, brighter influence of Sagittarius. This will be amplified the first year, brought in with trumpets, when Jupiter joins Pluto in Sagittarius as well. (Coincidentally, 1995 is the year that the satellite Galileo is scheduled to rendezvous with Jupiter.) Perhaps, with this expansive shift in energy, cures will be found for the sexually transmitted diseases that have plagued us over the last decade.

Sagittarius is a sign concerned with the big picture and with how everything relates to everything else. It is the sign of wisdom, of philosophers, educators, teachers, priests, and gurus.

Sagittarius is connected to expansion through transportation. That means all kinds of new forms of transportation are possible—high-speed trains, automobiles powered by a new kind of fuel, different forms of air travel. Some astrologers are predicting more space travel (and possibly space visitors). Already, Ford is announcing a high-tech "World Car," which will be built and sold in the same form all over the world. An expensive and risky effort, this uniform global design is sure to characterize new marketing ventures in the late nineties, when open world trade will allow more contact between cultures than ever before. Historically, this was the time when Venice rose to world power, expanding its territory throughout the Mediterranean. In the 1750s, England became a major world power, gaining territory after winning the French and Indian War and establishing itself as a major force in India. In the thirteenth century, the Mongol empire, the largest in history, was at its height, spanning from the Siberian steppes to the Danube and the Arabian Sea. With the current world trade talks forging new relationships between governments, the result is sure to be an entirely different kind of international trade that transcends each country's individual concerns and ethnic biases.

Pluto pushes to extremes, so we'll see the extreme form of Sagittarius-ruled things. This sign is connected to higher education, philosophy, religion, and expansive thinking in general, and should be good for universities. We'll be much more concerned with the quality of education overall, and with educating our children to have higher aims and ideals. The mid-eighteenth century, a previous Pluto-in-Sagittarius time, was one of the great times for philosophy, when great philosophers challenged the prevailing religions and created the humanistic movements of the period. This was the time of Diderot, Rousseau, Hume, Voltaire, and the Encyclopedists, who foreshadowed the French Revolution. At an earlier time, the philosopher Thomas Aquinas attempted to reconcile reason with revelation in the mid-thirteenth century.

Religion is also Sagittarius territory, and with the planet of extremes activating religious and metaphysical issues, it's anyone's guess how this energy will manifest. Already we are experiencing edicts from the pope against sexual permissiveness, calling for a "higher vision," a new morality to guide youngsters who are without values. We will probably get the extremes of either side, with conservatives becoming more dogmatic and liberal metaphysical leaders also asserting themselves. Through the many spiritual and philosophical confrontations, we in the West must learn to deal with spiritual challenges as well as material ones. At this time, the West is apprehensive about dealing with the more spiritually oriented Islamic cultures, which should bring some interesting developments as this transit moves on. In previous years, Pluto in Sagittarius was the time of the Spanish Inquisition (early 1500s) and the Protestant Reformation.

In America, religious conservatives have been addressing Scorpio issues like abortion and homosexuality for the last decade. Now this sector of the Right is reaching out into education and other social arenas. The influence of religion on education and vice versa is sure to be a much-debated topic. So will the creation of values and ideals in our children, and motivating them to prepare for higher education.

Sagittarius influences several countries, and it is amazing how many are in the news at this writing, either as scenes of controversy (Dalmatia, Czechoslovakia, Hungary, Arabia), or as up-and-coming places (Australia, Chile, Provence in France, Spain, Singapore). With Hong Kong changing hands, it is possible that the headquarters of Far Eastern trade will now move to Singapore.

Sagittarius is the sign of optimism and risk taking. Expect a surge in gambling casinos, lotteries, and chance-taking ventures. The downside of this is that we must guard against overspending and too much risk taking without any practical grounding. It is very important that we understand how to manage money so it can do the most good.

This is one of the most animal-loving signs of the zodiac, so Pluto here should push our concern for animals to the limits. Expect animal-rights activism to hit a new high. Sports involving animals, especially horses, like racing, polo, horse shows, jumping, and rodeos should be super-popular.

As a sign that represents hunters, Sagittarius has an affinity for Native Americans. As we go to press, there is discussion about whether Native Americans should operate gambling casinos (also Sagittarius-ruled) on their reservations.

In the media, "global" is the key word, as networks go

worldwide via satellite. Expect more programming from foreign countries, with subtitles, and more CNN-type stations that give intensive round-the-globe reporting. Shopping via television will extend to worldwide shopping. You might be able to buy a suit made in Hong Kong or glassware directly from Italy via your television shopping channel. American television is already reaching out to viewers in different countries, especially with MTV Latino (Sagittarius rules Spain and strongly influences most Latin countries), its new Latin American TV network that will include twenty countries in the Caribbean and South America.

Sagittarius rules publishing, so it's no surprise that the very first book was printed in China in 576 A.D. under Pluto in Sagittarius. It's fascinating to speculate about how Pluto will transform the publishing business beyond recognition in the next twelve years. Perhaps future readers will buy this book on computer disk, complete with astrology programs to calculate their own charts. The whole field of desktop publishing has many ramifications for the publishing industry, as more players will be entering the industry and publishing on a smaller scale. At the same time, the way books are being sold is changing, with block-long book markets, cafes, and celebrity autograph signings revising our ideas of what a bookstore can and should be. Perhaps the bookstore–coffee house will become a new center of intellectual and philosophical discussion.

Will the printed word be conveyed by paper, by computer screen, by voice, or by "virtual reality," where you'll experience the contents via electronic simulation of reality? One thing's for sure—after this transit, publishing will take off in some exciting new directions.

On a deeper, evolutionary level, this is a time when those who have strongly held, inflexible beliefs and principles may realize that there are many different points of view that are equally valid. Over the past few years, there has been much dissolution of the boundaries between cultures, and now the actual cross-contact will begin, thanks to global media and new trade agreements. It is those cultures which are firmly grounded in traditional beliefs who will feel the transformational impact of other points of view, because it will be very difficult to remain isolated. The religious extremes that have caused wars in Czechoslovakia, the Middle East, and Ireland will no longer be able to operate as before. Thanks to the new global society, there will be much more exposure to other cultures, and mutual exchange of ideas and beliefs. And through these exchanges, we should be able to arrive at a more universal understanding and tolerance of each other's version of truth.

True, there will be many who will not want to risk their safe, established belief systems, or who will fiercely resist any challenges, as happened during the Spanish Inquisition. But the most positive way to use this transit is through an attitude of mutual sharing, realizing that differing belief systems have valuable insights to why we are here. By exposure to many diverse points of view through the new globalism of Pluto in Sagittarius, we should have a much better understanding of who we are as a world culture and what our higher purpose might be.

For each one of us, Pluto's passage through this sign of truth and high moral vision should bring us many experiences, though a clash of cultures, through philosophical discussions, and through unprecedented exposure to the rest of the world, which will force us to examine our own point of view. And by confronting our own belief systems, we should come closer to discovering an authentic individual personal truth for ourselves. Many of us will be shaken up and transformed; however, in doing so, we may also have a true experience of a higher power.

CHAPTER 3

Where's Pluto in Your Life?

With Pluto making the most waves this year, you'll want to know how it will affect your personal life and what kinds of happenings to expect. You don't need an astrologer to do this; you can make a very good estimate yourself, and learn some more about astrology while doing it. The object of this exercise will be to find the Sagittarius area of your astrological chart, which is where Pluto will be passing through.

First, you must find out your time of birth, preferably from your birth certificate or hospital records. Then, look up your rising sign in the chapter in this book.

Now you're ready to make an estimated astrological chart. We'll keep it as easy as possible. Draw a circle and divide it into twelve equal segments, like a clock. Write your rising sign down at the nine o'clock position, then list the other signs in sequence on each spoke of the wheel, working counterclockwise around the circle. For example, if you have Leo rising, then Virgo would be on the eight o'clock spoke, Libra on the seven o'clock spoke, Scorpio on the six o'clock spoke, Sagittarius on the five o'clock spoke, and so on around the wheel.

When you've completed your wheel, you'll have a rough approximation of the outline of your horoscope chart. It will not be exact, because there are many different systems of dividing the wheel, based on the precise moment of your birth. Each chart is a unique portrait of a moment in time, after all. However, this chart can be quite useful in helping you determine what Pluto is plotting in your life.

Each segment of the wheel, in astrology language, is called a "house" and represents an area of your life. The spokes are called "cusps" and the sign on the cusp is the one that influences happenings in that house. Each house is numbered, starting with the rising sign, which governs the first house, then working downward, counterclockwise around the wheel. Again, assuming Leo is the rising sign, the second house would have Virgo on the cusp, the third would be Libra, and so on. Sagittarius, our key house this year, would be on the 5th-house cusp. So our Leo-rising reader would have major emphasis on the 5th-house matters this year.

To make life even easier for you, here's a list of rising signs and their Sagittarius houses:

Aries rising—ninth house
Taurus rising—eighth house
Gemini rising—seventh house
Cancer rising—sixth house
Leo rising—fifth house
Virgo rising—fourth house
Libra rising—third house
Scorpio rising—second house
Sagittarius rising—first house
Capricorn rising—twelfth house
Aquarius rising—eleventh house
Pisces rising—tenth house

Pluto is a transformative planet; therefore, the events in your life that it activates are designed to bring up beliefs or circumstances that have been holding you back or limiting you in some way, and either resolve or eliminate these issues. You change with Pluto in such a way that there's no going back. However, the point is to help you evolve, to bring up those deep, hidden areas from Pluto's underworld "cave" for reexamination, and to eliminate or change them if necessary. Look upon this time of soul searching as a process that has been made necessary by the course of your life, not something that just happened out of the blue. It was precipitated by your previous attitudes and patterns. So rather than resist the elimination of old, outmoded patterns or cling to what has provided you with security, your best strategy is to examine why you are being asked to make this transformation. What deep, underlying concepts of reality are you required to change? What is getting in the way of becoming all you are meant to be?

As we've mentioned before, each house represents an area of your life. The following interpretations should help you determine where Pluto may transform your personal experience in the coming years. Keep in mind that Pluto works slowly, therefore the actual transformation may not be apparent for several years.

Another point to remember, since the houses in your chart usually occur later in the sign (rather than beginning at the actual first degree of the sign), is that Pluto is now traveling through the house *before* the one with the Sagittarius cusp. For instance, if Sagittarius is on your fifth-house cusp, it will be some time before Pluto actually travels over that cusp—at the moment, it is still in the fourth house. However, because the Sagittarius house will be transformed next, you should consider the changes that have happened over the past twelve years in the Scorpio area of your life, for a preview of what Pluto can do in the following house.

Pluto in the First House

This is a time when you make a break from the past. Whatever has been holding you back, whatever is outworn, outmoded, or outgrown, has to go. This powerful transit begins a new cycle in your evolution that involves a transformation in your outward identity, a challenge to add new dimensions to your personality. Often there is an actual physical transformation—you will look different to others. This could come from a conscious decision to change your appearance via plastic surgery or body building. Or you may suddenly look older, lose your hair, put on or lose weight. Some may go through a physical transition, such as menopause or pregnancy, or experience an illness that gives you a sense of your own mortality. Life-or-death questions about how you're going to survive in the future are possible.

In this house, Pluto will bring up the kind of situations that challenge your independence. For instance, you might break off relationships that are too confining, or become more assertive because of the new confidence gained from deep psychological or spiritual work.

Pluto in the Second House

Your sense of values and material resources now feel the transforming touch of Pluto. You'll ask yourself what is really important in life and why. There may be an increase or decrease in your material resources. You may decide to change the way you earn your living if your job is not truly meaningful to you. If your work is simply providing you with security, you may either be forced to change it or you may have a strong compulsion to do what you really want to do. If you are not using your own personal resources, you may find new ways to do so that will change your life in some way. Many of you will sell off property or possessions that have been weighing you down. Others will change how you handle finances or discover hidden sources of income.

Pluto in the Third House

Why do you think like you do? This process will transform the way you think, communicate, reach out to others. There could be a big difference in your perceptions of the world around you and the people in it. You may question and change some of the opinions and assumptions you've held for years. You may find yourself attacking others' ideas. Or, instead of agreeing with you, those who enter your life now could oppose your ideas. The challenge is to find out where you're coming from, bring in new information, and find out what has caused you to hold your strongest beliefs. Since your desire now is for deep knowledge, this is an excellent time for intensive study that will alter your perspective. Relatives and happenings on the local scene may have a very strong influence now.

Pluto in the Fourth House

This is your center, the place you call home, your deep sense of security and your ideas of family. Are you "at home" where you are? If you are too dependent, Pluto's transit can create some very uncomfortable times. However, through the experience of examining what makes you feel emotionally secure, and overcoming dependencies that have been holding you back, you'll emerge a much more productive individual. It is also a time to examine fears of abandonment and intimate family relationships, especially with your mother.

Pluto in the Fifth House

This is the time to ask if you're truly expressing yourself creatively. How are you giving of yourself to others? Here Pluto enforces the transformation of one's creative potential and self-expression. Many will do this through having a child or relating to a child in some way, or bringing out the creative "child within." If you already have children, your relationship with them could be transformed as deep feelings emerge.

Pluto can also transform the way you get recognition. Do others in your life give you the love and attention that encourages you to express yourself? If not, you may look for love elsewhere through an intense love affair, where you get swept away by romantic feelings, or you may have a series of affairs to provide you with all the attention you crave.

Pluto in the Sixth House

Does your life work? Or do you need to create new systems that support your ideas and can make them happen? If you're unfocused, with your energies scattered and your life cluttered, Pluto will make this clear to you. This transit brings much self-scrutiny and self-criticism. You may feel compelled to perfect your skills and techniques, to reorganize your life. Any areas that are out of control will be manifested. Health or diet issues become priorities, and any kind of self-indulgence or physical abuse over the years could surface as illness now. But this is an excellent opportunity to make changes that revitalize your body and create a healthier lifestyle for the future.

Pluto in the Seventh House

Is the one you love really holding you back? Now is when you'll find out. Here Pluto transforms close relationships, partnerships, and commitments you make to others. You'll feel the need to create a new way of being together with someone, a way that allows you both to grow. This is your chance to resolve issues that have been limiting the relationship, or if they can't be resolved, to break up. But, rather than taking sudden action, it is important to examine the deeper reasons why the relationship isn't working out, so both partners can understand that it has completed its mission in your lives and move on with no recriminations.

Pluto in the Eighth House

This is the power house, where you examine what you must give up to achieve a higher goal. Pluto here transforms how you exercise power over others. This is sure to be a very charismatic time, when you examine your own relationship to both internal and external power. It is a time when you empower yourself by facing your fears, risking insecurity, and moving forward. You may also feel powerless, at times, in the grip of forces you can't control. Since this is the house of strong sexual urges and mergers, you may find yourself in a relationship that's "bigger than both of us." On a material level, you'll transform the way you handle the powers that be: the IRS, banks, debts, credit cards.

Pluto in the Ninth House

Here is where you'll be confronting the limits in the systems you believe in. And, since this is the natural Sagittarius-ruled house, this should be a *very* powerful year, with both Pluto and Jupiter activating this area. You may feel compelled to free yourself from any obligations that keep you from expanding now. You'll be required to be on the move, stretching your limits and transforming your concept of reality through exposure to new ideas and interacting with people from many different cultures, with teachers or with religious leaders. As a result, you may change your direction in life or literally move to another location. The big question will be: What is truth for you? When you find out, you may become a teacher who shows others the way.

Pluto in the Tenth House

What does success mean to you? Is your choice career giving you the chance to express who you are and what you believe? Are you being true to yourself in the way you influence others? For those who are not happy with their position either on the job or in some other public capacity, Pluto here could transform your career or the way you take power in society. You might enter public life, become a boss, or restructure your career so that it is more relevant to your inner needs. If you've been a private "inside" person, you may surprise others by taking a more visible role in the outside world. Or you may quit a job or end a relationship that is keeping you from pursuing new goals you have set for yourself.

Pluto in the Eleventh House

Pluto here transforms how you deal with society at large. Who you identify with and why, or where you feel you belong are the deep issues that arise. You might transform your life by working with groups in some way. You may become more socially active or involved with clubs, teams, or professional organizations. You may question why you are so invested in a particular group, or in such an active social life, and you may change the groups you belong to. You may acquire a new political interest. Or you may sever long-standing associations with groups which are no longer relevant to your goals or beliefs.

Pluto in the Twelfth House

The last house of the zodiac is the place of spiritual consciousness, where you are inspired and where you have the most potential for divine illumination. It's also the place where you get "high" via natural or potentially abusive substances. In this house, you have no brakes or structures to keep you from enlightenment or chaos. (That's why it's often called "the house of self-undoing.") Institutions, which are ruled by this house, are places where you go when you are helpless and must be protected or isolated from the outside world, such as convents, hospitals, or prisons. However, when Pluto passes through this place of transformational insights, it's a wonderful time to do deep psychological or spiritual work. You may find that you need more time alone than usual and have more vivid dreams. Now you can tap the collective unconscious and effect a powerful transformation on others with the creative work you do. Some of our most transformative artists (Madonna and Michael Jackson, for instance) were born with this Pluto position.

CHAPTER 4

Introduction to Astrology—Questions and Answers

Even though astrology is a very precise art, the basic principles are not that difficult to learn. And once you know the basics, you can begin to penetrate beyond your sun sign into the realm of influence of the other planets. You'll find that the more you know, the more you'll want to explore further! Here are the questions most beginning astrology students ask.

- **What is a sign and how is it different from a constellation?**

A sign is actually a thirty-degree division of a circular belt of sky called the zodiac, which means "circle of animals" in Greek. The zodiac corresponds to the apparent path of the sun, moon, and planets around the earth. Of course, we know that the earth and other planets orbit around the sun, but astrology takes the planet where we are located as a reference point.

Originally, each division was marked by a constellation, most of which were named after animals (the lion, bull, goat, ram) or sea creatures (fishes, crab), but as the earth's axis changed over thousands of years, so did the stellar signposts. However the thirty-degree signs retained the names and symbolism of their original markers. In other words, a sign is always the same thirty-degree segment of the zodiac, but the original constellations have moved with time.

As the sun, moon, and planets appear to move (from our observation here on earth) around the zodiac, they pass through each sign. A person born while the sun is passing through a sign is said to be a member of that sign. An Aries, for instance, was born while the sun was passing through the Aries portion of the zodiac.

- **I've heard that Pisces is a water sign, Aquarius is an air sign, and so on. What does that mean and how were these definitions determined?**

It's important to remember that the definitions of the signs were not determined by guesswork or chosen at random. They evolved systematically from several components that interrelate. These four different criteria are a sign's element, its quality, its polarity or sex, and its order on the zodiac belt. These all work together to tell us what the sign is like and how it behaves.

The system is magically mathematical: The number twelve—as in the twelve signs of the zodiac—is divisible by four, by three, and by two. Perhaps it is no coincidence that there are four elements, three qualities, and two polarities. These follow each other in sequence around the zodiac, starting with Aries.

The four elements (earth, air, fire, and water) are the building blocks of astrology. The use of an element to describe a sign probably dates from man's first attempts to categorize what and who he saw in the world. In ancient times, it was believed that all things were composed of combinations of earth, air, fire, and water. This included the human character, which was fiery/choleric, earthy/melancholy, airy/sanguine, or watery/phlegmatic. The elements also correspond to our emotional (water), physical (earth), mental (air), and spiritual (fire) natures. The energies of each of the elements were then observed to relate to the time of year when the sun was passing through a certain segment of the zodiac.

The fire signs—Aries, Leo, and Sagittarius—embody the characteristics of that element. Optimism, warmth, hot tempers, enthusiasm, and spirit are typical of these signs. Taurus, Virgo, and Capricorn are earthy—more grounded, physical, materialistic, organized, and deliberate than fire people. Air signs—Gemini, Libra, and Aquarius—are mentally oriented communicators. Water signs—Cancer, Scorpio, and Pisces—are emotional, creative, and caring.

Think of what each element does to the others: water puts out fire or evaporates with heat. Air fans the flames or blows them out. Earth smothers fire, drifts and erodes with too much wind, becomes mud or fertile soil with water. Those are often perfect analogies for the relationships between signs of these elements! This astro-chemistry was one of the first ways man described his relationships. Fortunately, no one is entirely air or fire. We all have a bit, or a lot, of each element in our horoscopes; this unique mix defines each astrological personality.

Within each element, there are three qualities, which describe how the sign behaves, how it works. Cardinal signs are the activists, the go-getters. These signs—Aries, Cancer, Libra, and Capricorn—begin each season. Fixed signs are the builders that happen in the middle of the season. You'll find that Taurus, Leo, Scorpio, and Aquarius are gifted with focused concentration, stubbornness, and stamina. Mutable signs—Gemini, Virgo, Sagittarius, and Pisces—are catalysts for change at the end of each season; these are flexible, adaptable, mobile signs.

The polarity of a sign is it's positive or negative "charge." It can be masculine, active, positive, or yang like the air and fire signs. Or it can be feminine, reactive, negative, or yin like the water and earth signs. The polarities of each sign alternate around the zodiac, like a giant battery.

Finally, we consider the sign's place in the order of the zodiac. This is vital to the balance of all the forces and the transmission of energy moving through the signs. Notice that each sign is quite different from its neighbors on either side. Yet each seems to grow out of its predecessor like links in a chain and transmits a synthesis of energy gathered along the chain to the following sign, beginning with the fire-powered active positive charge of Aries. Keep this in mind as you read through the descriptions.

ARIES: Fire element, cardinal quality, masculine polarity, first sign

Aries, the harbinger of spring, starts off the zodiac with a powerful charge. This is the youngest sign, the perennial baby, focused on the ego. Aries rushes forward, impatiently, always wanting to be first. This sign is active and assertive in everything it does.

TAURUS: Earth element, fixed quality, feminine polarity, second sign

Taurus is a growing period, a time to acclimate to the physical world and to explore the territory nearby. Taurus distinguishes between what's mine and what belongs to others. It is a sign that nurtures, that slows down and builds step by step after a fast start.

GEMINI: Air sign, mutable quality, masculine polarity, third sign

The third sign, Gemini, is ready to reach out actively to others, to communicate. This is an assertive, changeable, sociable sign that gathers information and breaks new ground.

CANCER: Water sign, cardinal quality, feminine polarity, fourth sign

After reaching out to others, comes an emotionally active sign with the feminine drive to nurture and bear fruit. Cancer, the first water sign, uses the emotions, and the first use of emotions is to nurture, protect, and mother others during the initial growing period of summer.

LEO: Fire sign, fixed quality, masculine polarity, fifth sign

After nurturing others, it is time to lead them into the world in the masculine sense. Leo is a sign to lean on, a bright and steady energy that asserts itself, builds strength and self-confidence.

VIRGO: Earth sign, mutable quality, feminine polarity, sixth sign

Time to stop, analyze. After the confident surge of Leo comes the practical down-to-earth Virgo, that makes sure everything is working well. It serves others by analyzing, teaching, criticizing, and improving what has been done.

LIBRA: Air sign, cardinal quality, masculine polarity, seventh sign

An active mental sign, Libra constantly weighs and balances objectively; sees both sides of the question; and asserts itself to maintain equilibrium and ideals of justice, balance, beauty.

SCORPIO: Water sign, fixed quality, feminine polarity, eighth sign

Coming after the mentally active Libra, we have the decisive, fixed sign of emotional extremes, of commitment. Scorpio is the proverbial still-waters-run-deep sign. It penetrates to the core, tends to be all or nothing. In this sign is the intense desire to procreate, the fascination with control and power.

SAGITTARIUS: Fire sign, mutable quality, masculine polarity, ninth sign

Here is a catalyst for growth, expansion, and change. This sign manifests fire's quest for spiritual development. This is a restless sign—a traveler always on the go who expands by relating to others and prepares the way for our relating to the world.

CAPRICORN: Earth sign, cardinal quality, feminine polarity, tenth sign

Now it is time to move into the world, to organize so we can function on a large scale, to organize. Capricorn is a dutiful sign that is conscious of the expectations of others, of one's status in the scheme of things.

AQUARIUS: Air sign, fixed quality, masculine polarity, eleventh sign

This mental sign is concerned with the correct social values, actively promoting the welfare of groups, discovering new inventions. It comes during the quiet time of winter, the right time for concentrated objective scientific thought, mass communication, planning for the future.

PISCES: Water sign, mutable quality, feminine polarity, twelfth sign

This sign's constantly changing emotions reflect the knowledge obtained in the trip through the other signs and prepare for the rebirth of spring in Aries. This sensitive sign must digest the impressions gathered; it's a creative time of dreams, and a time of contributing to others through service and caring.

- **Besides my "sun sign," how many other signs do I have?**

In compiling your astrological database, we consider eight planets, besides the moon and sun. Some astrologers also use asteroids, the moon's nodes, and certain sensitive points of the zodiac. The phrase "as above, so below" is often used to describe a chart as a microcosm of the universe. The three closest planets to the earth—Mercury, Mars, Venus, and the moon—affect your personal character. The next-farthest out—Jupiter and Saturn—affect influences from others, turning points and outside events, and significant cycles in your life. As we get farther out, the slower-moving planets—Uranus, Neptune, and Pluto—deal with mass trends that effect your whole generation. The zodiac, with its constellations of stars, represents the universal influences.

In the western systems of astrology, we confine our charts to the planets and stars within the zodiac. We would not consider the influence of the Big Dipper or Orion or black holes and supernovas.

The sign the planet is passing through at the time of your birth and that sign's location in the sky determine the way the planet will manifest itself in your life. For instance Mars in aggressive, impatient Aries will show a completely different energy than Mars in dreamy, creative Pisces.

The planets' influence in your horoscope is intensified if they are close together, or affecting another planet, which is called an "aspect." This term refers to a distance between two forces within the 360 degrees of the zodiac circle. Some aspects, such as the "trine" (120 degrees apart) and the "sextile" (60 degrees apart) are considered easy and harmonious. Others, such as the "square" (90 degrees) and the "opposition" (180 degrees) are tense, causing friction and conflict or, more positively, challenges.

Two or more planets traveling close together in the same sign (within ten degrees of each other) is called a "conjunction." Depending on the planets, the conjunction can be difficult or very beneficial. The sun works well with Mercury, Venus, and Jupiter. Mars, Uranus, and Saturn are best left alone. A conjunction will give much more importance to the sign it inhabits. When there are several planets crowding one sign, the activities of that area will dominate the horoscope.

• What is a "ruling planet?"

Each sign of the zodiac has a planet that corresponds to its energies. Mars rules the firey, assertive Aries. The sensual beauty and comfort-loving aspect of Venus rules Taurus, while the more idealistic side rules Libra. The quick-moving Mercury rules both Gemini and Virgo, showing its mental agility in Gemini and its critical, analytical side in Virgo. Emotional Cancer is ruled by the moon, while outgoing Leo is ruled by the sun. Scorpio was originally given Mars, but when Pluto was discovered in this century, its powerful magnetic energies were deemed more suitable to Scorpio. Disciplined Capricorn is ruled by Saturn. Expansive Sagittarius is ruled by Jupiter, unpredictable Aquarius by Uranus, and creative, impressionable Pisces by Neptune.

CHAPTER 5

Your Success Profile— Astrological Self-Help to Tap Your Potential

If you've ever wondered whether you're on the right track with your life, if you're making the most of what you've got, if you have undiscovered capabilities just waiting to make your fortune, look no further. If you're thinking about changing directions, trying on a new career for size, here is a clear road map. Does this sound like a mailer for one of the popular self-help courses? In a way, it does. The fact is, that for centuries astrology has been used to help people discover themselves and make important decisions. And it's still one of the best ways to learn more about yourself and what you can do best.

To know yourself astrologically, however, you must go beyond your sun sign to examine a complete profile of your personality, including all the planets in their positions at the moment you were born. Besides the sun, there are nine other planets (in astrology, by the way, the sun and moon are usually referred to as planets) that work together to create the unique astrological personality that is yours alone. Each planet has a role to play in your total portrait and each is a great source of information for getting to know yourself. So if you've been just sticking with your sun sign, come along with us in this chapter and find out how much more there is to your astrological portrait.

For those of you who feel you're not typical of your sun sign, this chapter may show you why. Having several planets in another sign can color your personality strongly with that sign's characteristics. For instance, a Leo sun sign with

Venus, Mercury, and the moon in Virgo will come across as a much more conservative person than the Leo sun person who has Venus, Jupiter, and Mercury also placed in Leo.

And while you're studying the planets, you can use the charts in Chapter 7—"Look Up Your Planets," to get to know your friends, coworkers, loved ones, and that fascinating person who might be your soulmate.

The Sun: Your Confidence and Sense of Self

The sign of the sun when you were born is always given most importance. This is the sign that's center stage. It is the showoff sign that is the major indicator of your personality, your confidence, and your general sense of who you are. You can find out all about your sun sign in detail from the individual chapters at the end of the book. Astrologers focus on the sun sign in general books like these because the qualities of the sun are the most typical of people who were born when the sun was passing through a given sign. This is the common denominator. You may share other planets with someone, but it's your sun sign that will color your outward personality most strongly.

The Moon: What Do You Need?

Your moon sign reflects your subconscious needs and longings, as well as the kind of mothering and childhood conditioning you had. Your moon sign will tell you what you need to be emotionally happy (rather than what attracts you, which is Venus's territory).

Since accurate moon tables are too extensive to include in this book, we suggest you consult an astrologer or have a computer chart made to determine your correct moon sign.

MOON IN ARIES. Emotionally, you are independent and ardent. You are fulfilled by meeting challenges, overcoming obstacles, being "first." You have exceptional courage. You love the challenge of an emotional pursuit, and difficult situations in love only intensify your excitement. As the legendary film star Bette Davis, an archetypical Aries, once asked, "If it's too easy, where's the challenge?" But the catch-22 is that after you attain your goal to conquer whatever or whomever you're pursuing, your ardor is likely to cool down rapidly. To avoid continuous treat-'em-rough situations, work on developing patience and tolerance.

MOON IN TAURUS. Solid, secure, comfortable situations and relationships are fulfilling to you. You need plenty of open displays of affection, lots of hugs and touching. You'll also gravitate to those who provide you with material comforts as well as sensual pleasures. Your emotions are steady and nurturing in this strong moon sign, but could lean toward stubbornness when pushed. You could miss out on some of life's excitement by sticking to the safe, straight and narrow road.

MOON IN GEMINI. You need constant emotional stimulation and enjoy an outgoing, diversified lifestyle. You could have difficulty with commitment, and therefore may marry more than once or have a love life of changing partners. An outgoing, interesting, talented partner could merit your attention, however. You could spread yourself too thin to accomplish major goals, but watch a tendency to be emotionally fragmented. Find a creative way to express the range of your feelings, possibly through developing writing, speaking, or other communicative talents.

MOON IN CANCER. This is the most powerful moon position, one that can seem even stronger than the sun in the horoscope. You are the zodiac nurturer who needs to be needed. You have an excellent memory and an intuitive understanding of the needs of others. You are happiest at home and may work in a home officc or turn your corner of the company into a home away from home. Work that supplies food and shelter, nurtures children, or involves occult studies and psychology could take advantage of this lunar position.

MOON IN LEO. You need to be treated like royalty! Strong support, loyalty, and loud applause win your heart. You rule over your territory and resent anyone who intrudes on your turf. Your attraction to the finer things in people and in your lifestyle could give you a snobbish outlook. But basically you have a warm, passionate, loyal, and emotional nature that gives generously to those you deem worthy. Children and leadership roles that express your creativity can bring you great satisfaction.

MOON IN VIRGO. This moon often draws you to situations where you play the role of healer, teacher, or critic. You may find it difficult to accept others as they are or enjoy what you have. Because you must analyze before you can give emotionally, the Virgo moon can seem hard on others and equally tough on yourself. Be aware that you may have impossible standards, and take it easier on others. A little tolerance goes a long way, and so does a bit of humor!

MOON IN LIBRA. Your emotional role is partnership oriented—you won't live or work alone for long! You may find it difficult to do things alone. You need the emotional balance of a strong "other." You thrive in an elegant, harmonious atmosphere, where you get attention and flattery. This moon needs to keep it light. Heavy emotions cause your Libran moon's scales to swing precariously. So does an overly possessive or demanding partner, so choose well. The right partner can make all the difference for the better in your life.

MOON IN SCORPIO. The moon is not totally comfortable in intense Scorpio, which is emotionally drawn to extremes and can be obsessive, suspicious, and jealous. You take disappointments very hard and are often drawn to issues of power and control. It's important to learn when to tone down those all-or-nothing feelings. Finding a healthy outlet in meaningful work could diffuse your intense needs. Medicine, occult work, police work, or psychology are good possibilities.

MOON IN SAGITTARIUS. This moon needs freedom—you can't stand to be possessed by anyone. You have emotional wanderlust and may need a constant dose of mental and spiritual stimulation. But you cope with the fluctuations of life with good humor and a spirit of adventure. You may find great satisfaction in exotic situations, foreign travels, philosophical and spiritual studies, rather than in intense one-on-one relationships.

MOON IN CAPRICORN. Here, the moon is cool and calculating—and very ambitious. You get a sense of security from achieving prestige and position in the outside world, rather than creating a cozy nest or cuddling romantically by the fire. Though you are dutiful toward those you love, your heart is in your climb to the top of the business or social ladder. Concrete achievement and improving your position in life bring you great satisfaction.

MOON IN AQUARIUS. This is a gregarious moon, happiest when surrounded by people. You're everybody's buddy, as long as no one gets too close. You'd rather stay pals. You make your own rules in emotional situations; you may have a radically different life-or love-style. Intimate relationships may feel too confining, for you need plenty of space.

MOON IN PISCES. This watery moon needs an emotional anchor to help you keep grounded in reality. Otherwise, you tend to escape to a fantasy world through intoxicating substances. Creative work could give you a far more productive way to express yourself and get away from it all. Working in a healing or helping profession is also good for you because you get satisfaction from helping the underdog. But, though you naturally attract people with sob stories, try to cultivate friends with a positive upbeat point of view.

Mercury: Your Mind Power

Mercury rules how your mind operates and how you communicate. Do you have a more disciplined, focused, one-track mind, or does your mind jump from idea to idea easily, perhaps a bit scattered? Or are you a visionary, poetic type? Do you communicate easily in speech or writing, or are you the type that spends a great deal of time thinking before you speak?

Since Mercury never moves more than a sign away from

the sun, check your sun sign and the signs preceding and following it to see which Mercury position most applies to you.

MERCURY IN ARIES never shies away from a confrontation. You say what you think; you are active and assertive. Your mind is sharp, alert, and impatient, but you may not be thorough.

MERCURY IN TAURUS is deliberate and thorough, with good concentration. You'll take the slow, methodical approach and leave no stone unturned. You'll see a problem through to the end, stick with a subject till you become an expert. You may talk very slowly, but in a melodious voice.

MERCURY IN GEMINI is a quick study. You can handle many subjects at once, jumping from one to the other easily. You may, however, spread yourself too thin. You express yourself easily both verbally and in writing. You are a "people person" who enjoys having others buzzing around and you are also skilled at communicating with a large audience.

MERCURY IN CANCER has great empathy for others—you can read their feelings. Your mind works intuitively rather than logically. And your thoughts are always colored by your emotions. You have an excellent memory and imagination.

MERCURY IN LEO has a flair for dramatic expression, and can hold the attention of others (and sometimes hog the limelight). This is also a placement of mental overconfidence. You think big and prefer to skip the details. However, this might make you an excellent salesperson or public speaker.

MERCURY IN VIRGO is a strong position. You're a natural critic, with an analytic, orderly mind. You pay attention to details and have a talent for thorough analysis and good organization, though you tend to focus on the practical side of things. Teaching and editing come naturally to you.

MERCURY IN LIBRA is a smooth talker, with a graceful gift of gab. Though gifted in diplomacy and debate, you may vacillate in making decisions, forever juggling the pros and cons. You speak in elegant, well-modulated tones.

MERCURY IN SCORPIO has a sharp mind that can be sarcastic and given to making cutting remarks. You have a penetrating insight and will stop at nothing to get to the heart of matters. You are an excellent and thorough investigator, researcher, or detective. You enjoy problems that challenge your skills in digging and probing.

MERCURY IN SAGITTARIUS has a great sense of humor but a tendency toward tactlessness. You enjoy telling others what you see as the truth "for their own good." This can either make you a great teacher or visionary, like poet Robert Bly, or it can make you dogmatic. When you feel you're in the right, you may expound endlessly on your own ideas. Watch a tendency to puff up ideas unrealistically (however, this talent could make you a super salesman).

MERCURY IN CAPRICORN has excellent mental discipline. You take a serious, orderly approach and play by the rules. You have a super-organized mind that grasps structures easily, though you may lack originality. You have a dry sense of humor.

MERCURY IN AQUARIUS is "exalted" and quite at home in this analytical sign. You have a highly original point of view, combined with good mental focus. An independent thinker, you'll break the rules, if this will help make your point. You are, however, fixed mentally, and reluctant to change your mind once it is made up. Therefore, you could sometimes come across as a "know it all."

MERCURY IN PISCES has a poetic mind that is receptive to psychic, intuitive influences. You may be vague, unclear in your expression and forgetful of details and find it difficult to work within a structure, but you are strong on creative communication and thinking. You'll express yourself in a very sympathetic, caring way. You should find work that uses your imaginative talents.

What Do You React To? What Attracts You? Look for Venus

Venus will show what turns a person on. It is the planet of romantic love, pleasure, and artistry. It shows your tastes and what you'll attract to you without trying. Venus will show you how to charm others in a way that's suited to you.

You can find your Venus placement on the chart in this book. Look for the year of your birth in the lefthand column, then follow the line across the page until you read the time of your birthday. The sign heading that column will be your Venus. If you were born on a day when Venus was changing signs, check the signs preceding or following that day. Here are the roles your Venus plays—and sings.

VENUS IN ARIES. Scarlett O'Hara probably had Venus here! You love a challenge that adds spice to life; you might even pick a fight now and then to "shake 'em up." Since a good chase revs up your romantic motor, you could abandon a romance if the going becomes too smooth. You're first on the block with the newest styles, and first out the door if you're bored or ordered around.

VENUS IN TAURUS. Venus is literally at home in Taurus. It's a terrific placement for a "material girl" or boy, an interior designer or a musician. You love to surround yourself with the very finest smells, tastes, sounds, visuals, textures. You'd run from an austere lifestyle or uncomfortable surroundings. Creature comforts turn you on. And so does a beautiful, secure nest—and nest egg. Not one to rush about, you take time to enjoy your pleasures and treasures.

VENUS IN GEMINI. You're a sparkler, like singer Cher, who loves the night life, with constant variety, and a frequent change of scenes and loves. You like lots of stimulation, a varied social life; you are better at light flirtations than at serious romances. You may be attracted to younger, playful lovers who have the pep and energy to keep up with you.

VENUS IN CANCER. You can be "daddy's girl" or "mama's boy," like the late Liberace. You love to be babied, coddled, and protected in a cozy, secure home. You are attracted to those who make you feel secure, well provided for. You could also have a secret love life or clandestine arrangement with a "sugar daddy." You love to "mother" others as well.

VENUS IN LEO. You're an "uptown" girl or boy who loves "Putting on the Ritz," where you can consort with elegant people, dress extravagantly, and be the center of attention. Think of Coco Chanel, who piled on the jewelry and decorated tweed suits with gold braid. You dress and act like a star, but you might often be more attracted to hangers-on and flatterers, rather than to those who can offer you a relationship with solid value.

VENUS IN VIRGO. This Venus is attracted to perfect order, but underneath your pristine white dress is some naughty black lace! You fall for those who you can make over or improve in some way. You may also fancy those in the medical profession. Here Venus may express itself best through some kind of service, by giving loving support. You may find it difficult to show your true feelings, to really let go in intimate moments. "I Can't Get No Satisfaction" could sometimes be your theme song.

VENUS IN LIBRA. "I Feel Pretty" sings this Venus. You love a beautiful, harmonious, luxurious atmosphere. Many artists and musicians thrive with this Venus, with its natural feeling for the balance of colors and sounds. In love, you make a very compatible partner in a supportive relationship where there are few confrontations. You can't stand arguments or argumentative people. The good looks of your partner may also be a deciding factor.

VENUS IN SCORPIO. "All or Nothing at All" could be your theme song. This Venus wants "Body and Soul." You're a natural detective who's attracted to a mystery. You know how to keep a secret, and have quite a few of your own. This is a very intense placement, where you can be preoccupied with sex and power. Living dangerously adds spice to your life, but don't get burned. All that's intense appeals to you: heady perfume, deep rich colors, dark woods, spicy foods.

VENUS IN SAGITTARIUS. "On the Road Again" sums up your Venus personality. Travel, athletics, New Age philosophies, and a casual, carefree lifestyle appeal to you. You are attracted to exciting, idealistic types who give you plenty of space. Large animals, especially horses, are part of your life. You probably have a four-wheel drive vehicle or a motorized skateboard—anything to keep moving.

VENUS IN CAPRICORN. "Diamonds Are a Girl's Best Friend" could characterize this ambitious Venus. You may seem cool and calculating, but underneath you're insecure and want a substantial relationship you can count on. It wouldn't hurt if your beloved could help you up the ladder professionally, either. This Venus is often attracted to objects and people of a different generation (like Clark Gable, you could marry someone much older—or younger)—antiques; traditional clothing (sometimes worn in a very "today" way, like Diane Keaton); and dignified, conservative behavior are trademarks.

VENUS IN AQUARIUS. "Just Friends, Lovers No More" is often what happens with Venus in Aquarius. You love to be surrounded by people, but are uncomfortable with intense emotions (steer clear of Venus in Scorpio!). You like a spontaneous lifestyle, full of surprises. You make your own rules in everything you do, including love. The avant-garde, high technology, and possibly unusual sexual experiences attract you.

VENUS IN PISCES. "Why not Take All of Me?" sings this exalted Venus, who loves to give. You may have a collection of stray animals, lost souls, the underprivileged, the lonely. (Try to assess their motives in a clear light.) You're a natural for theater, film, anything involving fantasy. Psychic or spiritual life also draws you, as does selfless service for a needy cause.

Your Drive and Motivation Come From Mars

Mars shows what you'll go for. This planet is your driving force, your active sexuality, what makes you run, your kind of energy. To find your Mars, refer to the Mars chart in this book. If the following description of your Mars sign doesn't ring true, you may have been born on a day when Mars was changing signs, so check the adjacent sign descriptions.

MARS IN ARIES runs in high gear, showing the full force of its energy. You have a fiery, explosive disposition, but are also very courageous, with enormous drive. You'll tackle problems head on and mow down anything that stands in your way. Though you're supercharged and can jump-start others, you are short on follow-through, especially when a situation requires diplomacy, patience, and tolerance.

MARS IN TAURUS could claim the motto, "Persistence alone is omnipotent." You're in it for the long haul, and you win the race with a slow, steady pace. Gifted with stamina and focus, this Mars may not be first out of the gate, but you're sure to finish. You tend to wear away or outlast your foes rather than bowl them over. Like Bruce Willis, this Mars is supersensual sexually—you take your time and enjoy yourself all the way. You'll probably accumulate many collections and material possessions.

MARS IN GEMINI holds the philosophy that "two loves are better than one," which could mean trouble. Your restless nature searches out stimulation and will switch rather than fight. Your life gets complicated, but that only makes it more interesting for you. You have a way with words and can "talk" with your hands. Since you tend to go all over the lot in your interests, you may have to work to develop focus and concentration.

MARS IN CANCER is given, in its fall, to moods and can be quite crabby. This may be due to a fragile sense of security. You are quite self-protective and secretive about your life, which might make you appear untrustworthy or manipulative to others. Try not to take things so much to heart—cultivate a sense of impersonality or detachment. Sexually, you are tender and sensitive, a very protective lover.

MARS IN LEO fills you with self-confidence and charisma. You'll use your considerable drive to get attention, coming on strong with show-biz flair, like Cher, who has this placement. In fact, you'll head right for the spotlight. Sexually, you're a giver—but you do demand the royal treatment in return. You enjoy giving orders and can create quite a scene if you're disobeyed. At some point, you may have to learn some lessons in humility.

MARS IN VIRGO is a worker bee, a "Felix Unger" character who notices every detail. This is a thorough, painstaking Mars that worries a great deal about making mistakes—this "worrier" tendency may lead to very tightly strung nerves under your controlled facade. Your energy can be expressed positively in a field like teaching or editing, but your tendency to fault-find could make you a hard-to-please lover. Learning to delegate and praise, rather than do everything perfectly yourself, could make you easier to live with. You enjoy good mental companionship, with less emphasis on sex and no emotional turmoil. If you do find the perfect lover, you'll tend to take care of that person.

MARS IN LIBRA is a passive-aggressor who avoids confrontations and charms people into doing what you want. You are best off in a position where you can exercise your great diplomatic skills. Mars is in its detriment in Libra, and expends much energy deciding which course of action to take. However, setting a solid goal in life—perhaps one that expresses your passion for beauty, justice, or art—could give you the vantage point you need to achieve success. In love, like Michael Douglas, you'll go for beauty in your partner and surroundings.

MARS IN SCORPIO has a powerful drive that could become an obsession. So learn to use this energy wisely and well, for Mars in Scorpio hates to compromise, loves with all-or-nothing fever (while it lasts), and can get jealous or manipulative if you don't get your way! But your powerful concentration and nonstop stamina is an asset in challenging fields like medicine or scientific research. You're the master planner, a super-strategist who, when well directed, can achieve important goals, like actors Larry Hagman and Bill Cosby, and scientist Jonas Salk.

MARS IN SAGITTARIUS is the conquering hero set off on a crusade. You're great at getting things off the ground. Your challenge is to consider the consequences of your actions. In love with freedom, you don't always make the best marriage partner. "Love 'em and leave 'em" could be your motto. You may also gravitate toward risk and adventure, and may have great athletic skill. You're best off in a situation where you can express your love of adventure, philosophy, and travel, or where you can use artistic talents to elevate the lives of others, like Johann Sebastian Bach.

MARS IN CAPRICORN is exalted, a "chief executive" placement that gives you a drive for success and the discipline to achieve it. You deliberately aim for status and a high position in life, and you'll keep climbing, despite the odds. This Mars will work for what you get. You are well organized and persistent—a winning combination. Sexually, you have a strong, earthy drive, but you may go for someone who can be useful to you, rather than someone flashy or fascinating.

MARS IN AQUARIUS Is a visionary and often a revolutionary who stands out from the crowd. You are innovative and highly original in your methods. Sexually, you could go for unusual relationships, like Hugh Hefner or Howard Hughes. You have a rebellious streak and like to shake people up a bit. Intimacy can be a problem—you may keep lots of people around you or isolate yourself to keep others from getting too close.

MARS IN PISCES likes to play different roles. Your ability to tune in and project others' emotions makes you a natural actor. There are many film and television personalities with this placement, such as Mary Tyler Moore, Jane Seymour, Cybill Shepherd, Burt Reynolds, and Jane Fonda. You understand how to use glamour and illusion for your own benefit. You can switch emotions on and off quickly, and you're especially good at getting sympathy. You'll go for romance, though real-life relationships never quite live up to your fantasies.

Your Enthusiasm and Sales Ability Come from Jupiter

Are you enthusiastic, optimistic, willing to take a risk? Look for Jupiter. This planet is often viewed as the "Santa Claus" of the horoscope, a jolly, happy planet that brings good luck, gifts, success, and opportunities. Jupiter also embodies the functions of the higher mind, where you do complex, expansive thinking, and deal with the big overall picture rather than with the specifics (the province of Mercury).

Be sure to look up your Jupiter "lucky spot" in the tables in this book. But bear in mind that Jupiter gives growth without discrimination or discipline. A person with a strong Jupiter may be weak in common sense. This is also the place where you could have too much of a good thing, resulting in extravagance, excess pounds, laziness, or carelessness.

JUPITER IN ARIES. You have big ambitions and won't settle for second place. You are luckiest when you are pioneering an innovative project, when you are pushing to be "first." You can break new ground with this placement, but watch a tendency to be pushy and arrogant. You'll also need to learn patience and follow through in the house where Jupiter falls in your horoscope.

JUPITER IN TAURUS. You have expensive tastes and like to surround yourself with the luxuries money can buy. You acquire beauty and comfort in all its forms. You could tend to expand physically from overindulgence in good tastes! Dieting could be a major challenge. Land and real estate are especially lucky for you.

JUPITER IN GEMINI. You love to be in the center of a whirlwind of activity, talking a blue streak, with all phone lines busy. You have great facility in expressing yourself verbally or in writing. Work that involves communicating or manual dexterity is especially lucky for you. Watch a tendency to be too restless—slow down from time to time. Try not to spread yourself too thin.

JUPITER IN CANCER. This Jupiter has a big safe-deposit box, an attic piled to overflowing with boxes of treasures. You may still have your christening dress or your beloved high school sweater. This Jupiter loves to accumulate things, to save for a rainy day, or to gather collections. Negatively, you could be a hoarder with closets full of things you'll never use. Protective, nurturing Jupiter in Cancer often has many mouths to feed, human or animal. Naturally, this placement produces great restauranteurs and hotel keepers. The shipping business is also a good bet.

JUPITER IN LEO. Naturally warm, romantic, and playful, you can't have too much attention or applause. You bask in the limelight while others are still trying to find the stage. Politics or show business—anywhere you can perform for an audience—are lucky for you. You love the good life and are happy to share your wealth with others. Negatively, you could be extravagant and tend to hog center stage. Let others take a bow from time to time. Also, be careful not to overdo or overspend.

JUPITER IN VIRGO. You like to work! In fact, work can be more interesting than play for you. You have a sharp eye for details and pick out every flaw! Be careful not to get caught up in nitpicking. You expect nothing short of perfection from others. Finding practical solutions to problems and helping others make the most of themselves are better uses for this Jupiter. Consider a health field such as nutrition, medicine, or health education.

JUPITER IN LIBRA. You function best when you have a stimulating partner. You also need harmonious, beautiful surroundings. Chances are, you have closets full of fashionable clothes. The serious side of this Jupiter has an excellent sense of fair play, and can be a good diplomat or judge. Careers in law, the arts, or fashion are favored.

JUPITER IN SCORPIO. You love the power of handling other people's money—or lives. Others see you as having nerves of steel. You have luck in detective work, sex-related ventures, psychotherapy, research, the occult, or tax work—anything that involves a mystery. You're always going to extremes, as testing the limits gives you a thrill.

Your timing is excellent—you'll wait for the perfect moment to make your moves. Negatively, this Jupiter could use power to achieve selfish ends.

JUPITER IN SAGITTARIUS. In its strongest place, Jupiter compels you to expand your mind, travel far from home, collect college degrees. This is the placement of the philosopher, the gambler, the animal trainer, the publisher. You have an excellent sense of humor and a cheerful disposition. This placement often works with animals, especially horses, in some way.

JUPITER IN CAPRICORN. You are luckiest working in an established situation, within a traditional structure. In the sign of caution and restraint, Jupiter is thrifty rather than a big spender. You accumulate duties and responsibilities, which is fine for business leadership. You'll expand in any area where you can achieve respect, prestige, or social position. People with this position are especially concerned that nothing be wasted. You might have great luck in a recycling or renovation business.

JUPITER IN AQUARIUS. You are lucky when doing good in the world. You are extremely idealistic and think in the most expansive terms about improving society at large. This is an excellent position for a politician or labor leader. You're everybody's buddy who can relate to people of diverse backgrounds. You are luckiest when you can operate away from rigid rules and conservative organizations.

JUPITER IN PISCES. You work best in a creative field or in one where you are helping the downtrodden. You exude sympathy and gravitate toward the underdog. Watch a tendency to be too self-sacrificing, overly emotional. You should also be careful not to overindulge in alcohol or drugs. Some lucky work areas: oil, perfume, dance, footwear, alcohol, pharmaceuticals, and the arts, especially film.

Can You Get the Job Done? Saturn Will Tell

Saturn is the planet of discipline, organization, and determination. It will show your ability to follow through and structure a project. It will also reveal your fears, and what you're afraid will be taken away from you.

Saturn has suffered from a bad reputation, always cast as the heavy in the horoscope. However, the flip side of Saturn is the teacher, the one whose class is the toughest in school, but, when you graduate, you never forget the lessons well learned. (They are the ones you came here on this planet to learn.) And the tests of Saturn, which come at regular seven-year exam periods, are the ones you need to pass to survive as a conscious, independent adult. Saturn gives us the grade we've earned—so, if we have studied and prepared for our tests, we needn't be afraid of the big bad wolf.

Your Saturn position can illuminate your fears, your hangups, your important lessons in life. Remember that Saturn is concerned with your maturity, what you need to know to survive in the world. Be sure to look it up in the Saturn chart in this book.

SATURN IN ARIES. "Don't push me around!" says this Saturn, which puts the brakes on Aries natural drive and enthusiasm. You'll have to learn to cooperate, tone down self-centeredness, and respect authorities, in order to get the job done. Bill Cosby, who has this placement, may have had the same lessons to learn.

SATURN IN TAURUS. "How am I going to pay the rent?" You'll have to stick out some lean periods and get control of your material life. Learn to use your talents to their fullest potential. In the same boat, Ben Franklin had the right idea: "A penny saved is a penny earned."

SATURN IN GEMINI. You're a deep thinker, with lofty ideals—a good position for scientific studies. You may be quite shy, speak slowly, or have fears about communicating, like Eleanor Roosevelt. Yet when you master these, you'll be able to sway the masses, just like she did. You'll tend to take shelter in abstract ideas, like Sigmund Freud, when dealing with emotional issues.

SATURN IN CANCER. Some very basic fears could center on your early home environment, overcoming a negative childhood influence to establish a sense of security.

You may fear being mothered or smothered and be tested in your female relationships. You may have to learn to be objective and distance yourself emotionally when threatened or when dealing with negative feelings such as jealousy or guilt. Bette Midler and Diane Keaton have this placement.

SATURN IN LEO. This placement can bring up ego problems. If you have not received the love you crave, you could be an overly strict, dictatorial parent. You may demand respect and a position of leadership at any cost. You may have to watch a tendency toward rigidity and withholding affection. You may have to learn to relax, have fun, lighten up!

SATURN IN VIRGO. You can be very hard on yourself, making yourself sick to your stomach by worrying about every little detail. You must learn to set priorities, discriminate, and laugh!

SATURN IN LIBRA. You may have your most successful marriage (or your first) later in life, because you must learn to stand on your own first. How to relate to others is one of your major lessons. Your great sense of fairness makes you a good judge or lawyer, or a prominent diplomat, like former Secretary of State Henry Kissenger.

SATURN IN SCORPIO. Your tests come when you handle situations involving control or power over others. You could fear depending on others financially or sexually, or there could be a blurring of the lines between sex and money. Sexual tests, periods of celibacy (resulting from fear of "merging" with another), or sex for money, are some ways this could manifest.

SATURN IN SAGITTARIUS. You accept nothing at face value. You are the opposite of the happy-go-lucky Sagittarius. With Saturn here, your beliefs must be fully examined and tested. Firsthand experience, without the guidance of dogma, gurus, or teachers, is your best education. This Saturn has little tolerance for another authority. You won't follow a dream unless you understand the idea behind it.

SATURN IN CAPRICORN. Saturn, which rules Capricorn, is sensitive to public opinion and achieving a high-status image. You are not a big risk taker because you do not want to compromise your position. In its most powerful place, Saturn is the teacher par excellence, giving structure and form to your life. Your persistence will assure you a continual climb to the top.

SATURN IN AQUARIUS. This is a Greta Garbo position, where you feel like an outsider, one who doesn't fit into the group. There may be a lack of trust in others, a kind of defensiveness that could engender defensiveness in return. Not a superficial social butterfly, your commitment to groups must have depth and humanitarian meaning.

SATURN IN PISCES. This position generates a feeling of helplessness, of being a victim of circumstances. You could underestimate yourself, lack a sense of self-power. However, this can give great wisdom if you can manage, like Edgar Cayce, to look inward, with contemplation and meditation, rather than outward, for solutions.

The Outer Planets: Uranus, Neptune, and Pluto

The three outer planets—Uranus, Neptune, and Pluto—are slow moving but powerful forces in our lives. Since they stay in a sign at least seven years, you'll share the sign placement with everyone you went to school with and probably your brothers and sisters. However, the specific place (house) in the horoscope where each one operates is yours alone, and depends on your moment in time—the exact time you were born. That's why it's important to have an exact birthchart. Look at the charts on pages 94–97 to find the signs of your outer planets.

Can You Work Independently? Are You a Rebel? An Original? Look at Uranus.

Uranus can be an excellent indicator of whether you stand out in a crowd. This is a brilliant, highly original, unpredictable planet who shakes us out of a rut and propels us forward.

URANUS IN ARIES. Yours was the generation that pioneered in electronics, developing the first computers and high-tech gadgets. Your powerful mixture of fire (Aries) and electricity (Uranus) propels you into exploring the unknown. Those of you born here, like Jacqueline Onassis, Andy Warhol, and Yoko Ono, probably have had sudden, violent changes in your lives and have a very headstrong, individualistic streak.

URANUS IN TAURUS. This generation became the "hippies" who rejected the establishment. The rise of communism and socialism happened during this period. You have bright ideas about making money and are a natural entrepreneur, but can have sudden financial shakeups.

URANUS IN GEMINI. The age of information begins. This generation was the first to be brought up on television. You stock up on cordless telephones, answering machines, faxes, modems, and car phones—any new way to communicate. You have an inquiring, curious, highly original mind. You're the talk-show person.

URANUS IN CANCER. You have unorthodox ideas about parenting, shelter, food, and child rearing. You are the "New Age" people, fascinated with the subconscious, memories, dreams, and psychic research. During this time period, the home was transformed with electronic gadgets. Many of you are sure to have home computers.

URANUS IN LEO. This period coincided with the rise of rock and roll and the heyday of Hollywood. Self-expression led to the exhibitionism of the Sixties. Electronic media was used skillfully for self-promotion and self-expression. This generation, now in your thirties, will have unusual love affairs and extraordinary children. You'll show the full force of your personality in a unique way.

URANUS IN VIRGO. This generation arrived at a time of student rebellions, the civil rights movement, and general acceptance of health foods. You'll be concerned with pollution and cleaning up the environment. You may revolutionize the healing arts, making nontraditional methods acceptable. This generation also has campaigned against the use of dangerous pesticides and smoking in public spaces.

URANUS IN LIBRA. Born at a time when the divorce rate soared and the women's liberation movement gained ground, this generation will have some revolutionary ideas about marriage and partnerships. You may have an on-again, off-again relationship, prefer unusual partners, or prefer to stay uncommitted. This generation will pioneer concepts in justice and revolutionize the arts.

URANUS IN SCORPIO. Uranus here shook up our sexual ideas. And this generation, just beginning to enter adulthood, will have unorthodox sex lives. You'll delve beneath the surface of life to explore life after death past lives and mediumship. This time period signaled the public awareness of the "New Age." Body and mind control will be an issue with the generation. You may make great breakthroughs in scientific research and the medical field, especially in surgery.

URANUS IN SAGITTARIUS. This generation rebels against orthodoxy and may invent some unusual modes of religion, education, or philosophy. In Sagittarius, Uranus will make breakthroughs in long-distance travel—these children may be the first to travel in outer space. When this placement happened earlier, the Wright Brothers began to fly and the aviator Charles Lindbergh was born.

URANUS IN CAPRICORN. For the past few years, Uranus is shaking up the established structures of society in Capricorn. Stock market ups and downs, the Berlin Wall crumbling, and new practical high-tech gadgets changed our lives. Long-established financial and technological structures, like Pan Am airlines, are suddenly disappearing. Those born with this placement will take an innovative approach to their careers. Capricorn likes tradition, while Uranus likes change. Therefore, this generation's task is to reconcile the two forces.

URANUS IN AQUARIUS. Uranus shines brightest in Aquarius, the sign it rules. During its previous transit, innovators such as Orson Welles and Leonard Bernstein were born, and breakthroughs in science and technology changed the way we view the world. Uranus will enter Aquarius again starting this year and lasting until 2002, when we can look forward to this planet performing at its most revolutionary, eccentric, and brilliant peak. Though this planet promises many surprises in store, we can be sure that the generation born during this time will be very concerned with global issues that are shared by all humanity, and with experimentation and innovation on every level.

URANUS IN PISCES. Many of the first television personalities were born with this placement, because this was the first generation to exploit the electronic media. This was the time of Prohibition (Pisces rules alcohol) and the development of the film industry (also Pisces-ruled). The next go-round, in the early 2000s, could bring on the Hollywood of the twenty-first century!

Are You Imaginative? What Are Your Dreams, Fantasies, Ideals? Neptune Will Tell

Neptune shows how well you and those of your generation create a world of illusion (very useful in creative work). Do you have an innate glamour you can tap? With Neptune, what you see is not what you get. Neptune is the planet of dissolution (it dissolves hard reality). It is not interested in the world at face value; it dons tinted glasses or blurs the facts with the haze of an intoxicating substance. Where Neptune is, you don't see things quite clearly. This planet's function is to express our visions, and it is most at home in Pisces, which it rules.

Neptune was in the following signs in this century:

NEPTUNE IN CANCER. Family ties were glamorized and extended to the nation. Motherhood and home cooking were cast in a rosy glow (Julia Child was born with this placement). People born then waved the flag, read Dr.

Spock, and watched Walt Disney. Many gave their lives for their homeland.

NEPTUNE IN LEO. Neptune in Leo brought the lavish spending and glamour of the 1920s, which blurred the harsh realities of the age. When Neptune left Leo and moved into Virgo in 1929, the stock market fell. This Neptune, which favored the entertainment industry, brought the golden age of Broadway and the rise of the star system. Those born with this placement have a flair for drama and may idealize fame without realizing there is a price to pay.

NEPTUNE IN VIRGO. Neptune in Virgo glamorizes health and fitness (Jane Fonda). This generation invented fitness videos, marathon running, and television sports. You may include psychotherapy as part of your mental-health regime. You glamorized the workplace and many became workaholics.

NEPTUNE IN LIBRA. Born at a time when "Ozzie and Harriet" was the marital ideal, this generation went on to glamorize "relating" in ways that idealized sexual equality and is still trying to find its balance in marriage. There have been many divorces as this generation tries to adapt traditional marriage to modern times and allow both sexes free expression.

NEPTUNE IN SCORPIO. This generation was born at a time which glamorized sex and drugs, and matured when the price was paid in AIDS and drug wars. The Berlin Wall was erected when they were born, torn down when they matured. Because of your intense powers of regeneration, part of your mission will be healing and transforming the earth after damage resulting from the delusions of the past is revealed.

NEPTUNE IN SAGITTARIUS. Spiritual and philosophical values were glamorized in the "New Age" period. Neptune brought out the truth-teller who revealed Watergate and unethical conduct in business. Space travel became a reality and children born with the placement could travel mentally or physically to other worlds.

NEPTUNE IN CAPRICORN. Now in Capricorn, Neptune brings illusions of material power, which were tested as Saturn passed by and were then shaken up by Uranus. It is a time when spiritual interests are commercialized and gain respectability. The business world, however, has been rocked with scandals and broken illusions, as management distances itself from the product and becomes engrossed in power plays. Those born during this period will embody these Neptune energies in some way and express them at maturity.

How Do You Handle Power? Find Pluto in Your Chart!

Pluto is slow-moving, covering only seven signs in the past century. It tells lots about how your generation handles power, what makes it seem "cool" to others. This planet brings deep subconscious feelings to light, digging out our secrets though painful probing, to effect a total transformation. Nothing escapes—or is sacred—with Pluto.

PLUTO IN GEMINI. Some of our most transformative writers were born with Pluto in Gemini, such as Hemingway and F. Scott Fitzgerald. Sex taboos were broken by other writers such as Henry Miller, D. H. Lawrence and James Joyce. Muckraking journalism became an agent for transformation. Psychoanalysis (talk therapy) was developed.

PLUTO IN CANCER. Motherhood, security, and the breast became fetishes for this generation; it was also the generation that saw the rise of women's rights and of dictators who swayed the masses with emotional appeals and the rise of nationalism. This generation is deeply sentimental, placing great value on emotional security. This was also the time of the depression, the deprivation of food and security. This is the sign of mother power; intense, emotional sympathy; and an understanding of where others are emotionally dependent. Power issues center around using the understanding of where others need mothering to either "feed" them psychologically or literally, or to manipulate them.

PLUTO IN LEO. Self-expression becomes a power play for this generation, which invented rock and roll. The rise of television and the development of the entertainment business emphasize Leo's transformative power. This was the generation that "did its own thing" and demanded sexual freedom. These people will go to great lengths to get attention and recognition. This desire for personal recognition can lead to self-aggrandizement and extremes of self-promotion, such as baring innermost secrets on a talk show or to a tabloid. This generation also produced some of the most flamboyant entrepreneurs of the 80s—the big-spending billionaires who lived in the grand style. Pluto in Leo loves to see itself in everything. As this generation ages, it will remain extremely visible and demanding of attention.

PLUTO IN VIRGO. This generation returned to traditional values and became workaholics. Fitness, health, and career interests took over mass consciousness. To increase efficiency, this generation stocked up on high-tech gadgets such as faxes, computer dictionaries, time planners, and portable telephones. This generation uses power by discrimination. These became the "yuppies" who want the best of everything. A keen, judgmental mind, good organizational skills, and an extremely dutiful attitude characterize their exercise of power.

PLUTO IN LIBRA. This generation is just beginning to come into its own. At their birthtime, there was landmark legislation on life-or-death issues such as abortion and euthanasia. The ERA and gay rights movements were coming into mass attention. Marriage is being redefined as an equal partnership and parental roles are being shared. There may be a compulsive need to be in a relationship and to link with others. This generation will exercise power in a diplomatic way, working well in partnerships rather than independently. This is more of a "we" person than an independent operator.

PLUTO IN SCORPIO. Pluto has been in its ruling sign of Scorpio for the past seven years, and during this time has come as close to earth as its irregular orbit will allow. So it is no wonder that we have experienced the full force of this tiny planet. Somewhere in each of our lives, we have felt Pluto's transforming power, especially in 1989, when Pluto was at its perhelion.

For those of you who have felt "nuked" by Pluto (Scorpios and those with Scorpio rising, especially), it may be helpful to remember one of the key symbols for Scorpio—the phoenix rising from the ashes. Pluto clears the decks in order to create anew. In the Scorpio area of your life, you will go through changes in order to be "born again" and to make way for a period of optimism and expansion. Scorpion themes such as sexuality, birth, and death—and the transcendence of death—will be reflected in the way this generation exercises power.

PLUTO IN SAGITTARIUS (January 17, 1995—2008). This should signal a time of great optimism and spiritual development, bringing the century to an exciting close. The generation born now will be expansive on a mass level. In Sagittarius, the traveler, there's a good possibility that Pluto, the planet of extremes, will make space travel a reality for many of us. Look for new dimensions in publishing, emphasis on higher education, and a concern with animal rights issues. Religion will have a new emphasis in our lives and we'll certainly be developing far-reaching philosophies designed to elevate our lives with a new sense of purpose.

CHAPTER 6

How Your Rising Sign Can Change Your Outward Image

At the moment you were born, when you assumed a physical body and became an independent person, an astrological sign—that is, a specific thirty-degree portion of the zodiac—was passing over the eastern horizon. Called your "rising sign" or ascendant, this sign is very important in your horoscope because it sets your horoscope (or "astrological life") in motion. In effect, it says, "Here I am!" as it announces your arrival in the world.

Rising signs change every two hours with the Earth's rotation. If you were born early in the morning when the sun was on the horizon (which makes your sun sign also your rising sign), then you will come across to others like the prototype of your sun sign. That is also why we call those born with their sun sign on the horizon a "double Aquarius" or a "double Virgo." You have twice as much input from that sign.

If you were born with another sign on the horizon, you will advertise yourself more like that other sign. This other sign will mask slightly—or completely disguise—your basic sun-sign character. If people have difficulty guessing your sun sign, this is probably the reason, particularly if you have a very outgoing ascendant, such a Leo ascendant, and a rather shy sun sign, like Virgo.

On the other hand, a rather conservative Capricorn ascendant can tone down the intensity of a Scorpio or make a jovial Sagittarian seem far more serious than he really is. Your rising sign is your "cover" or mask. Often a person will project just one facet of a rising sign. For instance, one person with a Sagittarius rising would be a lover of horses and a world traveler; another with the same ascendant would project the more spiritual side of this sign.

In your horoscope chart, the other signs follow the rising sign in sequence, rotating counterclockwise over the houses of your chart and coloring each one with their personality. Therefore, the rising sign sets up the tone of your chart. It rules the first house, which is the physical body (your appearance) and also influences your style, tastes, health, and physical environment (where you are most comfortable working and living).

You'll find your rising sign on the chart on pages 69-70. Since rising signs move rapidly, you should know your birthtime as close to the minute as possible. If you are unsure about the exact time, but know within a few hours, check the following descriptions to see which is most like the personality you project.

ARIES RISING. You'll be the most aggressive version of your sun sign, coming across as a go-getter—headed for the fast track, dynamic, energetic, and assertive. Billy Graham and Bette Midler show the sparkle and fire of this ascendant. But since you can also be somewhat impatient and combative, try to either consider where the other person is coming from or head for an area where your feistiness will be appreciated. With this ascendant, you may prefer the color red—or wear it a lot—instinctively grabbing for the red sweater or tie. Many of you walk with your head thrust forward like the ram. You may also have prominent eyebrows or a very wide browline. At some point in your life, you may acquire a facial scar or a head injury.

TAURUS RISING. There is nothing lightweight about the impression you give. You have a strong, steady presence; you are not easily dismissed. You are more sensual, patient, and pleasure oriented than others of your sign. You love good food and may be an excellent cook. Green thumbs are also common with this nature-loving ascendant. You may have a very unusual and memorable voice and great concentration and stamina, like TV news anchor Dan Rather. Though your frame is often stocky, with a tendency to put on weight, some curvaceous beauty queens and sex goddesses are born with this placement.

GEMINI RISING. You're a great talker, in constant motion. You're a quick thinker and fast learner, like comedienne Phyllis Diller and rock star and songwriter Bruce Springsteen. On the minus side, you could come across as nervous, scattered, a jack-of-all-trades. Play up your analytical mind and your ability to communicate and to adapt to different people and environments. This ascendant could also give you writing talent or an affinity for work that uses your hands, such as massage or piano playing. Learning a keyboard is second nature to you. You gesture often and probably have light coloring and fine features.

CANCER RISING. You may come across as sensitive and caring, one who enjoys taking care of others. You may seem a bit moodier than others of your sign and more self-protective, like actor John Travolta. You have very quick responses to emotional situations. You are also very astute businesswise, with a sharp sense of what will sell, like H. Ross Perot, a double Cancer. You may choose work dealing with hotels or shelter business, decorating or working with children. Physically, you may be a lunar type, with a large chest area, a round face, and delicate sensitive skin. Or you may be a "crab" type, with wide-set eyes and prominent bone structure.

LEO RISING. You project a regal air of authority, which instills confidence in your abilities. You come across as someone who can take charge. You are very poised in the spotlight and you know how to present yourself to play up your special star quality, like Ava Gardner, ballerina Cynthia Gregory, or Marilyn Monroe. You attract attention and you tend to take center stage graciously. In business, you can be the epitome of executive style.

VIRGO RISING. Your style may be rather conservative, restrained, and classic, but your intelligence and your analytical ability shine brightly. You seem well organized, with a no-nonsense air of knowing what you're doing. Never one to slack off, you're a hard worker who gets on with it. Your manner may be a bit aloof, and you can be critical of others who don't share your sense of mastery of your craft, of doing it to perfection. But this critical quality serves you well as an editor, writer, or teacher. You may also be drawn to the health or service fields. A high-profile example: George Bush.

LIBRA RISING. You come across as charming, attractive, well dressed, and diplomatic. Like Nancy Reagan, the first impression you give is one of social ease and harmony. You enjoy working with others and it shows. You thrive in partnerships and relationships, rather than going it alone. You may have aesthetic concerns, such as fashion or design, or you could gravitate to the diplomatic or legal fields. Physically, you'll have delicate, harmonious features; graceful gestures; and a lovely, often dimpled, smile.

SCORPIO RISING. Even if you don't say a word, your presence carries a charge of excitement and an air of mystery. Margaret Thatcher and Jacqueline Kennedy Onassis are terrific examples. Intense and charismatic, you'll make your presence felt with a penetrating gaze. Be careful not to come on too overwhelmingly strong. You might consider toning down your intensity, tempering it with a touch of humor. Less open than others of your sign, you can be very manipulative when chasing your goals. You project an air of subtle sexuality, of a secret agenda that could fascinate others. Sexual expression will be an important issue for you. You may wear a great deal of the "no-color," black.

SAGITTARIUS RISING. This ascendant can push normally home-loving signs to exotic locales. Always on the go, you have energy to burn. You're a bouncy, athletic version of your sign, like Ted Turner, with an upbeat personality that exudes cheerful optimism. You adore competitive sports that require lots of leg power. You may also be drawn to horses or horse-related activities. You are frank and direct in manner and don't hesitate to say what you think, even if it means stepping on some tender toes. Travel excites you—the more exotic the destination, the better. You may be attracted to idealistic or philosophical activities, or to teaching, publishing, or religious careers. Your sense of humor wins fans, but some of you may have to work on developing tact and diplomacy. Another famous example: Raquel Welch.

CAPRICORN RISING. You are the serious, hard-working type with a very sharp business sense. (*Cosmopolitan* editor Helen Gurley Brown, who has this ascendant, has called herself a "mouseburger"). But you could also have the traditional flair of Fred Astaire. A great organizer, you function well in a structured or corporate environment. Not a frivolous type, you aim to be taken seriously, like Paul Newman. You'll easily adapt to present the classiest impression appropriate to your business. You understand how to delegate and to use the talents of others, which could land you a leadership position. You prefer a traditional atmosphere, antiques, and possessions of "quiet quality." Take special care of your knees, teeth and bone structure, which are vulnerable areas.

AQUARIUS RISING. Like daredevil Evil Knievel, you're charismatic and individualistic—you know how to get attention, sometimes in a startling way that shakes everyone up. You'll dress to please yourself—never mind the dress code. Be sure to find a business that appreciates your eccentric side, one with a cause or principles you believe in. Your job should give you plenty of space and allow you to work independently. You'll make your own rules and probably won't take well to authority or outside discipline—you know what's best for you, anyway. You may be attracted to a high-tech career or to one that probes the depths of the mind in some way.

PISCES RISING. You'll express the most artistic, romantic, and imaginative side of your sun sign. Like Phil Donohue, you'll come across as empathetic, a good listener who is able to cue in to where others are coming from—a valuable interview asset. You may be quite dramatic, and present yourself as a "character," like baseball's Yogi Berra or author Norman Mailer. You are very happy on the water, or in a home that overlooks water. You might gravitate to the theater, dance or film worlds, or to any creative environment. Or you could take another Pisces tack and show your more spiritual side, dedicating yourself to helping others. Beautiful eyes and talented dancing feet are frequent gifts of this ascendant. One of your most vulnerable points is your supersensitivity to drugs, chemicals, or alcohol. High-profile example: Richard Pryor.

RISING SIGNS—A.M. BIRTHS

	1 AM	2 AM	3 AM	4 AM	5 AM	6 AM	7 AM	8 AM	9 AM	10 AM	11 AM	12 NOON
Jan 1	Lib	Sc	Sc	Sc	Sag	Sag	Cap	Cap	Aq	Aq	Pis	Ar
Jan 9	Lib	Sc	Sc	Sag	Sag	Sag	Cap	Cap	Aq	Pis	Ar	Tau
Jan 17	Sc	Sc	Sc	Sag	Sag	Cap	Cap	Aq	Aq	Pis	Ar	Tau
Jan 25	Sc	Sc	Sag	Sag	Sag	Cap	Cap	Aq	Pis	Ar	Tau	Tau
Feb 2	Sc	Sc	Sag	Sag	Cap	Cap	Aq	Pis	Pis	Ar	Tau	Gem
Feb 10	Sc	Sag	Sag	Sag	Cap	Cap	Aq	Pis	Ar	Tau	Tau	Gem
Feb 18	Sc	Sag	Sag	Cap	Cap	Aq	Pis	Pis	Ar	Tau	Gem	Gem
Feb 26	Sag	Sag	Sag	Cap	Aq	Aq	Pis	Ar	Tau	Tau	Gem	Gem
Mar 6	Sag	Sag	Cap	Cap	Aq	Pis	Pis	Ar	Tau	Gem	Gem	Cap
Mar 14	Sag	Cap	Cap	Aq	Aq	Pis	Ar	Tau	Tau	Gem	Gem	Can
Mar 22	Sag	Cap	Cap	Aq	Pis	Ar	Ar	Tau	Gem	Gem	Can	Can
Mar 30	Cap	Cap	Aq	Pis	Pis	Ar	Tau	Tau	Gem	Can	Can	Can
Apr 7	Cap	Cap	Aq	Pis	Ar	Ar	Tau	Gem	Gem	Can	Can	Leo
Apr 14	Cap	Aq	Aq	Pis	Ar	Tau	Tau	Gem	Gem	Can	Can	Leo
Apr 22	Cap	Aq	Pis	Ar	Ar	Tau	Gem	Gem	Gem	Can	Leo	Leo
Apr 30	Aq	Aq	Pis	Ar	Tau	Tau	Gem	Can	Can	Can	Leo	Leo
May 8	Aq	Pis	Ar	Ar	Tau	Gem	Gem	Can	Can	Leo	Leo	Leo
May 16	Aq	Pis	Ar	Tau	Gem	Gem	Can	Can	Can	Leo	Leo	Vir
May 24	Pis	Ar	Ar	Tau	Gem	Gem	Can	Can	Leo	Leo	Leo	Vir
June 1	Pis	Ar	Tau	Gem	Gem	Can	Can	Can	Leo	Leo	Vir	Vir
June 9	Ar	Ar	Tau	Gem	Gem	Can	Can	Leo	Leo	Leo	Vir	Vir
June 17	Ar	Tau	Gem	Gem	Can	Can	Can	Leo	Leo	Vir	Vir	Vir
June 25	Tau	Tau	Gem	Gem	Can	Can	Leo	Leo	Leo	Vir	Vir	Lib
July 3	Tau	Gem	Gem	Can	Can	Can	Leo	Leo	Vir	Vir	Vir	Lib
July 11	Tau	Gem	Gem	Can	Can	Leo	Leo	Leo	Vir	Vir	Lib	Lib
July 18	Gem	Gem	Can	Can	Can	Leo	Leo	Vir	Vir	Vir	Lib	Lib
July 26	Gem	Gem	Can	Can	Leo	Leo	Vir	Vir	Vir	Lib	Lib	Lib
Aug 3	Gem	Can	Can	Can	Leo	Leo	Vir	Vir	Vir	Lib	Lib	Sc
Aug 11	Gem	Can	Can	Leo	Leo	Leo	Vir	Vir	Lib	Lib	Lib	Sc
Aug 18	Can	Can	Can	Leo	Leo	Vir	Vir	Vir	Lib	Lib	Sc	Sc
Aug 27	Can	Can	Leo	Leo	Leo	Vir	Vir	Lib	Lib	Lib	Sc	Sc
Sept 4	Can	Can	Leo	Leo	Leo	Vir	Vir	Vir	Lib	Lib	Sc	Sc
Sept 12	Can	Leo	Leo	Leo	Vir	Vir	Lib	Lib	Lib	Sc	Sc	Sag
Sept 20	Leo	Leo	Leo	Vir	Vir	Vir	Lib	Lib	Sc	Sc	Sc	Sag
Sept 28	Leo	Leo	Leo	Vir	Vir	Lib	Lib	Lib	Sc	Sc	Sag	Sag
Oct 6	Leo	Leo	Vir	Vir	Vir	Lib	Lib	Sc	Sc	Sc	Sag	Sag
Oct 14	Leo	Vir	Vir	Vir	Lib	Lib	Lib	Sc	Sc	Sag	Sag	Cap
Oct 22	Leo	Vir	Vir	Lib	Lib	Lib	Sc	Sc	Sc	Sag	Sag	Cap
Oct 30	Vir	Vir	Vir	Lib	Lib	Sc	Sc	Sc	Sag	Sag	Cap	Cap
Nov 7	Vir	Vir	Lib	Lib	Lib	Sc	Sc	Sc	Sag	Sag	Cap	Cap
Nov 15	Vir	Vir	Lib	Lib	Sc	Sc	Sc	Sag	Sag	Cap	Cap	Aq
Nov 23	Vir	Lib	Lib	Lib	Sc	Sc	Sag	Sag	Sag	Cap	Cap	Aq
Dec 1	Vir	Lib	Lib	Sc	Sc	Sc	Sag	Sag	Cap	Cap	Aq	Aq
Dec 9	Lib	Lib	Lib	Sc	Sc	Sag	Sag	Sag	Cap	Cap	Aq	Pis
Dec 18	Lib	Lib	Sc	Sc	Sc	Sag	Sag	Cap	Cap	Aq	Aq	Pis
Dec 28	Lib	Lib	Sc	Sc	Sag	Sag	Sag	Cap	Aq	Aq	Pis	Ar

RISING SIGNS—P.M. BIRTHS

	1 PM	2 PM	3 PM	4 PM	5 PM	6 PM	7 PM	8 PM	9 PM	10 PM	11 PM	12 MID-NIGHT
Jan 1	Tau	Gem	Gem	Can	Can	Can	Leo	Leo	Vir	Vir	Vir	Lib
Jan 9	Tau	Gem	Gem	Can	Can	Leo	Leo	Leo	Vir	Vir	Vir	Lib
Jan 17	Gem	Gem	Can	Can	Can	Leo	Leo	Vir	Vir	Vir	Lib	Lib
Jan 25	Gem	Gem	Can	Can	Leo	Leo	Leo	Vir	Vir	Lib	Lib	Lib
Feb 2	Gem	Can	Can	Can	Leo	Leo	Vir	Vir	Vir	Lib	Lib	Sc
Feb 10	Gem	Can	Can	Leo	Leo	Leo	Vir	Vir	Lib	Lib	Lib	Sc
Feb 18	Can	Can	Can	Leo	Leo	Vir	Vir	Vir	Lib	Lib	Sc	Sc
Feb 26	Can	Can	Leo	Leo	Leo	Vir	Vir	Lib	Lib	Lib	Sc	Sc
Mar 6	Can	Leo	Leo	Leo	Vir	Vir	Vir	Lib	Lib	Sc	Sc	Sc
Mar 14	Can	Leo	Leo	Vir	Vir	Vir	Lib	Lib	Lib	Sc	Sc	Sag
Mar 22	Leo	Leo	Leo	Vir	Vir	Lib	Lib	Lib	Sc	Sc	Sc	Sag
Mar 30	Leo	Leo	Vir	Vir	Vir	Lib	Lib	Sc	Sc	Sc	Sag	Sag
Apr 7	Leo	Leo	Vir	Vir	Lib	Lib	Lib	Sc	Sc	Sc	Sag	Sag
Apr 14	Leo	Vir	Vir	Vir	Lib	Lib	Sc	Sc	Sc	Sag	Sag	Cap
Apr 22	Leo	Vir	Vir	Lib	Lib	Lib	Sc	Sc	Sc	Sag	Sag	Cap
Apr 30	Vir	Vir	Vir	Lib	Lib	Sc	Sc	Sc	Sag	Sag	Cap	Cap
May 8	Vir	Vir	Lib	Lib	Lib	Sc	Sc	Sag	Sag	Sag	Cap	Cap
May 16	Vir	Vir	Lib	Lib	Sc	Sc	Sc	Sag	Sag	Cap	Cap	Aq
May 24	Vir	Lib	Lib	Lib	Sc	Sc	Sag	Sag	Sag	Cap	Cap	Aq
June 1	Vir	Lib	Lib	Sc	Sc	Sc	Sag	Sag	Cap	Cap	Aq	Aq
June 9	Lib	Lib	Lib	Sc	Sc	Sag	Sag	Sag	Cap	Cap	Aq	Pis
June 17	Lib	Lib	Sc	Sc	Sc	Sag	Sag	Cap	Cap	Aq	Aq	Pis
June 25	Lib	Lib	Sc	Sc	Sag	Sag	Sag	Cap	Cap	Aq	Pis	Ar
July 3	Lib	Sc	Sc	Sc	Sag	Sag	Cap	Cap	Aq	Aq	Pis	Ar
July 11	Lib	Sc	Sc	Sag	Sag	Sag	Cap	Cap	Aq	Pis	Ar	Tau
July 18	Sc	Sc	Sc	Sag	Sag	Cap	Cap	Aq	Aq	Pis	Ar	Tau
July 26	Sc	Sc	Sag	Sag	Sag	Cap	Cap	Aq	Pis	Ar	Tau	Tau
Aug 3	Sc	Sc	Sag	Sag	Cap	Cap	Aq	Aq	Pis	Ar	Tau	Gem
Aug 11	Sc	Sag	Sag	Sag	Cap	Cap	Aq	Pis	Ar	Tau	Tau	Gem
Aug 18	Sc	Sag	Sag	Cap	Cap	Aq	Pis	Pis	Ar	Tau	Gem	Gem
Aug 27	Sag	Sag	Sag	Cap	Cap	Aq	Pis	Ar	Tau	Tau	Gem	Gem
Sept 4	Sag	Sag	Cap	Cap	Aq	Pis	Pis	Ar	Tau	Gem	Gem	Can
Sept 12	Sag	Sag	Cap	Aq	Aq	Pis	Ar	Tau	Tau	Gem	Gem	Can
Sept 20	Sag	Cap	Cap	Aq	Pis	Pis	Ar	Tau	Gem	Gem	Can	Can
Sept 28	Cap	Cap	Aq	Aq	Pis	Ar	Tau	Tau	Gem	Gem	Can	Can
Oct 6	Cap	Cap	Aq	Pis	Ar	Ar	Tau	Gem	Gem	Can	Can	Leo
Oct 14	Cap	Aq	Aq	Pis	Ar	Tau	Tau	Gem	Gem	Can	Can	Leo
Oct 22	Cap	Aq	Pis	Ar	Ar	Tau	Gem	Gem	Can	Can	Leo	Leo
Oct 30	Aq	Aq	Pis	Ar	Tau	Tau	Gem	Can	Can	Can	Leo	Leo
Nov 7	Aq	Aq	Pis	Ar	Tau	Tau	Gem	Can	Can	Can	Leo	Leo
Nov 15	Aq	Pis	Ar	Tau	Gem	Gem	Can	Can	Can	Leo	Leo	Vir
Nov 23	Pis	Ar	Ar	Tau	Gem	Gem	Can	Can	Leo	Leo	Leo	Vir
Dec 1	Pis	Ar	Tau	Gem	Gem	Can	Can	Can	Leo	Leo	Vir	Vir
Dec 9	Ar	Tau	Tau	Gem	Gem	Can	Can	Leo	Leo	Leo	Vir	Vir
Dec 18	Ar	Tau	Gem	Gem	Can	Can	Can	Leo	Leo	Vir	Vir	Vir
Dec 28	Tau	Tau	Gem	Gem	Can	Can	Leo	Leo	Vir	Vir	Vir	Lib

CHAPTER 7

Look Up Your Planets

The following tables are provided so that you can look up the signs of seven major planets—Venus, Mars, Saturn, Jupiter, Uranus, Neptune, and Pluto. We do not have room for tables for the moon and Mercury, which change signs often.

How to Use the Venus Table

Find the year of your birth in the vertical column on the left, then follow across the page until you find the correct date. The Venus sign is at the top of that column.

How to Use the Mars, Saturn, and Jupiter Tables

Find the year of your birth date on the left side of each column. The dates the planet entered each sign are listed on the right side of each column. (Signs are abbreviated to the first three letters.) Your birthday should fall on or between each date listed, and your planetary placement should correspond to the earlier sign of that period.

VENUS SIGNS 1901–2000

	Aries	Taurus	Gemini	Cancer	Leo	Virgo
1901	3/29-4/22	4/22-5/17	5/17-6/10	6/10-7/5	7/5-7/29	7/29-8/23
1902	5/7-6/3	6/3-6/30	6/30-7/25	7/25-8/19	8/19-9/13	9/13-10/7
1903	2/28-3/24	3/24-4/18	4/18-5/13	5/13-6/9	6/9-7/7	7/7-8/17 9/6-11/8
1904	3/13-5/7	5/7-6/1	6/1-6/25	6/25-7/19	7/19-8/13	8/13-9/6
1905	2/3-3/6 4/9-5/28	3/6-4/9 5/28-7/8	7/8-8/6	8/6-9/1	9/1-9/27	9/27-10/21
1906	3/1-4/7	4/7-5/2	5/2-5/26	5/26-6/20	6/20-7/16	7/16-8/11
1907	4/27-5/22	5/22-6/16	6/16-7/11	7/11-8/4	8/4-8/29	8/29-9/22
1908	2/14-3/10	3/10-4/5	4/5-5/5	5/5-9/8	9/8-10/8	10/8-11/3
1909	3/29-4/22	4/22-5/16	5/16-6/10	6/10-7/4	7/4-7/29	7/29-8/23
1910	5/7-6/3	6/4-6/29	6/30-7/24	7/25-8/18	8/19-9/12	9/13-10/6
1911	2/28-3/23	3/24-4/17	4/18-5/12	5/13-6/8	6/9-7/7	7/8-11/8
1912	4/13-5/6	5/7-5/31	6/1-6/24	6/24-7/18	7/19-8/12	8/13-9/5
1913	2/3-3/6 5/2-5/30	3/7-5/1 5/31-7/7	7/8-8/5	8/6-8/31	9/1-9/26	9/27-10/20
1914	3/14-4/6	4/7-5/1	5/2-5/25	5/26-6/19	6/20-7/15	7/16-8/10
1915	4/27-5/21	5/22-6/15	6/16-7/10	7/11-8/3	8/4-8/28	8/29-9/21
1916	2/14-3/9	3/10-4/5	4/6-5/5	5/6-9/8	9/9-10/7	10/8-11/2
1917	3/29-4/21	4/22-5/15	5/16-6/9	6/10-7/3	7/4-7/28	7/29-8/21
1918	5/7-6/2	6/3-6/28	6/29-7/24	7/25-8/18	8/19-9/11	9/12-10/5
1919	2/27-3/22	3/23-4/16	4/17-5/12	5/13-6/7	6/8-7/7	7/8-11/8
1920	4/12-5/6	5/7-5/30	5/31-6/23	6/24-7/18	7/19-8/11	8/12-9/4
1921	2/3-3/6 4/26-6/1	3/7-4/25 6/2-7/7	7/8-8/5	8/6-8/31	9/1-9/25	9/26-10/20
1922	3/13-4/6	4/7-4/30	5/1-5/25	5/26-6/19	6/20-7/14	7/15-8/9
1923	4/27-5/21	5/22-6/14	6/15-7/9	7/10-8/3	8/4-8/27	8/28-9/20
1924	2/13-3/8	3/9-4/4	4/5-5/5	5/6-9/8	9/9-10/7	10/8-11/12
1925	3/28-4/20	4/21-5/15	5/16-6/8	6/9-7/3	7/4-7/27	7/28-8/21

Libra	Scorpio	Sagittarius	Capricorn	Aquarius	Pisces
8/23-9/17	9/17-10/12	10/12-1/16	1/16-2/9	2/9	3/5-3/29
			11/7-12/5	12/5-1/11	
10/7-10/31	10/31-11/24	11/24-12/18	12/18-1/11	2/6-4/4	1/11-2/6
					4/4-5/7
8/17-9/6	12/9-1/5			1/11-2/4	2/4-2/28
11/8-12/9					
9/6-9/30	9/30-10/25	1/5-1/30	1/30-2/24	2/24-3/19	3/19-4/13
		10/25-11/18	11/18-12/13	12/13-1/7	
10/21-11/14	11/14-12/8	12/8-1/1/06			1/7-2/3
8/11-9/7	9/7-10/9	10/9-12/15	1/1-1/25	1/25-2/18	2/18-3/14
	12/15-12/25	12/25-2/6			
9/22-10/16	10/16-11/9	11/9-12/3	2/6-3/6	3/6-4/2	4/2-4/27
			12/3-12/27	12/27-1/20	
11/3-11/28	11/28-12/22	12/22-1/15			1/20-2/14
8/23-9/17	9/17-10/12	10/12-11/17	1/15-2/9	2/9-3/5	3/5-3/29
			11/17-12/5	12/5-1/15	
10/7-10/30	10/31-11/23	11/24-12/17	12/18-12/31	1/1-1/15	1/16-1/28
				1/29-4/4	4/5-5/6
11/19-12/8	12/9-12/31		1/1-1/10	1/11-2/2	2/3-2/27
9/6-9/30	1/1-1/4	1/5-1/29	1/30-2/23	2/24-3/18	3/19-4/12
	10/1-10/24	10/25-11/17	11/18-12/12	12/13-12/31	
10/21-11/13	11/14-12/7	12/8-12/31		1/1-1/6	1/7-2/2
8/11-9/6	9/7-10/9	10/10-12/5	1/1-1/24	1/25-2/17	2/18-3/13
	12-6/12-30	12/31			
9/22-10/15	10/16-11/8	1/1-2/6	2/7-3/6	3/7-4/1	4/2-4/26
		11/9-12/2	12/3-12/26	12/27-12/31	
11/3-11/27	11/28-12/21	12/22-12/31		1/1-1/19	1/20-2/13
8/22-9/16	9/17-10/11	1/1-1/14	1/15-2/7	2/8-3/4	3/5-3/28
		10/12-11/6	11/7-12/5	12/6-12/31	
10/6-10/29	10/30-11/22	11/23-12/16	12/17-12/31	1/1-4/5	4/6-5/6
11/9-12/8	12/9-12/31		1/1-1/9	1/10-2/2	2/3-2/26
9/5-9/30	1/1-1/3	1/4-1/28	1/29-2/22	2/23-3/18	3/19-4/11
	9/31-10/23	10/24-11/17	11/18-12/11	12/12-12/31	
10/21-11/13	11/14-12/7	12/8-12/31		1/1-1/6	1/7-2/2
8/10-9/6	9/7-10/10	10/11-11/28	1/1-1/24	1/25-2/16	2/17-3/12
	11/29-12/31				
9/21-10/14	1/1	1/2-2/6	2/7-3/5	3/6-3/31	4/1-4/26
	10/15-11/7	11/8-12/1	12/2-12/25	12/26-12/31	
11/3-11/26	11/27-12/21	12/22-12/31		1/1-1/19	1/20-2/12
8/22-9/15	9/16-10/11	1/1-1/14	1/15-2/7	2/8-3/3	3/4-3/27
		10-12/11-6	11/7-12/5	12/6-12/31	

VENUS SIGNS 1901–2000

	Aries	Taurus	Gemini	Cancer	Leo	Virgo
1926	5/7-6/2	6/3-6/28	6/29-7/23	7/24-8/17	8/18-9/11	9/12-10/5
1927	2/27-3/22	3/23-4/16	4/17-5/11	5/12-6/7	6/8-7/7	7/8-11/9
1928	4/12-5/5	5/6-5/29	5/30-6/23	6/24-7/17	7/18-8/11	8/12-9/4
1929	2/3-3/7	3/8-4/19	7/8-8/4	8/5-8/30	8/31-9/25	9/26-10/19
	4/20-6/2	6/3-7/7				
1930	3/13-4/5	4/6-4/30	5/1-5/24	5/25-6/18	6/19-7/14	7/15-8/9
1931	4/26-5/20	5/21-6/13	6/14-7/8	7/9-8/2	8/3-8/26	8/27-9/19
1932	2/12-3/8	3/9-4/3	4/4-5/5	5/6-7/12	9/9-10/6	10/7-11/1
			7/13-7/27	7/28-9/8		
1933	3/27-4/19	4/20-5/28	5/29-6/8	6/9-7/2	7/3-7/26	7/27-8/20
1934	5/6-6/1	6/2-6/27	6/28-7/22	7/23-8/16	8/17-9/10	9/11-10/4
1935	2/26-3/21	3/22-4/15	4/16-5/10	5/11-6/6	6/7-7/6	7/7-11/8
1936	4/11-5/4	5/5-5/28	5/29-6/22	6/23-7/16	7/17-8/10	8/11-9/4
1937	2/2-3/8	3/9-4/17	7/7-8/3	8/4-8/29	8/30-9/24	9/25-10/18
	4/14-6/3	6/4-7/6				
1938	3/12-4/4	4/5-4/28	4/29-5/23	5/24-6/18	6/19-7/13	7/14-8/8
1939	4-25/5/19	5/20-6/13	6/14-7/8	7/9-8/1	8/2-8/25	8/26-9/19
1940	2/12-3/7	3/8-4/3	4/4-5/5	5/6-7/4	9/9-10/5	10/6-10/31
			7/5-7/31	8/1-9/8		
1941	3/27-4/19	4/20-5/13	5/14-6/6	6/7-7/1	7/2-7/26	7/27-8/20
1942	5/6-6/1	6/2-6/26	6/27-7/22	7/23-8/16	8/17-9/9	9/10-10/3
1943	2/25-3/20	3/21-4/14	4/15-5/10	5/11-6/6	6/7-7/6	7/7-11/8
1944	4/10-5/3	5/4-5/28	5/29-6/21	6/22-7/16	7/17-8/9	8/10-9/2
1945	2/2-3/10	3/11-4/6	7/7-8/3	8/4-8/29	8/30-9/23	9/24-10/18
	4/7-6/3	6/4-7/6				
1946	3/11-4/4	4/5-4/28	4/29-5/23	5/24-6/17	6/18-7/12	7/13-8/8
1947	4/25-5/19	5/20-6/12	6/13-7/7	7/8-8/1	8/2-8/25	8/26-9/18
1948	2/11-3/7	3/8-4/3	4/4-5/6	5/7-6/28	9/8-10/5	10/6-10/31
			6/29-8/2	8/3-9/7		
1949	3/26-4/19	4/20-5/13	5/14-6/6	6/7-6/30	7/1-7/25	7/26-8/19
1950	5/5-5/31	6/1-6/26	6/27-7/21	7/22-8/15	8/16-9/9	9/10-10/3
1951	2/25-3/21	3/22-4/15	4/16-5/10	5/11-6/6	6/7-7/7	7/8-11/9

Libra	Scorpio	Sagittarius	Capricorn	Aquarius	Pisces
10/6-10/29	10/30-11/22	11/23-12/16	12/17-12/31	1/1-4/5	4/6-5/6
11/10-12/8	12/9-12/31	1/1-1/7	1/8	1/9-2/1	2/2-2/26
9/5-9/28	1/1-1/3	1/4-1/28	1/29-2/22	2/23-3/17	3/18-4/11
	9/29-10/23	10/24-11/16	11/17-12/11	12/12-12/31	
10/20-11/12	11/13-12/6	12/7-12/30	12/31	1/1-1/5	1/6-2/2
8/10-9/6	9/7-10/11	10/12-11/21	1/1-1/23	1/24-2/16	2/17-3/12
	11/22-12/31				
9/20-10/13	1/1-1/3	1/4-2/6	2/7-3/4	3/5-3/31	4/1-4/25
	10/14-11/6	11/7-11/30	12/1-12/24	12/25-12/31	
11/2-11/25	11/26-12/20	12/21-12/31		1/1-1/18	1/19-2/11
8/21-9/14	9/15-10/10	1/1-1/13	1/14-2/6	2/7-3/2	3/3-3/26
		10/11-11/5	11/6-12/4	12/5-12/31	
10/5-10/28	10/29-11/21	11/22-12/15	12/16-12/31	1/1-4/5	4/6-5/5
11/9-12/7	12/8-12/31		1/1-1/7	1/8-1/31	2/1-2/25
9/5-9/27	1/1-1/2	1/3-1/27	1/28-2/21	2/22-3/16	3/17-4/10
	9/28-10/22	10/23-11/15	11/16-12/10	12/11-12/31	
10/19-11/11	11/12-12/5	12/6-12/29	12/30-12/31	1/1-1/5	1/6-2/1
8/9-9/6	9/7-10/13	10/14-11/14	1/1-1/22	1/23-2/15	2/16-3/11
	11/15-12/31				
9/20-10/13	1/1-1/3	1/4-2/5	2/6-3/4	3/5-3/30	3/31-4/24
	10/14-11/6	11/7-11/30	12/1-12/24	12/25-12/31	
11/1-11/25	11/26-12/19	12/20-12/31		1/1-1/18	1/19-2/11
8/21-9/14	9/15-10/9	1/1-1/12	1/13-2/5	2/6-3/1	3/2-3/26
		10/10-11/5	11/6-12/4	12/5-12/31	
10/4-10/27	10/28-11/20	11/21-12/14	12/15-12/31	1/1-4/4	4/6-5/5
11/9-12/7	12/8-12/31		1/1-1/7	1/8-1/31	2/1-2/24
9/3-9/27	1/1-1/2	1/3-1/27	1/28-2/20	2/21-3/16	3/17-4/9
	9/28-10/21	10/22-11/15	11/16-12/10	12/11-12/31	
10/19-11/11	11/12-12/5	12/6-12/29	12/30-12/31	1/1-1/4	1/5-2/1
8/9-9/6	9/7-10/15	10/16-11/7	1/1-1/21	1/22-2/14	2/15-3/10
	11/8-12/31				
9/19-10/12	1/1-1/4	1/5-2/5	2/6-3/4	3/5-3/29	3/30-4/24
	10/13-11/5	11/6-11/29	11/30-12/23	12/24-12/31	
11/1-1/25	11/26-12/19	12/20-12/31		1/1-1/17	1/18-2/10
8/20-9/14	9/15-10/9	1/1-1/12	1/13-2/5	2/6-3/1	3/2-3/25
		10/10-11/5	11/6-12/5	12/6-12/31	
10/4-10/27	10/28-11/20	11/21-12/13	12/14-12/31	1/1-4/5	4/6-5/4
11/10-12/7	12/8-12/31		1/1-1/7	1/8-1/31	2/1-2/24

VENUS SIGNS 1901–2000

	Aries	Taurus	Gemini	Cancer	Leo	Virgo
1952	4/10-5/4	5/5-5/28	5/29-6/21	6/22-7/16	7/17-8/9	8/10-9/3
1953	2/2-3/13	3/4-3/31	7/8-8/3	8/4-8/29	8/30-9/24	9/25-10/18
	4/1-6/5	6/6-7/7				
1954	3/12-4/4	4/5-4/28	4/29-5/23	5/24-6/17	6/18-7/13	7/14-8/8
1955	4/25-5/19	5/20-6/13	6/14-7/7	7/8-8/1	8/2-8/25	8/26-9/18
1956	2/12-3/7	3/8-4/4	4/5-5/7	5/8-6/23	9/9-10/5	10/6-10/31
			6:24-8/4	8/5-9/8		
1957	3/26-4/19	4/20-5/13	5/14-6/6	6/7-7/1	7/2-7/26	7/7-8/19
1958	5/6-5/31	6/1-6/26	6/27-7/22	7/23-8/15	8/16-9/9	9/10-10/3
1959	2/25-3/20	3/21-4/14	4/15-5/10	5/11-6/6	6/7-7/8	7/9-9/20
					9/21-9/24	9/25-11/9
1960	4/10-5/3	5/4-5/28	5/29-6/21	6/22-7/15	7/16-8/9	8/10-9/2
1961	2/3-6/5	6/6-7/7	7/8-8/3	8/4-8/29	8/30-9/23	9/24-10/17
1962	3/11-4/3	4/4-4/28	4/29-5/22	5/23-6/17	6/18-7/12	7/13-8/8
1963	4/24-5/18	5/19-6/12	6/13-7/7	7/8-7/31	8/1-8/25	8/26-9/18
1964	2/11-3/7	3/8-4/4	4/5-5/9	5/10-6/17	9/9-10/5	10/6-10/31
			6/18-8/5	8/6-9/8		
1965	3/26-4/18	4/19-5/12	5/13-6/6	6/7-6/30	7/1-7/25	7/26-8/19
1966	5/6-6/31	6/1-6/26	6/27-7/21	7/22-8/15	8/16-9/8	9/9-10/2
1967	2/24-3/20	3/21-4/14	4/15-5/10	5/11-6/6	6/7-7/8	7/9-9/9
					9/10-10/1	10/2-11/9
1968	4/9-5/3	5/4-5/27	5/28-6/20	6/21-7/15	7/16-8/8	8/9-9/2
1969	2/3-6/6	6/7-7/6	7/7-8/3	8/4-8/28	8/29-9/22	9/23-10/17
1970	3/11-4/3	4/4-4/27	4/28-5/22	5/23-6/16	6/17-7/12	7/13-8/8
1971	4/24-5/18	5/19-6/12	6/13-7/6	7/7-7/31	8/1-8/24	8/25-9/17
1972	2/11-3/7	3/8-4/3	4/4-5/10	5/11-6/11		
			6/12-8/6	8/7-9/8	9/9-10/5	10/6-10/30
1973	3/25-4/18	4/18-5/12	5/13-6/5	6/6-6/29	7/1-7/25	7/26-8/19
1974						
	55-5/31	6/1-6/25	6/26-7/21	7/22-8/14	8/15-9/8	9/9-10/2
1975	2/24-3/20	3/21-4/13	4/14-5/9	5/10-6/6	6/7-7/9	7/10-9/2
					9/3-10/4	10/5-11/9

Libra	Scorpio	Sagittarius	Capricorn	Aquarius	Pisces
9/4-9/27	1/1-1/2	1/3-1/27	1/28-2/20	2/21-3/16	3/17-4/9
	9/28-10/21	10/22-11/15	11/16-12/10	12/11-12/31	
10/19-11/11	11/12-12/5	12/6-12/29	12/30-12/31	1/1-1/5	1/6-2/1
8/9-9/6	9/7-10/22	10/23-10/27	1/1-1/22	1/23-2/15	2/16-3/11
	10/28-12/31				
9/19-10/13	1/1-1/6	1/7-2/5	2/6-3/4	3/5-3/30	3/31-4/24
	10/14-11/5	11/6-11/30	12/1-12/24	12/25-12/31	
11/1-11/25	11/26-12/19	12/20-12/31		1/1-1/17	1/18-2/11
8/20-9/14	9/15-10/9	1/1-1/12	1/13-2/5	2/6-3/1	3/2-3/25
		10/10-11/5	11/6-12/16	12/7-12/31	
10/4-10/27	10/28-11/20	11/21-12/14	12/15-12/31	1/1-4/6	4/7-5/5
11/10-12/7	12/8-12/31		1/1-1/7	1/8-1/31	2/1-2/24
9/3-9/26	1/1-1/2	1/3-1/27	1/28-2/20	2/21-3/15	3/16-4/9
	9/27-10/21	10/22-11/15	11/16-12/10	12/11-12/31	
10/18-11/11	11/12-12/4	12/5-12/28	12/29-12/31	1/1-1/5	1/6-2/2
8/9-9/6	9/7-12/31		1/1-1/21	1/22-2/14	2/15-3/10
9/19-10/12	1/1-1/6	1/7-2/5	2/6-3/4	3/5-3/29	3/30-4/23
	10/13-11/5	11/6-11/29	11/30-12/23	12/24-12/31	
11/1-11/24	11/25-12/19	12/20-12/31		1/1-1/16	1/17-2/10
8/20-9/13	9/14-10/9	1/1-1/12	1/13-2/5	2/6-3/1	3/2-3/25
		10/10-11/5	11/6-12/7	12/8-12/31	
10/3-10/26	10/27-11/19	11/20-12/13	2/7-2/25	1/1-2/6	4/7-5/5
			12/14-12/31	2/26-4/6	
11/10-12/7	12/8-12/23		1/1-1/6	1/7-1/30	1/31-2/23
9/3-9/26	1/1	1/2-1/26	1/27-2/20	2/21-3/15	3/16-4/8
	9/27-10/21	10/22-11/14	11/15-12/9	12/10-12/31	
10/18-11/10	11/11-12/4	12/5-12/28	12/29-12/31	1/1-1/4	1/5-2/2
8/9-9/7	9/8-12/31		1/1-1/21	1/22-2/14	2/15-3/10
9/18-10/11	1/1-1/7	1/8-2/5	2/6-3/4	3/5-3/29	3/30-4/23
	10/12-11/5	11/6-11/29	11/30-12/23	12/24-12/31	
	11/25-12/18	12/19-12/31		1/1-1/16	1/17-2/10
10/31-11/24					
8/20-9/13		1/1-1/12	1/13-2/4	2/5-2/28	3/1-3/24
		10/9-11/5	11/6-12/7	12/8-12/31	
			1/30-2/28	1/1-1/29	
10/3-10/26	10/27-11/19	11/20-12/13	12/14-12/31	3/1-4/6	4/7-5/4
			1/1-1/6	1/7-1/30	1/31-2/23
11/10-12/7	12/8-12/31				

VENUS SIGNS 1901–2000

	Aries	Taurus	Gemini	Cancer	Leo	Virgo
1976	4/8-5/2	5/2-5/27	5/27-6/20	6/20-7/14	7/14-8/8	8/8-9/1
1977	2/2-6/6	6/6-7/6	7/6-8/2	8/2-8/28	8/28-9/22	9/22-10/17
1978	3/9-4/2	4/2-4/27	4/27-5/22	5/22-6/16	6/16-7/12	7/12-8/6
1979	4/23-5/18	5/18-6/11	6/11-7/6	7/6-7/30	7/30-8/24	8/24-9/17
1980	2/9-3/6	3/6-4/3	4/3-5/12	5/12-6/5	9/7-10/4	10/4-10/30
			6/5-8/6	8/6-9/7		
1981	3/24-4/17	4/17-5/11	5/11-6/5	6/5-6/29	6/29-7/24	7/24-8/18
1982	5/4-5/30	5/30-6/25	6/25-7/20	7/20-8/14	8/14-9/7	9/7-10/2
1983	2/22-3/19	3/19-4/13	4/13-5/9	5/9-6/6	6/6-7/10	7/10-8/27
					8/27-10/5	10/5-11/9
1984	4/7-5/2	5/2-5/26	5/26-6/20	6/20-7/14	7/14-8/7	8/7-9/1
1985	2/2-6/6	6/8-7/6	7/6-8/2	8/2-8/28	8/28-9/22	9/22-10/16
1986	3/9-4/2	4/2-4/26	4/26-5/21	5/21-6/15	6/15-7/11	7/11-8/7
1987	4/22-5/17	5/17-6/11	6/11-7/5	7/5-7/30	7/30-8/23	8/23-9/16
1988	2/9-3/6	3/6-4/3	4/3-5/17	5/17-5/27	9/7-10/4	10/4-10/29
			5/27-8/6	8/6-9/7		
1989	3/23-4/16	4/16-5/11	5/11-6/4	6/4-6/29	6/29-7/24	7/24-8/18
1990	5/4-5/30	5/30-6/25	6/25-7/20	7/20-8/13	8/13-9/7	9/7-10/1
1991	2/22-3/18	3/18-4/13	4/13-5/9	5/9-6/6	6/6-7/11	7/11-8/21
					8/21-10/6	10/6-11/9
1992	4/7-5/1	5/1-5/26	5/26-6/19	6/19-7/13	7/13-8/7	8/7-8/31
1993	2/2-6/6	6/6-7/6	7/6-8/1	8/1-8/27	8/27-9/21	9/21-10/16
1994	3/8-4/1	4/1-4/26	4/26-5/21	5/21-6/15	6/15-7/11	7/11-8/7
1995	4/22-5/16	5/16-6/10	6/10-7/5	7/5-7/29	7/29-8/23	8/23-9/16
1996	2/9-3/6	3/6-4/3	4/3-8/7	8/7-9/7	9/7-10/4	10/4-10/29
1997	3/23-4/16	4/16-5/10	5/10-6/4	6/4-6/28	6/28-7/23	7/23-8/17
1998	5/3-5/29	5/29-6/24	6/24-7/19	7/19-8/13	8/13-9/6	9/6-9/30
1999	2/21-3/18	3/18-4/12	4/12-5/8	5/8-6/5	6/5-7/12	7/12-8/15
					8/15-10/7	10/7-11/9
2000	4/6-5/1	5/1-5/25	5/25-6/13	6/13-7/13	7/13-8/6	8/6-8/31

Libra	Scorpio	Sagittarius	Capricorn	Aquarius	Pisces
9/1-9/26	9/26-10/20	1/1-1/26	1/26-2/19	2/19-3/15	3/15-4/8
		10/20-11/14	11/14-12/6	12/9-1/4	
10/17-11/10	11/10-12/4	12/4-12/27	12/27-1/20		1/4-2/2
8/6-9/7	9/7-1/7			1/20-2/13	2/13-3/9
9/17-10/11	10/11-11/4	1/7-2/5	2/5-3/3	3/3-3/29	3/29-4/23
		11/4-11/28	11/28-12/22	12/22-1/16	
10/30-11/24	11/24-12/18	12/18-1/11			1/16-2/9
8/18-9/12	9/12-10/9	10/9-11/5	1/11-2/4	2/4-2/28	2/28-3/24
			11/5-12/8	12/8-1/23	
10/2-10/26	10/26-11/18	11/18-12/12	1/23-3/2	3/2-4/6	4/6-5/4
			12/12-1/5		
11/9-12/6	12/6-1/1			1/5-1/29	1/29-2/22
9/1-9/25	9/25-10/20	1/1-1/25	1/25-2/19	2/19-3/14	3/14-4/7
		10/20-11/13	11/13-12/9		
10/16-11/9	11/9-12/3	12/3-12/27			1/4-2/2
8/7-9/7	9/7-1/7			1/20-3/13	2/13-3/9
9/16-10/10	10/10-11/3	1/7-2/5	2/5-3/3	3/3-3/28	3/28-4/22
		11/3-11/28	11/28-12/22	12/22-1/15	
10/29-11/23	11/23-12/17	12/17-1/10			1/15-2/9
8/18-9/12	9/12-10/8	10/8-11/5	1/10-2/3	2/3-2/27	2/27-3/23
			11/5-12/10	12/10-1/16	
10/1-10/25	10/25-11/18	11/18-12/12	1/16-3/3	3/3-4/6	4/6-5/4
			12/12-1/5		
8/21-12/6	12/6-12/31	12/21-1/25/92		1/5-1/29	1/29-2/22
8/31-9/25	9/25-10/19	10/19-11/13	1/25-2/18	2/18-3/13	3/13-4/7
			11/13-12/8	12/8-1/3	
10/16-11/9	11/9-12/2	12/2-12/26	12/26-1/19		1/3-2/2
8/7-9/7	9/7-1/7			1/19-2/12	2/12-3/8
9/16-10/10	10/10-11/13	1/7-2/4	2/4-3/2	3/2-3/28	3/28-4/22
		11/3-11/27	11/27-12/21	12/21-1/15	
10/29-11/23	11/23-12/17	12/17-1/10/97			1/15-2/9
8/17-9/12	9/12-10/8	10/8-11/5	1/10-2/3	2/3-2/27	2/27-3/23
			11/5-12/12	12/12-1/9	
9/30-10/24	10/24-11/17	11/17-12/11	1/9-3/4	3/4-4/6	4/6-5/3
11/9-12/5	12/5-12/31	12/31-1/24		1/4-1/28	1/28-2/21
8/31-9/24	9/24-10/19	10/19-11/13	1/24-2/18	2/18-3/12	3/13-4/6
			11/13-12/8	12/8	

MARS SIGN 1901–2000

1901	MAR	1	Leo
	May	11	Vir
	JUL	13	Lib
	AUG	31	Scp
	OCT	14	Sag
	NOV	24	Cap
1902	JAN	1	Aqu
	FEB	8	Pic
	MAR	19	Ari
	APR	27	Tau
	JUN	7	Gem
	JUL	20	Can
	SEP	4	Leo
	OCT	23	Vir
	DEC	20	Lib
1903	APR	19	Vir
	MAY	30	Lib
	AUG	6	Scp
	SEP	22	Sag
	NOV	3	Cap
	DEC	12	Aqu
1904	JAN	19	Pic
	FEB	27	Ari
	APR	6	Tau
	MAY	18	Gem
	JUN	30	Can
	AUG	15	Leo
	OCT	1	Vir
	NOV	20	Lib
1905	JAN	13	Scp
	AUG	21	Sag
	OCT	8	Cap
	NOV	18	Aqu
	DEC	27	Pic
1906	FEB	4	Ari
	MAR	17	Tau
	APR	28	Gem
	JUN	11	Can
	JUL	27	Leo
	SEP	12	Vir
	OCT	30	Lib
	DEC	17	Scp
1907	FEB	5	Sag
	APR	1	Cap
	OCT	13	Aqu
	NOV	29	Pic
1908	JAN	11	Ari
	FEB	23	Tau
	APR	7	Gem
	MAY	22	Can
	JUL	8	Leo
	AUG	24	Vir
	OCT	10	Lib
	NOV	25	Scp
1909	JAN	10	Sag
	FEB	24	Cap
	APR	9	Aqu
	MAY	25	Pic
	JUL	21	Ari
	SEP	26	Pic
	NOV	20	Ari
1910	JAN	23	Tau
	MAR	14	Gem
	MAY	1	Can
	JUN	19	Leo
	AUG	6	Vir
	SEP	22	Lib
	NOV	6	Scp
	DEC	20	Sag
1911	JAN	31	Cap
	MAR	14	Aqu
	APR	23	Pic

	JUN	2	Ari
	JUL	15	Tau
	SEP	5	Gem
	NOV	30	Tau
1912	JAN	30	Gem
	APR	5	Can
	MAY	28	Leo
	JUL	17	Vir
	SEP	2	Lib
	OCT	18	Scp
	NOV	30	Sag
1913	JAN	10	Cap
	FEB	19	Aqu
	MAR	30	Pic
	MAY	8	Ari
	JUN	17	Tau
	JUL	29	Gem
	SEP	15	Can
1914	MAY	1	Leo
	JUN	26	Vir
	AUG	14	Lib
	SEP	29	Scp
	NOV	11	Sag
	DEC	22	Cap
1915	JAN	30	Aqu
	MAR	9	Pic
	APR	16	Ari
	MAY	26	Tau
	JUL	6	Gem
	AUG	19	Can
	OCT	7	Leo
1916	MAY	28	Vir
	JUL	23	Lib
	SEP	8	Scp
	OCT	22	Sag
	DEC	1	Cap
1917	JAN	9	Aqu
	FEB	16	Pic
	MAR	26	Ari
	MAY	4	Tau
	JUN	14	Gem
	JUL	28	Can
	SEP	12	Leo
	NOV	2	Vir
1918	JAN	11	Lib
	FEB	25	Vir
	JUN	23	Lib
	AUG	17	Scp
	OCT	1	Sag
	NOV	11	Cap
	DEC	20	Aqu
1919	JAN	27	Pic
	MAR	6	Ari
	APR	15	Tau
	MAY	26	Gem
	JUL	8	Can
	AUG	23	Leo
	OCT	10	Vir
	NOV	30	Lib
1920	JAN	31	Scp
	APR	23	Lib
	JUL	10	Scp
	SEP	4	Sag
	OCT	18	Cap
	NOV	27	Aqu
1921	JAN	5	Pic
	FEB	13	Ari
	MAR	25	Tau
	MAY	6	Gem
	JUN	18	Can
	AUG	3	Leo
	SEP	19	Vir
	NOV	6	Lib
	DEC	26	Scp
1922	FEB	18	Sag
	SEP	13	Cap
	OCT	30	Aqu
	DEC	11	Pic

1923	JAN	21	Ari
	MAR	4	Tau
	APR	16	Gem
	MAY	30	Can
	JUL	16	Leo
	SEP	1	Vir
	OCT	18	Lib
	DEC	4	Scp
1924	JAN	19	Sag
	MAR	6	Cap
	APR	24	Aqu
	JUN	24	Pic
	AUG	24	Aqu
	OCT	19	Pic
	DEC	19	Ari
1925	FEB	5	Tau
	MAR	24	Gem
	MAY	9	Can
	JUN	26	Leo
	AUG	12	Vir
	SEP	28	Lib
	NOV	13	Scp
	DEC	28	Sag
1926	FEB	9	Cap
	MAR	23	Aqu
	MAY	3	Pic
	JUN	15	Ari
	AUG	1	Tau
1927	FEB	22	Gem
	APR	17	Can
	JUN	6	Leo
	JUL	25	Vir
	SEP	10	Lib
	OCT	26	Scp
	DEC	8	Sag
1928	JAN	19	Cap
	FEB	28	Aqu
	APR	7	Pic
	MAY	16	Ari
	JUN	26	Tau
	AUG	9	Gem
	OCT	3	Can
	DEC	20	Gem
1929	MAR	10	Can
	MAY	13	Leo
	JUL	4	Vir
	AUG	21	Lib
	OCT	6	Scp
	NOV	18	Sag
	DEC	29	Cap
1930	FEB	6	Aqu
	MAR	17	Pic
	APR	24	Ari
	JUN	3	Tau
	JUL	14	Gem
	AUG	28	Can
	OCT	20	Leo
1931	FEB	16	Can
	MAR	30	Leo
	JUN	10	Vir
	AUG	1	Lib
	SEP	17	Scp
	OCT	30	Sag
	DEC	10	Cap
1932	JAN	18	Aqu
	FEB	25	Pic
	APR	3	Ari
	MAY	12	Tau
	JUN	22	Gem
	AUG	4	Can
	SEP	20	Leo
	NOV	13	Vir
1933	JUL	6	Lib
	AUG	26	Scp
	OCT	9	Sag
	NOV	19	Cap
	DEC	28	Aqu
1934	FEB	4	Pic

	MAR	14	Ari
	APR	22	Tau
	JUN	2	Gem
	JUL	15	Can
	AUG	30	Leo
	OCT	18	Vir
	DEC	11	Lib
1935	JUL	29	Scp
	SEP	16	Sag
	OCT	28	Cap
	DEC	7	Aqu
1936	JAN	14	Pic
	FEB	22	Ari
	APR	1	Tau
	MAY	13	Gem
	JUN	25	Can
	AUG	10	Leo
	SEP	26	Vir
	NOV	14	Lib
1937	JAN	5	Scp
	MAR	13	Sag
	MAY	14	Scp
	AUG	8	Sag
	SEP	30	Cap
	NOV	11	Aqu
	DEC	21	Pic
1938	JAN	30	Ari
	MAR	12	Tau
	APR	23	Gem
	JUN	7	Can
	JUL	22	Leo
	SEP	7	Vir
	OCT	25	Lib
	DEC	11	Scp
1939	JAN	29	Sag
	MAR	21	Cap
	MAY	25	Aqu
	JUL	21	Cap
	SEP	24	Aqu
	NOV	19	Pic
1940	JAN	4	Ari
	FEB	17	Tau
	APR	1	Gem
	MAY	17	Can
	JUL	3	Leo
	AUG	19	Vir
	OCT	5	Lib
	NOV	20	Scp
1941	JAN	4	Sag
	FEB	17	Cap
	APR	2	Aqu
	MAY	16	Pic
	JUL	2	Ari
1942	JAN	11	Tau
	MAR	7	Gem
	APR	26	Can
	JUN	14	Leo
	AUG	1	Vir
	SEP	17	Lib
	NOV	1	Scp
	DEC	15	Sag
1943	JAN	26	Cap
	MAR	8	Aqu
	APR	17	Pic
	MAY	27	Ari
	JUL	7	Tau
	AUG	23	Gem
1944	MAR	28	Can
	MAY	22	Leo
	JUL	12	Vir
	AUG	29	Lib
	OCT	13	Scp
	NOV	25	Sag
1945	JAN	5	Cap
	FEB	14	Aqu
	MAR	25	Pic
	MAY	2	Ari
	JUN	11	Tau

	JUL	23	Gem
	SEP	7	Can
	NOV	11	Leo
	DEC	26	Can
1946	APR	22	Leo
	JUN	20	Vir
	AUG	9	Lib
	SEP	24	Scp
	NOV	6	Sag
	DEC	17	Cap
1947	JAN	25	Aqu
	MAR	4	Pic
	APR	11	Ari
	MAY	21	Tau
	JUL	1	Gem
	AUG	13	Can
	OCT	1	Leo
	DEC	1	Vir
1948	FEB	12	Leo
	MAY	18	Vir
	JUL	17	Lib
	SEP	3	Scp
	OCT	17	Sag
	NOV	26	Cap
1949	JAN	4	Aqu
	FEB	11	Pic
	MAR	21	Ari
	APR	30	Tau
	JUN	10	Gem
	JUL	23	Can
	SEP	7	Leo
	OCT	27	Vir
	DEC	26	Lib
1950	MAR	28	Vir
	JUN	11	Lib
	AUG	10	Scp
	SEP	25	Sag
	NOV	6	Cap
	DEC	15	Aqu

1951	JAN	22	Pic
	MAR	1	Ari
	APR	10	Tau
	MAY	21	Gem
	JUL	3	Can
	AUG	18	Leo
	OCT	5	Vir
	NOV	24	Lib
1952	JAN	20	Scp
	AUG	27	Sag
	OCT	12	Cap
	NOV	21	Aqu
	DEC	30	Pic
1953	FEB	8	Ari
	MAR	20	Tau
	MAY	1	Gem
	JUN	14	Can
	JUL	29	Leo
	SEP	14	Vir
	NOV	1	Lib
	DEC	20	Scp
1954	FEB	9	Sag
	APR	12	Cap
	JUL	3	Sag
	AUG	24	Cap
	OCT	21	Aqu
	DEC	4	Pic
1955	JAN	15	Ari
	FEB	26	Tau
	APR	10	Gem
	MAY	26	Can
	JUL	11	Leo
	AUG	27	Vir
	OCT	13	Lib
	NOV	29	Scp
1956	JAN	14	Sag
	FEB	28	Cap
	APR	14	Aqu
	JUN	3	Pic

	DEC	6	Ari
1957	JAN	28	Tau
	MAR	17	Gem
	MAY	4	Can
	JUN	21	Leo
	AUG	8	Vir
	SEP	24	Lib
	NOV	8	Scp
	DEC	23	Sag
1958	FEB	3	Cap
	MAR	17	Aqu
	APR	27	Pic
	JUN	7	Ari
	JUL	21	Tau
	SEP	21	Gem
	OCT	29	Tau
1959	FEB	10	Gem
	APR	10	Can
	JUN	1	Leo
	JUL	20	Vir
	SEP	5	Lib
	OCT	21	Scp
	DEC	3	Sag
1960	JAN	14	Cap
	FEB	23	Aqu
	APR	2	Pic
	MAY	11	Ari
	JUN	20	Tau
	AUG	2	Gem
	SEP	21	Can
1961	FEB	5	Gem
	FEB	7	Can
	MAY	6	Leo
	JUN	28	Vir
	AUG	17	Lib
	OCT	1	Scp
	NOV	13	Sag
	DEC	24	Cap
1962	FEB	1	Aqu
	MAR	12	Pic
	APR	19	Ari
	MAY	28	Tau
	JUL	9	Gem
	AUG	22	Can
	OCT	11	Leo
1963	JUN	3	Vir
	JUL	27	Lib
	SEP	12	Scp
	OCT	25	Sag
	DEC	5	Cap
1964	JAN	13	Aqu
	FEB	20	Pic
	MAR	29	Ari
	MAY	7	Tau
	JUN	17	Gem
	JUL	30	Can
	SEP	15	Leo
	NOV	6	Vir
1965	JUN	29	Lib
	AUG	20	Scp
	OCT	4	Sag
	NOV	14	Cap
	DEC	23	Aqu
1966	JAN	30	Pic
	MAR	9	Ari
	APR	17	Tau
	MAY	28	Gem
	JUL	11	Can
	AUG	25	Leo
	OCT	12	Vir
	DEC	4	Lib
1967	FEB	12	Scp
	MAR	31	Lib
	JUL	19	Scp
	SEP	10	Sag
	OCT	23	Cap
	DEC	1	Aqu
1968	JAN	9	Pic

Year	Month	Day	Sign
	FEB	17	Ari
	MAR	27	Tau
	MAY	8	Gem
	JUN	21	Can
	AUG	5	Leo
	SEP	21	Vir
	NOV	9	Lib
	DEC	29	Scp
1969	FEB	25	Sag
	SEP	21	Cap
	NOV	4	Aqu
	DEC	15	Pic
1970	JAN	24	Ari
	MAR	7	Tau
	APR	18	Gem
	JUN	2	Can
	JUL	18	Leo
	SEP	3	Vir
	OCT	20	Lib
	DEC	6	Scp
1971	JAN	23	Sag
	MAR	12	Cap
	MAY	3	Aqu
	NOV	6	Pic
	DEC	26	Ari
1972	FEB	10	Tau
	MAR	27	Gem
	MAY	12	Can
	JUN	28	Leo
	AUG	15	Vir
	SEP	30	Lib
	NOV	15	Scp
	DEC	30	Sag
1973	FEB	12	Cap
	MAR	26	Aqu
	MAY	8	Pic
	JUN	20	Ari
	AUG	12	Tau
	OCT	29	Ari
	DEC	24	Tau
1974	FEB	27	Gem
	APR	20	Can
	JUN	9	Leo
	JUL	27	Vir
	SEP	12	Lib
	OCT	28	Scp
	DEC	10	Sag
1975	JAN	21	Cap
	MAR	3	Aqu
	APR	11	Pic
	MAY	21	Ari
	JUL	1	Tau
	AUG	14	Gem
	OCT	17	Can
	NOV	25	Gem
1976	MAR	18	Can
	MAY	16	Leo
	JUL	6	Vir
	AUG	24	Lib
	OCT	8	Scp
	NOV	20	Sag
1977	JAN	1	Cap
	FEB	9	Aqu
	MAR	20	Pic
	APR	27	Ari
	JUN	6	Tau
	JUL	17	Gem
	SEP	1	Can
	OCT	26	Leo
1978	JAN	26	Can
	APR	10	Leo
	JUN	14	Vir
	AUG	4	Lib
	SEP	19	Scp
	NOV	2	Sag
	DEC	12	Cap
1979	JAN	20	Aqu
	FEB	27	Pic

Year	Month	Day	Sign
	APR	7	Ari
	MAY	16	Tau
	JUN	26	Gem
	AUG	8	Can
	SEP	24	Leo
	NOV	19	Vir
1980	MAR	11	Leo
	MAY	4	Vir
	JUL	10	Lib
	AUG	29	Scp
	OCT	12	Sag
	NOV	22	Cap
	DEC	30	Aqu
1981	FEB	6	Pic
	MAR	17	Ari
	APR	25	Tau
	JUN	5	Gem
	JUL	18	Can
	SEP	2	Leo
	OCT	21	Vir
	DEC	16	Lib
1982	AUG	3	Scp
	SEP	20	Sag
	OCT	31	Cap
	DEC	10	Aqu
1983	JAN	17	Pic
	FEB	25	Ari
	APR	5	Tau
	MAY	16	Gem
	JUN	29	Can
	AUG	13	Leo
	SEP	30	Vir
	NOV	18	Lib
1984	JAN	11	Scp
	AUG	17	Sag
	OCT	5	Cap
	NOV	15	Aqu
	DEC	25	Pic
1985	FEB	2	Ari
	MAR	15	Tau
	APR	26	Gem
	JUN	9	Can
	JUL	25	Leo
	SEP	10	Vir
	OCT	27	Lib
	DEC	14	Scp
1986	FEB	2	Sag
	MAR	28	Cap
	OCT	9	Aqu
	NOV	26	Pic
1987	JAN	8	Ari
	FEB	20	Tau
	APR	5	Gem
	MAY	21	Can
	JUL	6	Leo
	AUG	22	Vir
	OCT	8	Lib
	NOV	24	Scp
1988	JAN	8	Sag
	FEB	22	Cap
	APR	6	Aqu
	MAY	22	Pic
	JUL	13	Ari
	OCT	23	Pic
	NOV	1	Ari
1989	JAN	19	Tau
	MAR	11	Gem
	APR	29	Can
	JUN	16	Leo
	AUG	3	Vir
	SEP	19	Lib
	NOV	4	Scp
	DEC	18	Sag
1990	JAN	29	Cap
	MAR	11	Aqu
	APR	20	Pic
	MAY	31	Ari
	JUL	12	Tau

	AUG	31	Gem
	DEC	14	Tau
1991	JAN	21	Gem
	APR	3	Can
	MAY	26	Leo
	JUL	15	Vir
	SEP	1	Lib
	OCT	16	Scp
	NOV	29	Sag
1992	JAN	9	Cap
	FEB	18	Aqu
	MAR	28	Pic
	MAY	5	Ari
	JUN	14	Tau
	JUL	26	Gem
	SEP	12	Can
1993	APR	27	Leo
	JUN	23	Vir
	AUG	12	Lib
	SEP	27	Scp
	NOV	9	Sag
	DEC	20	Cap
1994	JAN	28	Aqu
	MAR	7	Pic
	APR	14	Ari
	MAY	23	Tau
	JUL	3	Gem
	AUG	16	Can
	OCT	4	Leo
	DEC	12	Vir
1995	JAN	22	Leo
	MAY	25	Vir
	JUL	21	Lib
	SEP	7	Scp
	OCT	20	Sag
	NOV	30	Cap
1996	JAN	8	Aqu
	FEB	15	Pic
	MAR	24	Ari
	MAY	2	Tau
	JUN	12	Gem
	JUL	25	Can
	SEP	9	Leo
	OCT	30	Vir
1997	JAN	3	Lib
	MAR	8	Vir
	JUN	19	Lib
	AUG	14	Scp
	SEP	28	Sag
	NOV	9	Cap
	DEC	18	Aqu
1998	JAN	25	Pic
	MAR	4	Ari
	APR	13	Tau
	MAY	24	Gem
	JUL	6	Can
	AUG	20	Leo
	OCT	7	Vir
	NOV	27	Lib
1999	JAN	26	Scp
	MAY	5	Lib
	JUL	5	Scp
	SEP	2	Sag
	OCT	17	Cap
	NOV	26	Aqu
2000	JAN	4	Pic
	FEB	12	Ari
	MAR	23	Tau
	MAY	3	Gem
	JUN	16	Can
	AUG	1	Leo
	SEP	17	Vir
	NOV	4	Lib
	DEC	23	Scp

JUPITER SIGN 1901–2000

Year	Month	Day	Sign
1901	JAN	19	Cap
1902	FEB	6	Aqu
1903	FEB	20	Pic
1904	MAR	1	Ari
	AUG	8	Tau
	AUG	31	Ari
1905	MAR	7	Tau
	JUL	21	Gem
	DEC	4	Tau
1906	MAR	9	Gem
	JUL	30	Can
1907	AUG	18	Leo
1908	SEP	12	Vir
1909	OCT	11	Lib
1910	NOV	11	Scp
1911	DEC	10	Sag
1913	JAN	2	Cap
1914	JAN	21	Aqu
1915	FEB	4	Pic
1916	FEB	12	Ari
	JUN	26	Tau
	OCT	26	Ari
1917	FEB	12	Tau
	JUN	29	Gem
1918	JUL	13	Can
1919	AUG	2	Leo
1920	AUG	27	Vir
1921	SEP	25	Lib
1922	OCT	26	Scp
1923	NOV	24	Sag
1924	DEC	18	Cap
1926	JAN	6	Aqu
1927	JAN	18	Pic
	JUN	6	Ari
	SEP	11	Pic
1928	JAN	23	Ari
	JUN	4	Tau
1929	JUN	12	Gem
1930	JUN	26	Can
1931	JUL	17	Leo
1932	AUG	11	Vir
1933	SEP	10	Lib
1934	OCT	11	Scp
1935	NOV	9	Sag
1936	DEC	2	Cap
1937	DEC	20	Aqu
1938	MAY	14	Pic
	JUL	30	Aqu
	DEC	29	Pic
1939	MAY	11	Ari
	OCT	30	Pic
	DEC	20	Ari
1940	MAY	16	Tau
1941	MAY	26	Gem
1942	JUN	10	Can
1943	JUN	30	Leo
1944	JUL	26	Vir
1945	AUG	25	Lib
1946	SEP	25	Scp
1947	OCT	24	Sag
1948	NOV	15	Cap
1949	APR	12	Aqu
	JUN	27	Cap
	NOV	30	Aqu
1950	APR	15	Pic
	SEP	15	Aqu
	DEC	1	Pic
1951	APR	21	Ari
1952	APR	28	Tau
1953	MAY	9	Gem
1954	MAY	24	Can
1955	JUN	13	Leo
	NOV	17	Vir
1956	JAN	18	Leo
	JUL	7	Vir
	DEC	13	Lib

1957 FEB 19 Vir
AUG 7 Lib
1958 JAN 13 Scp
MAR 20 Lib
SEP 7 Scp
1959 FEB 10 Sag
APR 24 Scp
OCT 5 Sag
1960 MAR 1 Cap
JUN 10 Sag
OCT 26 Cap
1961 MAR 15 Aqu
AUG 12 Cap
NOV 4 Aqu
1962 MAR 25 Pic
1963 APR 4 Ari
1964 APR 12 Tau
1965 APR 22 Gem
SEP 21 Can
NOV 17 Gem
1966 MAY 5 Can
SEP 27 Leo
1967 JAN 16 Can
MAY 23 Leo
OCT 19 Vir
1968 FEB 27 Leo
JUN 15 Vir
NOV 15 Lib
1969 MAR 30 Vir
JUL 15 Lib
DEC 16 Scp
1970 APR 30 Lib
AUG 15 Scp
1971 JAN 14 Sag
JUN 5 Scp
SEP 11 Sag
1972 FEB 6 Cap
JUL 24 Sag
SEP 25 Cap

1973 FEB 23 Aqu
1974 MAR 8 Pic
1975 MAR 18 Ari
1976 MAR 26 Tau
AUG 23 Gem
OCT 16 Tau
1977 APR 3 Gem
AUG 20 Can
DEC 30 Gem
1978 APR 12 Can
SEP 5 Leo
1979 FEB 28 Can
APR 20 Leo
SEP 29 Vir
1980 OCT 27 Lib
1981 Nov 27 Scp
1982 DEC 26 Sag
1984 JAN 19 Cap
1985 FEB 6 Aqu
1986 FEB 20 Pic
1987 MAR 2 Ari
1988 MAR 8 Tau
JUL 22 Gem
NOV 30 Tau
1989 MAR 11 Gem
JUL 30 Can
1990 AUG 18 Leo
1991 SEP 12 Vir
1992 OCT 10 Lib
1993 NOV 10 Scp
1994 DEC 9 Sag
1996 JAN 3 Cap
1997 JAN 21 Aqu
1998 FEB 4 Pic
1999 FEB 13 Ari
JUN 28 Tau
OCT 23 Ari
2000 FEB 14 Tau
JUN 30 Gem

SATURN SIGN 1903–2000

1903	JAN	19	Aqu
1905	APR	13	Pic
	AUG	17	Aqu
1906	JAN	8	Pic
1908	MAR	19	Ari
1910	MAY	17	Tau
	DEC	14	Ari
1911	JAN	20	Tau
1912	JUL	7	Gem
	NOV	30	Tau
1913	MAR	26	Gem
1914	AUG	24	Can
	DEC	7	Gem
1915	MAY	11	Can
1916	OCT	17	Leo
	DEC	7	Can
1917	JUN	24	Leo
1919	AUG	12	Vir
1921	OCT	7	Lib
1923	DEC	20	Scp
1924	APR	6	Lib
	SEP	13	Scp
1926	DEC	2	Sag
1929	MAR	15	Cap
	MAY	5	Sag
	NOV	30	Cap
1932	FEB	24	Aqu
	AUG	13	Cap
	NOV	20	Aqu
1935	FEB	14	Pic
1937	APR	25	Ari
	OCT	18	Pic
1938	JAN	14	Ari
1939	JUL	6	Tau
	SEP	22	Ari
1940	MAR	20	Tau
1942	MAY	8	Gem
1944	JUN	20	Can
1946	AUG	2	Leo
1948	SEP	19	Vir
1949	APR	3	Leo
	MAY	29	Vir
1950	NOV	20	Lib
1951	MAR	7	Vir
	AUG	13	Lib
1953	OCT	22	Scp
1956	JAN	12	Sag
	MAY	14	Scp
	OCT	10	Sag
1959	JAN	5	Cap
1962	JAN	3	Aqu
1964	MAR	24	Pic
	SEP	16	Aqu
	DEC	16	Pic
1967	MAR	3	Ari
1969	APR	29	Tau
1971	JUN	18	Gem
1972	JAN	10	Tau
	FEB	21	Gem
1973	AUG	1	Can
1974	JAN	7	Gem
	APR	18	Can
1975	SEP	17	Leo
1976	JAN	14	Can
	JUN	5	Leo
1977	NOV	17	Vir
1978	JAN	5	Leo
	JUL	26	Vir
1980	SEP	21	Lib
1982	NOV	29	Scp
1983	MAY	6	Lib
	AUG	24	Scp

1985	NOV	17	Sag	1994	JAN	28	Pic
1988	FEB	13	Cap	1996	APR	7	Ari
	JUN	10	Sag	1998	JUN	9	Tau
	NOV	12	Cap		OCT	25	Ari
1991	FEB	6	Aqu	1999	MAR	1	Tau
1993	MAY	21	Pic	2000	AUG	10	Gem
	JUN	30	Aqu		OCT	16	Tau

How to Use the Uranus, Neptune, and Pluto Tables

Find your birthday in the list following each sign.

Look up your Uranus placement by finding your birthday on the following lists.

URANUS IN ARIES BIRTH DATES

March 31–November 4, 1927
January 13, 1928–June 6, 1934
October 10, 1934–March 28, 1935

URANUS IN TAURUS BIRTH DATES

June 6, 1934–October 10, 1935
March 28, 1935–August 7, 1941
October 5, 1941–May 15, 1942

URANUS IN GEMINI BIRTH DATES

August 7–October 5, 1941
May 15, 1949–August 30, 1948
November 12, 1948–June 10, 1949

URANUS IN CANCER BIRTH DATES

August 30–November 12, 1948
June 10, 1942–August 24, 1955
January 28–June 10, 1956

URANUS IN LEO BIRTH DATES

August 24, 1955–January 28, 1956
June 10, 1956–November 1, 1961
January 10–August 10, 1962

URANUS IN VIRGO BIRTH DATES

November 1, 1961–January 10, 1962
August 10, 1962–September 28, 1968
May 20, 1969–June 24, 1969

URANUS IN LIBRA BIRTH DATES

September 28, 1968–May 20, 1969
June 24, 1969–November 21, 1974
May 1–September 8, 1975

URANUS IN SCORPIO BIRTH DATES

November 21, 1974–May 1, 1975
September 8, 1975–February 17, 1981
March 20–November 16, 1981

URANUS IN SAGITTARIUS BIRTH DATES

February 17–March 20, 1981
November 16, 1981–February 15, 1988
May 27, 1988–December 2, 1988

URANUS IN CAPRICORN BIRTH DATES

December 20, 1904–January 30, 1912
September 4–November 12, 1912
February 15–May 27, 1988
December 2, 1988–April 1, 1995
June 9, 1995–January 12, 1996

URANUS IN AQUARIUS BIRTH DATES

January 30–September 4, 1912
November 12, 1912–April 1, 1919
August 16, 1919–January 22, 1920

URANUS IN PISCES BIRTH DATES

April 1–August 16, 1919
January 22, 1920–March 31, 1927
November 4, 1927–January 13, 1928

Look up your Neptune placement by finding your birthday on the following lists.

NEPTUNE IN CANCER BIRTH DATES

July 19–December 25, 1901
May 21, 1902–September 23, 1914
December 14, 1914–July 19, 1915
March 19–May 2, 1916

NEPTUNE IN LEO BIRTH DATES

September 23–December 14, 1914
July 19, 1915–March 19, 1916
May 2, 1916–September 21, 1928
February 19, 1929–July 24, 1929

NEPTUNE IN VIRGO BIRTH DATES

September 21, 1928–February 19, 1929
July 24, 1929–October 3, 1942
April 17–August 2, 1943

NEPTUNE IN LIBRA BIRTH DATES

October 3, 1942–April 17, 1943
August 2, 1943–December 24, 1955
March 12–October 9, 1956
June 15–August 6, 1957

NEPTUNE IN SCORPIO BIRTH DATES

December 24, 1955–March 12, 1956
October 9, 1956–June 15, 1957
August 6, 1957–January 4, 1970
May 3–November 6, 1970

NEPTUNE IN SAGITTARIUS BIRTH DATES

January 4–May 3, 1970
November 6, 1970–January 19, 1984
June 23–November 21, 1984

NEPTUNE IN CAPRICORN BIRTH DATES

January 19, 1984–June 23, 1984
November 21, 1984–January 29, 1998

Find your Pluto placement in the following list:
Pluto in Gemini—Late 1800s until May 28, 1914
Pluto in Cancer—May 26, 1914–June 14, 1939
Pluto in Leo—June 14, 1939–August 19, 1957
Pluto in Virgo—August 19, 1957–October 5, 1971
April 17, 1972–July 30, 1972
Pluto in Libra—October 5, 1971–April 17, 1972
July 30, 1972–August 28, 1984
Pluto in Scorpio—August 28, 1984–January 17, 1995
Pluto in Sagittarius—starting January 17, 1995

CHAPTER 8

Astrology's Glyphs and the Myths Behind Them

Your horoscope chart is written in a special language known to astrologers all over the world. An astrologer in South America could read it as easily as an astrologer in Moscow could. However, if you don't know the meaning of the symbols covering your chart, the language of "astrologese" might look like a difficult code to crack.

If you have ordered one of the popular computer astrology programs, or if you have ordered your chart from one of the many computer services, you'll want to learn the meaning of the symbols. You probably know a few already, like the one for your sun sign, and the moon. It's easy to learn the meaning of the symbols, or "glyphs," for the other signs and planets.

Those little characters, twelve symbols for the astrological signs and 10 for planets, each contain information about their identity—and the hidden meaning of what they represent—within their design. Some are so obvious they give themselves away, like the symbol for the moon. Others take a bit of detective work, like a game of hide-and-seek. But the meaning is expressed right there in that combination of circles, wavy lines, and crosses. In fact, those readers who have already memorized the glyphs may not have realized how much of their meaning is revealed.

Let's start with the symbols for the planets. Look for them inside the "houses" (wedge-shaped segments) of your chart.

Glyphs for the Planets

Almost all the glyphs of the planets are derived from a combination of three basic forms—the circle, the half-circle or arc, and the cross (though this may not be immediately apparent because several symbols have become highly stylized over the years). Each element has a special meaning in relation to the others, which adds to the significance of the completed glyph.

The circle, with no beginning or end, is one of the oldest symbols of spirit or spiritual forces. All of the early diagrams of the heavens—spiritual territory—are shown in circular form. The arc or semicircle is the receptive symbol of the soul. The soul is finite, yet there is spiritual potential. The vertical line symbolizes movement from heaven to earth. The horizontal line describes temporal movement, in time and in space. Superimposed together, they become the cross, symbolizing manifestation in the material world.

THE SUN GLYPH ☉

The sun is always shown by this powerful solar symbol, a circle with a point in the center. It is you, your spiritual center, your infinite personality incarnating into the finite cycles of birth and death.

This symbol was brought into common use in the 16th century, after a German occultist and scholar, Cornelius Agrippa (1486–1535) wrote a book called *De Occulta Philosophia,* which became accepted as the standard work in its field. Agrippa collected many medieval astrological and magical symbols in this book, which were used by astrologers thereafter, copied from those found in Agrippa's book. In the light of what we have written about Pluto in Sagittarius in other chapters in this book, it's especially interesting that Agrippa's influential philosophical treatise was written during a previous time when Pluto was in Sagittarius (the sign that rules philosophy).

THE MOON GLYPH ☽

The easiest symbol to spot on a chart, the moon glyph is a left-facing arc stylized into the crescent moon, which perfectly captures the reactive, receptive, emotional nature of the moon.

As part of a circle, the arc symbolizes the potential fulfillment of the entire circle. It is the life force that is still incomplete. Unlike the circle, it is in a receptive state.

THE MERCURY GLYPH ☿

With a stretch of the imagination, can't you see the winged cap of Mercury the messenger? You might also think of the upturned crescent as little antennae that tune in and transmit messages from the sun, signifying that Mercury is the way you communicate, the way your mind works. The upturned arc is receiving energy into the spirit or solar disk, which will later be translated into action on the material plane, symbolized by the cross. All the elements are equally sized—because Mercury is neutral and doesn't play favorites—this planet symbolizes objective, detached, dispassionate thinking.

THE VENUS GLYPH ♀

Here the relationship is between two elements, the circle of spirit above the cross of matter. Spirit is elevated over matter, pulling it upward. Venus asks, "What is beautiful? What do you like best, what do you love to have done to you?" Venus determines both your ideal of beauty and what feels good sensually. It governs your own allure and power to attract, as well as what attracts and pleases you.

THE MARS GLYPH ♂

In this glyph, the cross of matter is stylized into an arrowhead pointed up and outward, propelled by the circle of spirit. You can deduce that Mars embodies your spiritual energy projected into the outer world. It's your assertiveness, your initiative, your aggressive drive, what you like to do to others, your temper. Your task is to use your outgoing Mars energy wisely and well.

THE JUPITER GLYPH ♃

Jupiter is the basic cross of matter, with a large stylized crescent perched on the left side of the horizontal, temporal plane. You might think of the crescent as an open hand—one meaning of Jupiter is "luck," what's handed to you. You don't work for what you get from Jupiter—it comes to you if you're open to it.

The Jupiter glyph might also remind you of a jumbo jet plane with a huge tail fin, about to take off. This is the planet of travel, mental and spiritual, of expanding your horizons via new ideas, new spiritual dimensions, and new places. Jupiter embodies the optimism and enthusiasm of the traveler about the embark on an exciting adventure.

THE SATURN GLYPH ♄

Flip Jupiter upside down and you've got Saturn. (This might not be immediately apparent, because Saturn is usually stylized into an "h" form like the one shown here.) But the principle it expresses is the opposite of Jupiter's expansive tendencies. Saturn pulls you back to earth—the receptive arc is pushed down underneath the cross of matter. Before there is any expansion, the duties and obligations of the material world must be considered. Saturn says, "Stop, wait, finish your chores before you take off!"

Saturn's glyph also resembles the sickle of old "Father Time." Saturn was first known as Chronos, the Greek god of time, for time brings all matter to an end. When it was the most distant planet (before the discovery of Uranus), it was thought to be the place where time stopped. After the soul, having departed from earth, journeyed back to the outer reaches of the universe, it finally stopped at Saturn, at the end of time.

THE URANUS GLYPH ♅

The glyph for Uranus is often stylized to form a capital "H" after Sir William Herschel, the name of the planet's discoverer. But the more esoteric version curves the two pillars of the H into crescent antennae, like satellite discs receiving signals from space, perched on the material plane of the cross of matter and pushed from below by the circle of the spirit (a bit like an orbiting satellite). Uranus channels the highest energy of all, the white electrical light of the universal spiritual sun. This pure electrical energy picks up impulses from the deepest reaches of the universe. Because it doesn't follow the ordinary drumbeat, it can't be controlled or predicted (which is also true of those who are strongly influenced by this eccentric planet). This light of spirit is manifested through the balance of polarities (the two arms of the glyph).

THE NEPTUNE GLYPH ♆

Neptune's glyph is usually stylized to look like a trident, the weapon of the Roman god Neptune. However, on a more esoteric level, it shows the large upturned crescent of the soul pierced through by the cross of matter. Neptune nails down, or materializes, soul energy, bringing impulses from the soul level into manifestation. That is why Neptune is associated with imagination, making an image of the soul. Neptune works through feeling, sensitivity and mystical capacity to bring the divine into the earthly realm.

THE PLUTO GLYPH ⯓ or ♇

Pluto is written two ways. One is a composite of the letters PL, the first two letters of the word Pluto and coincidentally the initials of Percival Lowell, one of the planet's discoverers. The other, more esoteric symbol is a small circle above a large open crescent surmounting the cross of matter. This depicts Pluto's power to regenerate—you might imagine from this glyph a new little spirit emerging from the sheltering cup of the soul. Pluto rules the forces of life and death—after a Pluto experience, you are transformed, reborn in some way.

Sci-fi fans might visualize this glyph as a small satellite

being launched. It was shortly after Pluto's discovery that we learned how to harness the nuclear forces that made space exploration possible. Pluto rules the transformative power of atomic energy, which totally changed our lives and from which there was no turning back.

The Glyphs for the Signs

On your chart, the glyphs for the sign will appear after the planet. You'll see something like (moon) 23 (Taurus) 44. That means that the moon is located at 23 degrees of Taurus, 44 minutes. At the dividing points (or cusps) between the houses on your chart, you'll also see a symbol for the sign that rules each house.

Glyphs for the signs are much harder to define visually than those of the planets. Many have been passed down from ancient Egyptian and Chaldean civilizations with few modifications. Others have been adapted over the centuries. In deciphering many of the glyphs, you'll often find the dual nature of a sign revealed that is not always obvious from sun-sign descriptions. The Gemini glyph is much like a Roman numeral for two, and reveals the sign's longing for the twin soul. The Cancer glyph may be interpreted as either nurturing, like the breast, or self-protective, like the crab. Libra's glyph embodies the duality of the spirit balanced with material reality. The Sagittarius glyph shows that the aspirant must also carry along the earthy animal nature. The Capricorn sea goat climbs high, yet is pulled back by the deep waters of the unconscious. Aquarius embodies the double waves of detachment and friendliness. And finally the two fishes of Pisces, forever tied together, show the duality of the soul and spirit that must be reconciled.

THE ARIES GLYPH ♈

Since the symbol for Aries is the ram, this glyph's most obvious association is with a ram's horns, which characterizes one aspect of the Aries personality—an aggressive, me-first, leaping-head-first attitude. But the symbol may have other meanings for you, too. Some astrologers liken it to a fountain of energy, which Aries people also embody. The first sign of the zodiac bursts on the scene eagerly, ready to go. Another analogy is to the eyebrows and nose of the human head, which Aries rules, and the thinking power that is initiated in the brain.

One theory of the origin of this symbol links it to the Egyptian god Amun, represented by a ram. As Amon-Ra, this god was believed to embody the creator of the universe, the leader of all the other gods. This relates easily to the position of Aries as the leader (or first sign) of the zodiac, which begins at the spring equinox, a time of the year when nature is renewed.

THE TAURUS GLYPH ♉

This is another easy glyph to draw and identify. It takes little imagination to decipher the bull's head with long curving horns. Like the bull, the archetypal Taurus is slow to anger but ferocious when provoked, as well as stubborn, steady, and sensual. Another association is the larynx (and thyroid) of the throat area (ruled by Taurus) and the eustachian tubes running up to the ears, which coincides with the relationship of Taurus to the voice, song, and music. Many famous singer, musicians, and composers have prominent Taurus influences.

Many ancient religions involve a bull as a central figure in certain rites of fertility or initiation, usually symbolizing the victory of man over his animal nature. Another possible origin is in the sacred bull of Egypt, who embodied the incarnate form of Osiris, god of death and resurrection. In early Christian imagery, the Taurean bull represented St. Luke.

THE GEMINI GLYPH ♊

The standard glyph immediately calls to mind the Roman numeral for two and the symbol for Gemini, the "twins." In almost all images for this sign, the relationship between two persons is emphasized. This is the sign of communication, human contact brings with it the desire to share. Many of the figurative images for Gemini show twins with their arms around each other, emphasizing that they are sharing the same ideas and the same ground. In the glyph, the top line indicates mental communication, while the bottom line indicates shared physical space.

The most prevalent Gemini legend is that of the twin sons, Castor and Pollux, one of whom had a mortal father, while the other was the son of Zeus, king of the gods. When it came time for the mortal twin to die, his grief-stricken brother pleaded with Zeus, who agreed to let them spend half the year on earth, in mortal form, and half in immortal life with the gods on Mt. Olympus. This reflects the basic nature of humankind, which possesses an immortal soul, yet is also subject to the limits of mortality.

THE CANCER GLYPH ♋

Two convenient images relate to the Cancer glyph. The easiest to picture is the curving claws of the Cancer symbol, the crab. Like the crab, Cancer's element is water. This sensitive sign also has a hard protective shell to protect its tender interior. It is wily to escape predators, scampering sideways and hiding shyly under rocks. The crab also responds to the cycles of the moon, as do all shellfish. The other image is that of two female breasts, which Cancer rules, showing that this is a sign that nurtures and protects others as well as itself.

In ancient Egypt, Cancer was also represented by the scarab beetle, a symbol of regeneration and eternal life.

THE LEO GLYPH ♌

Lions have belonged to the sign of Leo since earliest times, and it is not difficult to imagine the king of beasts with his sweeping manc and curling tail from this glyph. The upward sweep of the glyph easily describes the positive energy of Leos; the flourishing tail, their flamboyant qualities. Another analogy, which is a stretch, is that of a heart leaping up with joy and enthusiasm—also very typical of Leo. Notice that the Leo glyph seems to be an extension of Cancer's glyph; however, in the Cancer glyph, the figures are folding inward, protectively, while the Leo glyph expresses energy outward and there is no duality in the symbol (or in Leo). In early Christian imagery, the winged Leo lion represented St. Mark.

THE VIRGO GLYPH ♍

You can read much into this mysterious glyph. The initials of "Mary Virgin," female genitalia, and a young woman holding a staff of wheat are common interpretations. The "M" shape might also remind you that Virgo is ruled by Mercury. The cross beneath the symbol could indicate the grounded, practical nature of this earth sign.

The earliest zodiacs link Virgo with the Egyptian goddess Isis, who gave birth to the god Horus after her husband Osiris had been killed, in the archetype of a miraculous conception. There are many statues of Isis nursing her baby son, which are reminiscent of medieval Virgin and Child motifs. This sign has also been associated with the image of the Holy Grail, when the Virgo symbol was substituted with a chalice.

THE LIBRA GLYPH ♎

It is not difficult to read the standard image for Libra, the scales, into this glyph. There is another meaning, however, that is equally relevant: the setting sun as it descends over the horizon. Libra's natural position on the zodiac wheel is the descendant or sunset position (as Aries' natural position is the ascendant, or rising sign). Both images relate to Libra's personality. Libra is always weighing pros and cons for a balanced decision. In the sunset image, the sun (male) hovers over the horizontal Earth (female) before setting. Libra is the space between these lines, harmonizing yin and yang, spiritual and material, ideal and real worlds. The glyph has also been linked to the kidneys, which are ruled by Libra.

THE SCORPIO GLYPH ♏

With its barbed tail, this glyph is easy to identify with the sign of the Scorpion. It also represents the male sexual parts, over which the sign rules. However, some earlier symbols for Scorpio, such as the Egyptian, represent it as an erect serpent. You can also draw the conclusion that Mars is its ruler by the arrowhead.

Another image for Scorpio, which is not identifiable in this glyph, is the eagle. Scorpios can go to extremes, soaring like the eagle or self-destructing like the Scorpion. In early Christian imagery, which often used zodiacal symbols, the Scorpio eagle was chosen to symbolize the intense apostle St. John the Evangelist.

THE SAGITTARIUS GLYPH ♐

This glyph is one of the easiest to spot and draw—an upward pointing arrow lifting up a cross. The arrow is pointing skyward, while the cross represents the four elements of the material world, which the arrow must convey. Elevating materiality into spirituality is an important Sagittarius quality, which explains why this sign is associated with higher learning, religion, philosophy, travel—the aspiring professions. Sagittarians can also send barbed arrows of frankness in their pursuit of truth. (This is also the sign of the super-salesman.)

Sagittarius is symbolically represented by the centaur, a mythological creature who is half-man, half-horse, aiming his arrow toward the skies. Though Sagittarius is motivated by spiritual aspiration, it also must balance the powerful appetites of the animal nature. The centaur Chiron, a figure in Greek mythology, became a wise teacher, after many adventures and world travels.

THE CAPRICORN GLYPH ♑

One of the most difficult symbols to draw, this glyph may take some practice. It is a representation of the seagoat: a mythical animal that is a goat with a curving fish's tail. The goat part of Capricorn wants to leave the waters of the emotions and climb to the elevated areas of life. But the fish part is the unconscious, the deep chaotic psychic level that draws the goat back. Capricorn is often trying to escape the deep, feeling part of life by submerging himself in work, steadily climbing to the top. To some people, the glyph represents a seated figure with a bent knee, since Capricorn governs the knee area of the body.

An interesting aspect of this figure is how the sharp

pointed horns of this figure, which represent the penetrating, shrewd, conscious side of Capricorn, contrast with the swishing tail, which represents its serpentine, unconscious, emotional force. One Capricorn legend dates from Roman times. The earthy fertility god, Pan, tried to save himself from uncontrollable life forces by jumping into the Nile. His upper body then turned into a goat, while the lower part became a fish. Then Jupiter gave him a save have in the skies, as a constellation.

THE AQUARIUS GLYPH ♒

This ancient water symbol can be traced back to an Egyptian hieroglyph representing streams of life force. Symbolized by the water bearer, Aquarius is distributor of the waters of life—the magic liquid of regeneration. The two waves can also be linked to the positive and negative charges of the electrical energy that Aquarius rules, a sort of universal wavelength. Aquarius is tuned in intuitively to higher forces via this electrical force. The duality of the glyph could also refer to the dual nature of Aquarius, a sign that runs hot and cold, is friendly but also detached in the mental world of air signs.

In Greek legends, Aquarius was represented by Ganymedes, who was carried to heaven by an eagle in order to become the cup bearer of Zeus, and to supervise the annual flooding of the Nile. The sign became associated with aviation and notions of flight.

THE PISCES GLYPH ♓

Here is an abstraction of the familiar image of Pisces, two fishes swimming in opposite directions, bound together by a cord. The fishes represent spirit, which yearns for the freedom of heaven, while the soul remains attached to the desires of the temporal world. During life on earth, the spirit and the soul are bound together, and when they complement each other, instead of pulling in opposite directions, this facilitates the creative expression for which Pisceans are known. The ancient version of this glyph, taken from the Egyptians, had no connecting line, which was added in the fourteenth century.

Another interpretation is that the left fish indicates the

direction of involution or the beginning of a cycle; the right-hand fish, the direction of evolution, the way to completion of a cycle. It's an appropriate meaning for Pisces, the last sign of the zodiac.

CHAPTER 9

Ten Sure-fire Ways to Thrive in '95!

Wouldn't you like to use the power of the planets to help you achieve your goals? By flowing with the major planetary movements of 1995, you can master your own particular universe. Scheduling activities to coincide with the most favorable cosmic trends is a technique that rulers, presidents, and financiers have been using for centuries. Now you have the same kind of information that was once a highly guarded secret available right in this chapter.

Some very predictable movements of the planet Mercury, for instance, could cause your big plans to stall or go into reverse motion. Perhaps someone might not get an urgent message on time. Or a plane trip might be unaccountably delayed. Knowing what Mercury's up to in advance, you'll double check reservations, and give yourself plenty of options and a double dose of patience. Other planetary movements could bring a situation you've been barely tolerating to a dramatic head, causing tempers to flare. That's when your Dr. Jekyll turns into Mr. Hyde and comes out of hiding. However, these topsy-turvy times might also serve a useful purpose, by forcing you to slow down, reevaluate your life, or blast yourself out of a rut.

Several kinds of events can throw your daily life off track. One possible cause is a retrograding planet. Periodically, most planets seem to tread backward (retrograde) from our point of view on Earth. (Planets don't actually move backward; it just looks that way from here.) If you have a new project planned for those times, you'll know enough to provide for possible delays and tie-ups. On the other hand, you'll have much more success with the kinds of activities that require reaction rather than direct action. If you learn not to push against the tide, but to flow with it, you'll have a big advantage!

Here's our ten-point plan for getting the most out of '95:

1. Promote Yourself When You'll Be Most Attractive to Others

When Venus is in your sign, you can be sure that your charm will be appreciated. Since Venus spends about a month in each sign, time your big sales pitches for the month when it passes through your sun Sign. That's when to flirt up a storm with someone who hasn't been giving you the time of day. Socialize and network with potential clients and contacts. Wear the colors of your sun Sign and play up all your natural sun-sign charms. You'll be the flavor of the month! For example, from January 7 to February 4, Venus is passing through Sagittarius, so Sagittarians will be most appealing. But signs of the same fire-sign family as Sagittarius (Leo and Aries) will also benefit from Venus in Sagittarius. It's also good for air signs (Libra, Aquarius, and Gemini).

So it pays to look for the times when Venus is in your sign, putting a rosy glow on the signs most compatible with yours. For a brief review, fire and air signs generally click. Water and earth signs are generally compatible. The glow will "rub off" on you!

Your Venus Timetable for 1995

As the year begins: Venus is in Scorpio

January 7:	Venus moves to Sagittarius
February 4:	Venus to Capricorn
March 2:	Venus enters Aquarius
March 28:	Venus enters Pisces
April 22:	Venus to Aries
May 16:	Venus to Taurus
June 10:	Venus to Gemini
July 5:	Venus to Cancer
July 29:	Venus to Leo

August 23:	Venus to Virgo
September 16:	Venus to Libra
October 10:	Venus to Scorpio
November 3:	Venus to Sagittarius
November 27:	Venus to Capricorn
December 21:	Venus to Aquarius

2. Make Your Big Push When You'll Have Energy to Burn

Mars is often called the great motivator—it shows how to get where you want to go. It's your personal battery charger, so knowing where this planet is traveling at any given time can help you take the initiative and schedule your major moves for days when you can get ahead fast. At other times, you may be much better off kicking back and reacting to what's happening around you.

Your best times to forge ahead are during the weeks when Mars is traveling through your sun sign or your Mars sign (you can look your Mars Sign up in the chapter on how to find your planets). Also consider times when Mars is in a compatible sign (fire with air signs, or earth with water signs). You'll be sure to have plenty of fuel to get where you're going.

Hold your fire, however, from January 2 until March 24 this year, when Mars retrogrades back from Virgo to Leo, especially if your sun or Mars is in either of those signs. This is the time to exercise diplomacy, let someone else run with the ball, or fight city hall. You may feel that you are not accomplishing as much as you'd like. The key here for everybody when Mars retrogrades is patience. Slow down and work off any frustrations with constructive physical activity (get on that Stairmaster; start pumping iron). It's also best to postpone buying mechanical devices (Mars-ruled) and take extra care when handling sharp objects.

Your Mars Timetable for 1995

January 2:	* Mars turns retrograde in Virgo
January 22:	* Mars retrogrades back to Leo
March 24:	Mars turns direct in Leo

May 25:	Mars reenters Virgo
July 21:	Mars to Libra
September 7:	Mars to Scorpio
October 20:	Mars to Sagittarius
November 30:	Mars to Capricorn

3. Play Your Cards on Your Best Days Every Month and Your High Times Each Year

Your birthday is literally a new birth, when you begin a new solar cycle. This is truly the high time of the year, when the qualities of your sun sign predominate in the overall atmosphere. Take advantage of this time to get new projects under way, especially at the time of the new moon in your sign. This is a powerful time to try new things, to take off in a different direction.

For about two days every month, as the moon passes through your sun sign, the emotional energies are in tune with you. This is also an excellent time to make your moves. Use the moon listings, which accompany your daily forecasts in this book, to schedule key activities.

4. Take It Easy During Your Personal "Low" Times

There are two times during the year when you may feel you are out of sync with what's happening around you. One time is right before your birthday, when the sun is passing through the sign preceding yours. This is a slowdown time, before the annual rebirth on your birthday. You may be feeling a bit vulnerable and reflective, more like keeping to yourself than socializing. (That's good—it's what you're supposed to do at this time!) This is a time to toss away ideas that have outlived their usefulness and unproductive ways of using your time. If you reflect on where you're going and why, then this can be one of your most profitable times of the year. It's also the ideal time to meditate and spend time in more spiritual pursuits.

The other time of year when you may feel at odds with the world is when the sun is passing through the sign opposite yours. If you are a Pisces, for instance, you may feel a sense of unease when the sun is in down-to-earth Virgo, which favors efficient, routine work, rather than creative, imaginative activity. On the other hand, this may be the perfect time to get your life in order. When the full moon is in Pisces, which occurs during this period, you Pisceans may feel especially emotional, as if you're pulled in different directions.

During each month, when the moon passes through your opposite sign, play it cool, doing a few things you've been avoiding. Pisces could clean up clutter when the moon is in Virgo; Aries might be more diplomatic when the moon is in Libra. The idea is to look at the other side of the coin and act accordingly.

5. Gear Up for Saturn's Testing Times

You'll discover strengths you didn't know you had when Saturn comes calling! With a Saturn transit, obstacles appear and our dreams often get doused with a cold splash of reality. However, if these dreams have a chance of really happening, Saturn will provide the structure that will make them materialize. So don't knock Saturn! If you pass this planet's tests, you'll be a much stronger, more grown-up, and more capable person.

Important Saturn times are those when Saturn returns to the position it occupied when you were born, every twenty-eight years or so. At these times, if you don't think about duties and obligations, settling down, and taking on responsibilities, events may force you to do so. Other significant times are when Saturn crosses your rising sign and when it passes your natal sun.

Since Saturn will be traveling through the second half of Pisces all year long, those with Pisces placements will find that they're having some of Saturn's learning experiences. You might find that you are restricted or constrained in some area of your life. (If you're astrology aware, look up the house Saturn is passing through to discover what kind of experiences to expect.) If you ask yourself what the lessons are in these experiences, you might discover that they involve adjusting your dreams to reality and dealing with the responsibilities of being an adult. You'll grow up fast during a Saturn transit.

When Saturn retrogrades, from July 6 to November 21, all signs may feel a lack of discipline. It may be difficult to get things done when you'd rather indulge yourself. You're more likely to give in to daydreaming or overspending when Saturn's restraints are lifted. (Don't worry—you'll put your nose to the grindstone later!)

The best times of this year's Saturn transit could be when Saturn sextiles Neptune (the ruler of Pisces). This happens twice this year, on June 27 and August 17). During this favorable aspect, your dreams have a good chance of becoming realities. On the other hand, it's "chin-up" time in November, when first Jupiter (November 11) and then Mars (November 15) in Sagittarius form an unfriendly angle to Saturn. Things should get back on track after November 21, when Saturn swings into forward motion.

If Saturn is putting on the brakes in your life, remember that Father Time (Saturn) is a fair teacher. You'll get the grades you earn. This planet can be very kind to those who have progressed in maturity and learned their lessons well. It is those who need to learn discipline and responsibility (not the strong points of Sagittarius and Gemini) who will face the most difficult tests.

6. Outwit Mercury Mischief!

If there's one planet that is guaranteed to cause mischief with your scheduling, it's Mercury. This little planet, which rules communications, turns retrograde three times each year for three weeks at a time, when it wreaks havoc with computers, telephones, and traffic of all kinds. People don't get your message or they misunderstand you. Your answering machine breaks down. Computer terminals at your travel agency will somehow put you on the wrong flight. Then your baggage gets lost.

Your best ammunition against the woes of Mercury retrograde is a sense of humor. This diabolical little planet seems to be saying "Don't take it all so seriously!" If traveling, carry a good book or some work to do during delays. Put on your favorite tape when stuck in traffic. Keep your options open and double-check all reservations. Try not to sign contracts or make major purchases during this period. If you're traveling for pleasure, revisit favorite places, leaving exploring the unknown for another time.

This is also a time when people or things from the past could turn up again. You might reignite a former passion or plan a reunion with school buddies. While you're cleaning out your files, you might find an important document you'd lost. Look in the back of your closet—you could uncover a forgotten dress or jacket that could be recycled now. Revisit favorite places. Spend a weekend with your first love in a small hotel filled with memories. You might run into an old friend. At work, go for repeat business. Call up customers you haven't heard from in a while, look up old business contacts, renew subscriptions to professional journals.

This year, Mercury turns retrograde in air signs (Aquarius, Gemini, and Libra), so mark the dates on your calendar. Those born in air signs could feel especially confused or unfocused. Give yourself plenty of options; double-check all communication; and try not to make commitments, sign leases, or make contracts. Instead, use this time to reevaluate your plans and strategies. And remember, in just three weeks, it will be over!

Mercury Retrogrades for 1995

January 26:	Mercury turns retrograde in Aquarius
February 16:	Mercury direct in Aquarius
May 24:	Mercury turns retrograde in Gemini
June 17:	Mercury direct in Gemini
September 22:	Mercury turns retrograde in Libra
October 14:	Mercury direct in Libra

7. Could You Get Lucky This Year? Put Your Money on Sagittarius!

Jupiter represents the principle of expansion—think of hot-air balloons, Santa Claus, and "Luck Be a Lady Tonight." The flipside of Jupiter is that there are no limits—you can expand right off the planet, which is why Jupiter is also called the gateway to heaven. Many people pass on with a Jupiter transit or overextend themselves in some way. Jupiter promotes optimism and enthusiasm, as well as overconfidence, so you'll need a good set of brakes when this planet steps on the gas.

This year, Jupiter is especially strong as it passes through the sign it rules, Sagittarius. This makes for a blast of optimism, enthusiasm, and risk taking in Sagittarian-ruled things. Since Pluto is also powering up the beginning of Sagittarius, it's fair to bet on horses, publishing ventures, higher education, gambling, the travel business, and religious-themed products.

Doing foreign business? Consider Chile, Czechoslovakia, Saudi Arabia, Spain, Toronto, Provence (France), Singapore, Stuttgart (Germany), or Madagascar—all Sagittarius-influenced.

However, be careful of overoptimism during the April 1–August 2 period, when Jupiter will be retrograding, which can deflate enthusiasm and cause powers of persuasion to fall flat. There may be delays and foul-ups in Jupiter-ruled areas, so postpone your risk-taking adventures until after Jupiter turns direct!

Another period to note is the time around November 11, when Jupiter forms a tense aspect with Saturn, which will apply the brakes to any overinflated ventures. However, if your schemes pass Saturn's test, you can be sure they're winners!

Movements of Jupiter in 1995

April 1:	Jupiter turns retrograde in Sagittarius
August 2:	Jupiter direct in Sagittarius
November 11:	Jupiter in Sagittarius squares Saturn in Pisces

8. Oh, Those Ominous Eclipses!

Eclipses have had an ominous reputation since man first panicked at the blackout of one of the celestial lights. If you've ever witnessed a total solar eclipse, you'll agree it's an awesome spectacle. Even today, people in many parts of the world cling to their superstitions about the negative effects of eclipses. During the total solar eclipse of July 1991, villagers in Mexico painted fruit trees red and wore red ribbons and underwear to deflect "evil rays." Then everyone retreated inside to track the eclipse on TV.

Could you be eclipsed by an eclipse? Not if you know how to turn one of nature's most fascinating events to your advantage. Lunar eclipses happen at the time of a full moon, when emotions would normally come to a head and be released—this is the monthly climax of events. Then, after the full moon comes a winding-down period before the next new moon starts the cycle rolling again. At a lunar eclipse, however, the release, which is usually triggered by the tension of the sun opposing the moon, is intercepted by the Earth, which passes exactly between the two bodies and cuts off the exchange of energy, like a football player intercepting a long pass. The effect can be either confusion or clarity, as subconscious energies are let loose, bringing insights and events that can change the pattern of our lives. Whether this creates disorientation or divine insight depends on each individual's reaction. However, change is the key word.

When a solar eclipse occurs, the moon is the interfering body, blocking the sun's energy from the Earth. Since this always happens at the new moon, which begins the monthly cycle, the alignment of sun and moon energies becomes super-intense, with the moon's emotional nature taking over. It's not a time for objective clarity! Emotions can get out of hand as the ego (sun) goes into hiding. But what a time for spiritual or psychic experiences!

Because the exact alignments of eclipses create such a concentration of energy, everything from birds, animals, fish—even oysters—become disoriented. But if we look behind eclipse-related crises, we often find that there is some deep, positive force activated—a change that needed to happen.

How should you handle an eclipse? Mark your calendar the week before the eclipse, a few days after the previous quarter moon, when energies start to build up. Clearly this would not be a good time to make a serious commitment, an important decision, or a major purchase that requires measured, rational thinking. Generally, stick to low-stress activities, since your energy and immune system may be lower than usual. If at all possible, avoid surgery, risky sports, handling sharp or dangerous objects. And be especially careful with any form of drug or alcohol use.

However, if you'd like to catch someone off guard, this would be the time to do it! Let the competition make a move, while you sit patiently and wait until at least three days after the eclipse before you act.

New Moons, Full Moons, and Eclipses in 1995

January 1:	New moon in Capricorn
January 16:	Full moon in Cancer
January 30:	New moon in Aquarius
February 15:	Full moon in Leo
March 1:	New moon in Pisces
March 17:	Full moon in Virgo
March 31:	New moon in Aries
**April 15:	Full moon/lunar eclipse in Libra
**April 29:	New moon/solar eclipse in Taurus
May 14:	Full moon in Scorpio
May 29:	New moon in Gemini
June 13:	Full moon in Sagittarius
June 27:	New moon in Cancer
July 12:	Full moon in Capricorn
July 27:	New moon in Leo
August 10:	Full moon in Aquarius
August 26:	New moon in Virgo
September 9:	Full moon at Pisces
September 24:	New moon in Libra
**October 8:	Full moon/lunar eclipse in Aries
**October 24:	New moon/solar eclipse in Scorpio
November 7:	Full moon in Taurus
November 22:	New moon in Scorpio again
December 7:	Full moon in Gemini
December 21:	New moon in Sagittarius

9. Process What You Learned over the Last Two Years

The outer planets, Uranus and Neptune, have been making the news since 1993, when they lined up in Capricorn for a monumental happening that takes place only once every

171 years. Many of us experienced the fallout from natural shakeups—floods, wars, personal confusion—which served to break down traditional structures in all areas of our lives, redefine our priorities, and put us on new ground for the next century. Now, as both planets prepare to leave Capricorn, you should be making significant progress based on what you've learned over the past two years.

Pay attention when both these planets turn retrograde this year. At these times, watch for delays and setbacks in areas where there have been revolutionary changes in the last two years. This is a pause to gather energy for a great shift in the atmosphere next year. During late November and December, when Venus, Mars, and Mercury pass by Uranus and Neptune, their energies will be strongly activated once again. Expect the unexpected!

In June and August, Neptune's sextile to Saturn, which is passing through Neptune-ruled Pisces, could have a very constructive effect in our lives by providing an understanding of the lessons we learned over the past two years.

Uranus, often called the awakener, has certainly done its work over the past two years. This year, it begins to move into Aquarius, the sign it rules, where its influence is strongest. More than ever, it seems to say, "Make way for the new!" This is a transition time between the breaking up of old structures and the beginning of a more expansive and more advanced era. Uranus will confirm this as it nods to Pluto on April 10 and August 7, signaling a shift in energy that should bring hope to everyone.

Movements of Uranus in 1995

April 1:	Uranus enters Aquarius, its planetary ruler
April 10:	Uranus sextiles Pluto in Sagittarius
May 5:	Uranus turns retrograde in Aquarius
June 8:	Uranus retrogrades back to Capricorn
August 7:	Uranus in Capricorn Sextiles Pluto in Scorpio again
October 6:	Uranus turns direct in Capricorn

Movements of Neptune in 1995

April 27:	Neptune turns retrograde in Capricorn
June 27:	Saturn (Pisces) sextiles Neptune (Capricorn)

August 17:	Saturn (retrograding in Pisces) sextiles Neptune (Capricorn) for the second time.
October 5:	Neptune turns direct in Capricorn

10. Watch Pluto Switch on a New Kind of Power!

Pluto shows where the power is on a mass level. And if you have strong Sagittarius placements, you're sure to feel the intense transformative power of Pluto in the next few years. Everyone else could also benefit by some Pluto awareness. Though this tiny planet moves very slowly through the zodiac, it's an amazingly accurate barometer of what's really happening on a deep, subconscious level. Since we've covered the main event this year (Pluto's move into Sagittarius) in a separate chapter, this should serve as an extra reminder to tune in to Pluto and mark its movements on your calendar.

After moving into Sagittarius on January 17, giving us a taste of things to come, Pluto turns retrograde on March 3, moving back to Scorpio and, after turning direct on August 8, it finally enters Sagittarius on November 10. You may be able to feel the energy as it shifts from the intensity of Scorpio to the light, jovial optimism of Sagittarius. We'll all be transformed in our attitudes toward the very serious life-and-death issues that Scorpio rules. Now we can look forward to a spiritual shift with the potential to uplift our lives!

Movements of Pluto

**January 17:	Pluto enters Sagittarius, a major event
March 3:	Pluto turns retrograde in Sagittarius
April 10:	Uranus sextiles Pluto in Sagittarius
April 21:	Pluto retrogrades back to Scorpio
August 8:	Pluto turns direct in Scorpio
November 10:	Pluto enters Sagittarius

CHAPTER 10

Find Your Love in the Sun-Sign Personals

For some lucky people, the love of their lives is waiting in their favorite newspaper or magazine. There, in the back pages, could be a "successful entrepreneur looking for a curvaceous cutie." Further down the column is a "sensuous, brilliant blonde." Or how about the sports fan who's looking for someone who likes tennis and kayaking.

Since "personals" columns are taking up more and more classified ad space, many people must be getting together via the printed media. And some love seekers include either their own astrological sign, or the sign they'd most like to meet, in their qualifications.

Astrology-savvy sleuths might be able to detect a certain sign's style from the wording of the ad. Who but a Leo would be so confident in print? And doesn't that long list of qualifications sound like a Virgo's ad? But first, you have to know what a given sun sign's line might be. One easy way to do this is to guess which sign wrote the following ads. Then ask yourself who you'd be most likely to respond to it.

The ad writer's astrological identity will be revealed at the end of the chapter.

Women Seeking Men

1. RESCUE ME! I've been looking for love in all the wrong places. I need a special someone who is successful, sincere, and ready for a permanent commitment. I'm a magical dreamer who could invent some fantasies you'd love to fulfill. If you like affectionate, adorable, offbeat ladies, who are interested in music, art, and romantic candlelit dinners, I'll be happy to start over again with you.

2. LOOKING FOR THE REAL THING. Are you a steadfast, caring go-getter, who not only appreciates the best things in life but wants to have them! Are you the ritzy romantic who'll break down my reserve, the man of substance who can also make me laugh? I'm a hard-working, ambitious professional who'll make romance a high priority with an equally accomplished soulmate. I'll give you good value if you'll cater to my needs.

3. FIRE UP YOUR ENGINE! I'm looking for my knight riding a red Miata, Jeep or dirt bike. Let's hit the road and talk. I'm a feminine feminist, financially independent and frisky. I love the simple joy of wind in my hair, would rather have a mountaintop picnic than a posh night out. My guy is in good shape, has high energy, and is brave enough to have an equal relationship. Adventure and wild passion are ahead for us both.

4. PRESCRIPTION FOR PASSION. I'm waiting for a doting doctor with a logical mind and a poetic soul. You need tender loving care from a sweet-tempered nurse who is intelligent, informed, and a good conversationalist. I need a responsible, rational Romeo who's fit physically and financially. You should be a nonsmoker, brainy, funny, and confident, but also shy, gentle, and gallant. Since casual encounters are not my style, please be serious about having a meaningful relationship.

5. WOMAN OF DEPTH, looking for a man of substance. If you're smart, sexy, and do what you do with passion, we should meet. Why settle for less? This passionate, attractive, super-sensual seductress is looking for her match. I have some wild ideas, but old-fashioned values. I'm ready to be your one-and-only, so say good-bye to all your exes, and let's get back to basics together.

6. LET'S BE FRIENDS FIRST, LOVERS LATER. I'm a loving visionary who cares about making the world a better place. I'm looking for a Renaissance man who's unconventional, bright, and strong, who dances to his own tune, a like-minded lover who will hold me lightly. If you'd like to be the wind beneath my wings, let's get together and reach for the stars.

7. BIG SPENDER WANTS MILLIONAIRE IN TRAINING. Let's conquer the world together. I'm a warm, ultra-feminine head-turner who's as gorgeous in jeans as in a ball gown. If you deserve the best, look no further. My best man has George Hamilton's wardrobe, Bill Clinton's power, and Schwartzenegger's muscles. But if you've just got a heart of gold, you might still be The One for me.

8. I'M THRILLED BY CREATURE COMFORTS. Breakfast in bed, fresh flowers, gourmet dinners, velvet gowns. I'm looking for someone to share earthly pleasures and earthy passion. Let's indulge each other! I could make beautiful music with someone who's generous, sensual, and single. You'll be rewarded with all the cuddling and laughter you can handle!

9. ARE THERE ANY GUYS LEFT who like nice old-fashioned girls like me? I'm pretty, full figured, and want a solid relationship with a man of morals, manners, and means, who can take time to be loving and tender. Please be a family man who'll bring me home to mother, introduce me to your kids, wolf down the wonderful meals I'll cook for you, and hold hands under the full moon.

10. SPORTS FAN. Blond personal trainer, 5'10", looking for someone who likes football as much as I do. Interested in meeting upbeat, honest, athletic male for tennis or biking, as well as Monday-night TV games. If you love travel to exotic places, have a sharp mind in a fit body, I'll take a gamble on you. Let's go jogging or walk our dogs together. Who knows where we'll end up?

11. DESIGNING WOMAN SEEKS A LEADING MAN. If you appreciate the finer things in life (and can afford them), let me surround you with romance. I'm a beautiful balance of cool logic and vulnerability; I love togetherness, but also need my own well-decorated space. Please be an unencumbered potential mate with good looks, good manners, and a great lifestyle. If you believe success is better when shared, then I'm the elegant lady who can take you from here to eternity.

12. GOT A TWINKLE IN YOUR EYE? Then I'll be no trivial pursuit. If we can talk a good game, then we might be lifetime playmates. You've got a lot to say and a witty way to say it; you're a playful party-goer, a sharp dresser who can make me laugh. Would a sophisticated, brainy beauty, who'll never give you a dull moment, make you happy? Then let's talk!

Men Seeking Women

1. TRY A LITTLE TENDERNESS. I'm romantic; I love moonlight and old-fashioned girls. I'm looking for someone to share long walks by the sea, old movies, and cozy candlelit dinners we'll cook together. You should be gentle and feminine, soft spoken and affectionate, with family values. We'll go antiquing, make love in a canopy bed, share our secrets. I love children, good wine, good company. Intimacy is my specialty. Let me provide a warm, supportive nest for you.

2. YOUR BEST INVESTMENT. Established professional, very financially secure, seeks an attractive, classy, charming lady to get serious about. Am interested in raising a family. You should also be marriage minded, intelligent, and well educated. I offer you a life of art, music, and mental stimulation. Please be slim, between 25–35, and physically fit. You may be a career woman by day, but be a homebody by night.

3. READ MY LIPS. Young-looking, young-at-heart, divorced male with eclectic tastes. I'm looking for a stunning, spirited companion with a zest for life. Great sense of humor a must. I'm whimsical, unencumbered, fun-loving, and communicative. Be ready for laughter and loving combined. If you like a varied menu of activities with lots of spice and sweet words, can we talk?

4. DOES KAYAKING IN ALASKA LEAVE YOU COLD? If so, you're not the spirited, adventurous, outdoor gal I'm looking for. Be in good shape or willing to get there fast. You should also like camping, animals, and weekends away from it all. If you're an optimist who cares about making the world a better place; if you're a brainy, insightful lady with great legs, then let's try out that kayak! Keep your bags packed and your passport updated.

5. LIVE OUT YOUR FANTASIES. I'm the man you meet in your dreams, the one who knows your thoughts before you speak, who treats you like the special person you are. I'll listen to your innermost confidences, give you my shoulder to cry on. Please be sweet but strong willed. Let me be the dreamer, while you be the doer. If you've been overworking, I'll de-stress you with caresses, give you the romance you've been missing.

6. LET ME BE YOUR TEDDYBEAR. I'm looking for a curvaceous cutie to huddle and cuddle with. Be my favorite pet and we'll satisfy our appetites in the kitchen and bedroom. You won't have to diet for me! I like you full figured and fabulous, wearing silk blouses, fluffy sweaters, and French perfumes. If you're a peaceful, home-loving lady with feet on the ground, let's get together. If you're a great cook, even better.

7. BE MY PRETTY WOMAN. I'll show you how beautiful life can be. Let's be Nick and Nora, Fred and Ginger, Bill and Hillary. I'm slim and handsome, and I have a passion for the arts and fine dining. I love entertaining and am as comfortable in a tux as I am in a jogging suit. I'd like a committed relationship with my female counterpart, who's up on the latest fashions and exudes elegance. Come share my social whirl!

8. WHERE'S MY QUEEN OF HEARTS? I'm a handsome, high-powered executive looking for a princess to share my castle. I'd love to hear from a beautiful, intelligent, passionate woman who feels good about herself and would like to share life's pleasures with a very generous man. If you're a warm, sunny head-turner with a radiant smile, I'll give you the royal treatment.

9. ALL OR NOTHING AT ALL. A woman of depth and sensuality who'll be my body and soulmate. If you're a one-man woman who's ready to be cherished forever, I'd like to meet you. I could get serious about someone who is intensely feminine, proud and passionate, erotically inventive. Let's rendezvous in a haunted mansion, read each other's tarot cards and snack on caviar. Wear slinky black—or nothing at all—under your trenchcoat.

10. LOOKING FOR BEAUTY AND BRAINS. Successful M.D. seeks lady to share the best things in life. I'm looking for a foxy lady who exudes style, class, and great taste in all she does. Dazzle me with your brilliant mind and fascinate me with witty conversation. You should also be in great shape, slim, and health conscious. Be conservative in public, and an uninhibited vixen in private. For Ms. Perfect, I'll cure your insecurities and be your significant other.

11. I'M OPEN-MINDED AND WILLING TO TRY ANYTHING ONCE. Surprise me! I'm slightly eccentric—a Renaissance man with Tom Selleck's looks, Einstein's mind, and Yeltsin's guts. You're your own person, strong in spirit and body. Be adventurous, unconventional, open minded, and future oriented. Material girls need not apply. Be my best friend as well as my lover, and I'll be yours for keeps.

12. LIGHT MY FIRE! I'm a strong, confident macho man who's looking for a kindred spirit to share life's challenges. You should be athletic, energetic, and ready for lots of action. If you spark my interest, I'll give you plenty of fireworks—get ready to be swept off your feet, wooed, and pursued like you've never been before. My white charger's waiting for the right fair damsel.

Who Placed the Personal Ads?

Women Seeking Men

1. Pisces
2. Capricorn
3. Aries
4. Virgo
5. Scorpio
6. Aquarius
7. Leo
8. Taurus
9. Cancer
10. Sagittarius
11. Libra
12. Gemini

Men Seeking Women:

1. Cancer
2. Capricorn
3. Gemini
4. Sagittarius
5. Pisces
6. Taurus
7. Libra
8. Leo
9. Scorpio
10. Virgo
11. Aquarius
12. Aries

CHAPTER 11

Let the Stars Guide You to Your True-Love Type

Ladies, does the sensitivity of Tom Cruise and the smooth style of Harrison Ford appeal to you most? Or do you prefer the dash of Dennis Quaid and Alec Baldwin? Guys, do you dream of Kim Basinger? Or are Julia Roberts and Demi Moore more your type?

It's amazing how many celebrities embody the qualities of their sun sign. And it's amazing, too, what your favorite celebrity's sign can reveal about your potential soulmate. To prove (or disprove) this point, circle the celebrities that appeal to you on the following lists. Some are all-time classic film personalities; others might be the talk-show host you watch most often, or the celebrity you'd like most to have dinner with. You may be surprised to find out how many of your choices fall under one or two signs. Then look up the sun sign type at the end of the lists and learn more about who really turns you on (it could be quite a different sign than the one you expect)!

Type A: Dashing and Daring

MALES	**FEMALES**
Alec Baldwin	Ellen Barkin
Al Gore	Diana Ross
Gregory Peck	Emma Thompson
Spencer Tracy	Leeza Gibbons
Matthew Broderick	Paulina Porizkova
Timothy Dalton	Mariah Carey

Dennis Quaid	Reba McEntire
Warren Beatty	Shannon Doherty
David Letterman	Marilu Henner
Eddie Murphy	Ali MacGraw

Type B: Earthy Sensualists

MALES	FEMALES
Daniel Day Lewis	Michelle Pfeiffer
Jack Nicholson	Janet Jackson
Jay Leno	Candice Bergen
Randy Travis	Andie MacDowell
Al Pacino	Debra Winger
Pierce Brosnan	Shirley Maclaine
Tony Danza	Sheena Easton
David Byrne	Cher
Billy Joel	Bea Arthur
Emilio Estevez	Jessica Lange

Type C: Charm to Spare

MALES	FEMALES
Tom Berenger	Elle MacPherson
Clint Eastwood	Brooke Shields
Parker Stevenson	Isabella Rossellini
Donald Trump	Nicole Kidman
Tony Geary	Joan Rivers
Tristan Rogers	Kathleen Turner
Prince	Lisa Hartman
Johnny Depp	Phylicia Rashad
Paul McCartney	Joan Collins
John Goodman	Connie Selleca

Type D: Tender and Caring

FEMALES

Princess Diana
Linda Ronstadt
Kim Alexis
Meryl Streep
Diahann Carroll
Phoebe Cates
Isabelle Adjani
Jerry Hall
Angelica Huston
Brigitte Neilson

MALES

Tom Cruise
Harrison Ford
Geraldo Rivera
Bill Cosby
Jimmy Smits
Robin Williams
George Michael
John Tesh
Alex Trebek
Sylvester Stallone

Type E: Big-time Romantics

MALES

Mick Jagger
Arnold Schwartzenegger
President Bill Clinton
Steve Martin
Kenny Rogers
Peter Jennings
Magic Johnson
Robert de Niro
Robert Redford
Patrick Swayze

FEMALES

Madonna
Jackee
Whitney Houston
Lynda Carter
Delta Burke
Connie Chung
Kathie Lee Gifford
Deborah Norville
Iman
Loni Anderson

Type F: They Love Taking Care of You

FEMALES

Shelley Long
Joan Lunden
Raquel Welch
Sophia Loren
Jacqueline Bisset
Faith Ford

MALES

Richard Gere
Jeremy Irons
Harry Connick, Jr.
Billy Ray Cyrus
David Soul
Corbin Bernson

Rebecca DeMornay
Ann Archer
Amy Irving
Linda Gray

John Ritter
Sean Connery
Michael Keaton
Mark Harmon

Type G: The Beauty Lover

MALES

Michael Douglas
Armand Assante
Julio Iglesias
Marcello Mastroianni
Luciano Pavarotti
John Lithgow
Sting
Jesse Jackson
Bryant Gumbel
Charleton Heston

FEMALES

Susan Sarandon
Sigourney Weaver
Suzanne Somers
Cheryl Tiegs
Catherine Deneuve
Heather Locklear
Brigitte Bardot
Angela Lansbury
Julie Andrews
Deborah Kerr

Type H: Intense and Passionate

FEMALES

Jodie Foster
Goldie Hawn
Roseanne Arnold
Demi Moore
Julia Roberts
Whoopi Goldberg
Meg Ryan
Mary Elizabeth Mastrantonio
Mary Hart
Maria Shriver

MALES

Sam Sheppard
Dan Rather
Larry King
Kevin Kline
Harry Hamlin
Burt Lancaster
Richard Burton
Danny DeVito
Pat Sajak
Ted Turner

Type I: Call Me Lucky

MALES

Don Johnson
Billy Idol
Frank Sinatra
Jeff Bridges
John F. Kennedy, Jr.
Kirk Douglas
Michael Nouri
Richard Pryor
Phil Donohue
Woody Allen

FEMALES

Kim Basinger
Darryl Hannah
Jane Fonda
Sinead O'Connor
Bette Midler
Robin Givens
Susan Dey
Tina Turner
Teri Garr
Liv Ullman

Type J: Home Is Where the Heart Is

FEMALES

Katie Courec
Diane Sawyer
Diane Keaton
Kirstie Alley
Victoria Principal
Faye Dunaway
Susan Lucci
Dolly Parton
Marlene Dietrich
Ava Gardner

MALES

David Bowie
Elvis Presley
Rod Stewart
Denzel Washington
Ted Danson
Nicholas Cage
Mel Gibson
Kevin Costner
Cary Grant
Anthony Hopkins

Type K: Mr. or Ms. Charisma

MALES

Clark Gable
Michael Jordan
Axl Rose
Burt Reynolds
Tom Selleck
Garth Brooks

FEMALES

Geena Davis
Ann Jillian
Farrah Fawcett
Morgan Fairchild
Meg Tilly
Lana Turner

Lorenzo Lamas	Cybill Shepherd
Paul Newman	Jane Seymour
Richard Dean Anderson	Vanna White
John Travolta	Oprah Winfrey

Type L: The Fantasy Lover

FEMALES	MALES
Cindy Crawford	Michael Bolton
Drew Barrymore	Edward James Olmos
Bernadette Peters	William Hurt
Glenn Close	Raul Julia
Rue McClanahan	Chuck Norris
Sharon Stone	Billy Crystal
Paula Zahn	Erik Estrada
Faith Daniels	James Taylor
Sally Jessy Raphael	Harry Belafonte
Elizabeth Taylor	Willard Scott

• **IF MOST OF YOUR CHOICES ARE TYPE A, YOUR FANTASY SOULMATE IS ARIES.** These are the macho men and liberated women of the zodiac. You are probably also fascinated by such classic stars as Bette Davis, Marlon Brando, and Joan Crawford. Aries men are the type who sweep you off your feet, with plenty of enthusiasm. They may, however, cool down just as fast as they heated up. This sign has produced some noted playboys, including the founder of *Playboy* magazine, Hugh Hefner, as well as Warren Beatty and Marlon Brando. The women are some of the most exciting in the zodiac. These are assertive take-charge women who usually have dynamic careers. Obstacles only make life more challenging for lady Aries, who needs someone who'll let her take the lead—or have her own turf.

• **IF MOST ARE TYPE B, YOUR FANTASY SOULMATE IS TAURUS.** This sign experiences the world through the five senses—whatever or whoever feels good, tastes good, smells good, sounds good, looks good, is the one they love. This is the sign that stops to smell the roses, and probably planted them in the first place. This sign likes control, and stars of this sign, like Barbra Streisand and

Shirley Maclaine, usually call their own shots. Men of this sign, like Jack Nicholson and Daniel Day Lewis, have an earthy kind of sensuality. They're the type that responds to good food, comfort, and physical beauty in a woman. The gorgeous Taurus stars like Candice Bergen, Michelle Pfeiffer, and Andie McDowell have a flowerlike femininity that is down to earth and a bit maternal—someone you'd love to come home to.

• **IF MOST ARE TYPE C, YOUR FANTASY SOULMATE IS GEMINI.** Gemini celebrities are known for their great lines. When we say, "Can we talk?" or "Make my day," or when we mention "the art of the deal," we conjure up images of Joan Rivers, Clint Eastwood, or Donald Trump. Joan Collins's TV character on "Dynasty" was as famous for her quick wit as her beauty. Never bored or boring, Gemini values mental stimulation more than the physical pleasures or material rewards. One example is Gemini beauty Brooke Shields, who cut her career short to finish college. Rather than be typecast, Kathleen Turner and Isabella Rossellini experiment with many kinds of roles. Rare is the Gemini who has only one career or one marriage. George Bush was the exception—but he was married to Barbara, another Gemini. Variety is the key to Gemini's appeal, and it's also the secret to their ability to communicate with so many different kinds of people.

• **IF MOST ARE TYPE D, YOUR FANTASY SOULMATE IS CANCER.** Women born under this sign are among the most classically feminine and nurturing in the zodiac. However, that same caring nature can make them powerful mother figures, like Princess Diana, Nancy Reagan, and Imelda Marcos. If you're attracted to this type, you love their strong femininity and depth of feelings. Actresses like Meryl Streep and Angelica Huston have an intuitive understanding of character that helps them turn in award-winning performances. The Cancer male, like Robin Williams or Tom Cruise, also accesses that uncanny intuition. Here is a man who is more comfortable with women than any other sign. This man is a born romantic, whose understanding of a woman's emotions and insecurities makes him one of the zodiac's most tender and sympathetic lovers.

• **IF MOST ARE TYPE E, YOUR FANTASY SOUL-MATE IS LEO.** This sign does everything in a big way. They crave lots of attention, and you'd better be ready to provide it if you fall in love with this sign. President Bill Clinton and Arnold Schwartzenegger are prototypes of the larger-than-life Leo male. Though not on the list, Stormin' Norman Schwartzkopf is another. Even Leos who are less than impressive physically make their presence felt—Dustin Hoffman and Mick Jagger are two examples. The women of this sign are regal romantics who need a lover who knows how to pay court. Many Leo stars were beauty queens or involved with the pageants, like Delta Burke, Lynda Carter, and Kathie Lee Gifford. Many Leo stars are powerful enough to be known by only one name, like Madonna, Iman, Jackee, or Jackie O. If she can learn to share the spotlight sometimes, this sign makes a warm, loving mate who radiates positive energy.

• **IF MOST ARE TYPE F, YOUR FANTASY SOUL-MATE IS VIRGO.** It may come as a surprise that the sign of the virgin contains some of the sexiest celebrities, like Sophia Loren, Sean Connery, Raquel Welch, and Jaqueline Bisset. Yet these are not types who bestow affection lightly. There is always an idealism, a search for the perfect lover, behind their quest. The Virgo male type, like Jeremy Irons and Corbin Bernsen, appreciates brains as well as beauty—and that's a big part of his appeal. And this is one man that can sing about an "Achey Breakey Heart" (Billy Ray Cyrus) and have women lining up to cure it. Virgo women, sensuous though they may be, always have an air of discipline and discrimination. Like Raquel, they watch what they eat and exercise every day. But it's this blend of sensuality and practicality that makes this sign so appealing. If they take such good care of themselves, imagine how well they'll take care of you!

• **IF MOST ARE TYPE G, YOUR FANTASY SOUL-MATE IS LIBRA.** Libra is an aesthetic sign that is able to project an ideal kind of beauty, like Catherine Deneuve, Deborah Kerr, or Brigitte Bardot. When this sign's scales are balanced, Libra combines charm, style, and ideals of fairness. The men of this sign are often style setters, like Bryant Gumbel, Marcello Mastroianni, or Ralph Lauren, yet they always retain an air of detachment as they examine everyone and everything from many perspectives. The women are ultra-feminine but fight fiercely for justice, as shown by the Libran celebrities' roles. Sigourney Weaver in *Aliens* and Susan Sarandon in *Thelma and Louise* are two examples. And in real life, there are forceful Libra heroines like Eleanor Roosevelt and Margaret Thatcher.

• **IF MOST ARE TYPE H, YOUR FANTASY SOUL-MATE IS SCORPIO.** This category shows an attraction to intense characters. Both male and female Scorpios love to exercise power and control over others. You'll find many female Scorpio stars firmly holding the reins, involved in all aspects of their shows. Jodie Foster, Roseanne Arnold, and Goldie Hawn are all active players in the Hollywood power scene. Hillary Rodham Clinton wields Scorpio female political power. Scorpio men, like Kevin Kline, have strong sexual magnetism, even when playing comedy roles. Often they come across as low key, like Sam Sheppard or anchorman Dan Rather—but never underestimate their underlying drive. To intrigue a Scorpio, keep your air of mystery. Don't tell all. Scorpio loves to delve into your deep secrets.

• **IF MOST ARE TYPE I, YOUR FANTASY SOUL-MATE IS SAGITTARIUS.** When Frank Sinatra sings "I Did It My Way," he's singing the Sagittarius theme song. This sign hates to take orders and needs to keep some independence in any relationship. The male Sagittarius is a romantic wanderer, but so much fun that he's easier to forgive than other zodiac Don Juans. This sign is also compelled to voice its opinions, controversial as they may be. You may be attracted by the outspoken, sometimes outrageous qualities of Sagittarius stars like Sinead O'Connor, Bette Midler, and Phil Donohue. This sign is very sports minded, whether as a participant or spectator, and adores being on the road. Sagittarius women, like Jane Fonda and Liv Ullman, usually have interests that reach beyond their profession. Sagittarians are big risk takers, whether it be a new business venture or a night at the casino. Fortunately, luck usually smiles on this sign, perhaps because these folks are among the most optimistic positive thinkers of the zodiac.

• **IF MOST ARE TYPE J, YOUR FANTASY SOULMATE IS CAPRICORN.** It may come as a surprise that a sign that contains David Bowie, Rod Stewart, and Elvis Presley, could be called home loving and traditional. But male Capricorns like the little woman to stay in the background, helping them rise to the top, and they usually do not tolerate a two-career marriage for long. Women of this sign also combine ambition with traditional values. Dolly Parton has lovingly restored the backwoods cabin where she grew up. Throughout her long career, Marlene Dietrich returned to her husband's chicken farm and stayed married to the same man in spite of her legendary love life. This combination of the devoted girl or boy next door with worldly success is one thing that keeps Capricorn stars like Cary Grant, Ava Gardner, and Loretta Young on our mind.

• **IF MOST ARE TYPE K, YOUR FANTASY SOULMATE IS AQUARIUS.** Charisma is the word for the electric appeal of Aquarius, which grows ever stronger over high-tech media like television and video. This sign understands the secret of universal appeal. They're everyone's friend and can reach out to groups of people easily, like Oprah Winfrey or Paul Newman. The men of this sign easily embody an archetypal masculinity, like Clark Gable or Burt Reynolds. However, on a personal level they tend to be remote. There's always a fascinating elusive quality that can't quite be pinned down. To have a lasting relationship with this sign, you've got to be a friend as well a lover. It also helps if you share plenty of outside activities and interests—this is not a sign who'll focus on you alone.

• **IF MOST ARE TYPE L, YOUR FANTASY SOULMATE IS PISCES.** Pisces celebrities wrap their talent in an air of illusion. They rarely come on strong. Instead, they have an undefinable ease and glamour that lures admirers. Like the actors Michael Caine, Glen Close, or Raul Julia, Pisces artists seem to do what they do effortlessly, as if they're hardly trying. No one can guess the hard work behind their talented facade. They love to help the needy (and often attract people with problems). Pisces, like Elizabeth Taylor, will champion the most controversial causes. The Pisces female, like Cindy Crawford, epitomizes feminine glamour, but there is always a caring, emotional quality as well. The Pisces male is home loving and sensual. He's the dreamy kind of romantic, who will make you feel as if you're the center of his universe and that he understands everything you're going through. If he's in a field where he can use his creative talents, he's sure to be a success.

CHAPTER 12

The Astrology Bulletin—How to Make Your Own Astrology Connections

If you've caught the "astrology bug," you'll want to go even further than the scope of this book. Perhaps you'll begin by having your chart done, then deepen your knowledge by taking courses or attending conferences, subscribing to astrology-oriented magazines, or trying your hand at doing charts yourself on your personal computer. If you are buying a computer with astrology use in mind, you'll want to know where to find the right program for your needs and expertise.

To help you in your quest, here is what you can expect from a typical astrological reading, some tips on the newest computer programs, plus a resource list of reputable companies and organizations at the end of the chapter.

Whether you're new to astrology or already hooked, you'll find the more you get involved, the more you'll be fascinated by its accuracy and relevance to your life. And the more there is to challenge you!

When to Have a Reading

If you've been wondering about whether an astrological reading could give you the competitive edge in business, help you break through a personal dilemma, decide on the best day for a key event in your life, or help you make a career change, this may be the time to have a personal consultation. An astrologer might give you reassurance and validation at a turning point or crisis time in your life, or simply help you get where you want to go. Though you can learn much about astrology from books such as this one, or you can choose from a varied menu of computer readings (there are some quite sophisticated readings done by world-famous astrologers), nothing compares to a personal consultation with a professional astrologer who has analyzed thousands of charts and who can pinpoint the winning potential within yours. With your astrologer, you can address specific problems in your life that may be holding you back. For instance, if you are not getting along with your mate or coworker, you could leave the reading with some new insights and some constructive ways to handle the situation. There's no question that a good astrologer can help you create a more fulfilling future by understanding your own tendencies as well as your place in the cosmic scheme.

YOU'LL NEED TO GIVE THE ASTROLOGER THIS INFORMATION BEFOREHAND. Before your reading, a reputable astrologer will ask you for the date, time (as accurately as possible), and place of birth of the subject of the reading. A horoscope can be cast about anything that has a specific time and place. Most astrologers will enter this information into a computer, which will then calculate your chart in seconds. From the resulting chart, the astrologer will do an interpretation.

WHAT TO DO IF YOU ARE NOT SURE OF YOUR EXACT BIRTH TIME. If you don't know your exact birth time, you can usually find it filed at the Bureau of Vital Statistics at the city hall or county seat of the state where you were born. If you have no success in getting your time of birth, some astrologers specialize in rectification, using past events of your life to estimate an approximate birth time.

How to Find a Good Astrologer

Your first priority should be to choose a qualified astrologer. Rather than relying on hearsay or grandiose advertising claims, do this with the same care you would choose any trusted adviser such as a doctor, lawyer, or banker.

Unfortunately, anyone can claim to be an astrologer—to date, there is no licensing of astrologers or established professional criteria. However, there are nationwide organizations of serious, committed astrologers that can help you in your search.

Good places to start your investigation are organizations such as the American Federation of Astrologers or the National Council for Geocosmic Research (NCGR), which offers a program of study and certification. If you live near a major city, there is sure to be an active NCGR chapter or astrology club in your area—many are listed in astrology magazines available at your local newsstand. In response to many requests for referrals, the NCGR has compiled a directory of professional astrologers, which includes a glossary of terms and an explanation of specialties within the astrological field. Contact the NCGR headquarters (see the resource list at the end of this chapter) to order a copy.

As a potentially lucrative freelance business, astrology has always attracted self-styled experts who may not have the technique or the counseling experience to give an accurate, helpful reading. These astrologers can range from the well-meaning amateur to the charlatan or street-corner gypsy who has for many years given astrology a bad name. Be very wary of astrologers who claim to have occult powers or who make pretentious claims of celebrated clients or miraculous achievements. You can often tell from the initial phone conversation if the astrologer is legitimate. He or she should ask for your birthday time and place and conduct the conversation in a professional way. Any astrologer who gives a reading based only on your sun sign is highly suspect.

When you arrive at the reading, the astrologer should be prepared. The consultation should be conducted in a private, quiet place. The astrologer should be interested in your problems of the moment. A good reading involves feedback on your part, so if the reading is not relating to your concerns, you should let the astrologer know. You should feel free to ask questions and get clarification of technical terms. Thc reading should be an interaction between two people rather than a solo performance. The more you actively participate, rather than expecting the astrologer to carry the reading or come forth with oraclar predictions, the more meaningful your experience will be.

An astrologer should help you validate your current experience and be frank about possible negative happenings, but be helpful about pointing your life in the most positive direction.

In their approach to a reading, some astrologers may be more literal, some more intuitive. Those who have had counseling training may take a more psychological approach. Though some astrologers may seem to have an almost psychic ability, extrasensory perception or any other parapsychological talent is not necessary to be a good astrologer. A very accurate picture can be drawn from factual data.

An astrologer may do several charts for each client—one for the time of birth, one for the current date, and a "progressed" chart showing the evolution from the birth time to the present. According to your individual needs, there are many other possibilities, such as a chart for a different location, if you are contemplating a change of place. Relationships between any two people, things, or events can be interpreted with a "synastry" chart, which compares the chart of one birth date with the chart of another date. Another type of relationship chart is the composite chart, which uses the midpoints between planets in two individual charts to describe the relationship.

An astrologer will be particularly interested in transits—planets passing over the planets or sensitive points in your chart during the upcoming year, which signal important times for you.

Another option is a taped reading—the astrologer will mail you a previously taped reading based on your birth chart. This type of reading if more personal than a computer printout and can give you valuable insights, but it is not equivalent to a live reading, when you have a dialogue with the astrologer and can cover your specific interests.

Astrology on Your Home Computer

Your PC is an excellent tool for learning about astrology. There are basic programs especially for students, which cost under $100, such as "Chartwheels" from Astrolabe. No longer do you have to spend hours on tedious calculations or rely on guesswork when you set up a chart. The computer does this for you in seconds and runs off a great-looking chart.

Software is now available for every computer and for all levels of astrological expertise. Some will provide pages of interpretations. Others simply run off a chart with technical information. Others give you mind-boggling menus enabling you to choose from many different zodiacs, house systems, and types of charts. If, like most of our readers, you will only be using the program occasionally for fun, then you really don't need an expensive and complicated program. If you are motivated to study astrology in depth, however, you may want to investigate the more challenging programs.

There are several companies on the resource list at the end of this chapter that produce or distribute astrological software. Most are happy to offer support and advice. If you give them the make and model of your computer and your level of astrological knowledge, they will recommend a program and even help you get started. Some offer chart services to print up charts and interpretations for those who do not have a computer or do not want to invest in a program.

BUYING A COMPUTER TO DO ASTROLOGY. There are programs available for all operating systems, although most are created for IBM compatibles. At this writing, one of the top astrology software companies, Astrolabe, is offering thirty programs for IBM PC compatibles, thirteen for Macintoshes, and one for the Commodore Amiga. It also continues to stock some older programs for Apple II, earlier Commodores, and CPM-compatible machines, so don't despair if you are still working on a "dinosaur."

If you're buying a new computer and want to run state-of-the-art programs, most software vendors recommend an 80386 to 80486 processor chip, at least 640K RAM (though most current software runs on 512 K RAM), a speed of 16 megaHertz or faster, and DOS 3.3 or higher. A hard disk with 40 or more megabytes and at least one floppy are recommended. As for monitors, color displays are not necessary; however, there are some gorgeous graphic astrology charts coming out that will require an auto VGA. Otherwise, a high-resolution one-color monitor with a Hercules monographics card is fine.

If you are buying a new printer, graphics look sharpest on a laser printer, but many astrologers are very content with a 9- or 24-pin printer. Those of you who use Windows will find that several of the companies listed at the end of the chapter are now doing programs for this environment, with pull-down menus and graphics. "Solar Fire" from Astrolabe is one such program.

Where to Connect with Other Astrologers

Check your local metaphysical bookstore for flyers or a bulletin board posting astrological events in your area. Many New Age centers offer courses with astrologers visiting your area, when you can meet kindred souls.

You can contact other astrologers or learn about astrological happenings in your area and nationwide through computer networks which have astrological SIG's (Special Interest Groups). These are often reviewed or listed in astrology magazines, so, if you have a modem, why not tune in? If you already belong to a network or to Compuserve, check to see if there are astrology fans online.

Another way of finding an astrology class is to contact one of the regional astrology groups across the country that have regular meetings. Ask at your local metaphysical or New Age bookstore or look for listings in an astrology magazine such as *American Astrology* or *Dell's Horoscope.* Astrological organizations like the National Council for Geocosmic Research may give classes in your area. Several times a year, these organizations sponsor regional astrology conferences where you can meet some of the best teachers, as well as broaden your knowledge and socialize with other astrology fans.

Several astrologers are running mating-and-dating services, using astrological savvy to bring cosmically connected couples together. It is possible that one of your local astrologers is running a comparable service. This could be a "personals" column with astrological information about the participants that you then follow up on your own, or the astrologer may do a more personalized search for you, involving individual chart comparisons, personal interviews, and video interviews.

Some Other Ways to Study Astrology

First, consider attending one of the several yearly regional conferences sponsored by the major astrological organizations. Most offer programs at several levels of expertise. You could also connect with a teacher who would help you further your studies.

If you cannot go to conferences, you can still hear many of the lectures and workshops on tape cassetes in your home or car. See the resource list to order catalogues of regional and national conferences. Taped instruction is also advertised in the more specialized astrology magazines such as *Planet Earth* or *Mountain Astrologer.*

Another option, which might interest those who live in out-of-the-way places or who are unable to fit classes into their schedule, are study-by-mail courses that are offered by several astrological computing services and astrology magazines. Some courses will send you a series of tapes; others use workbooks or computer printouts.

An Astrology Resource List

Nationwide Astrology Organizations

(Conferences, Workshops, Local Meetings, Conference Tapes, Referrals)

National Council for Geocosmic Research
(For Directory of Professional Astrologers, classes, tape catalogue, and conference schedule.)
105 Snyder Avenue
Ramsey, NJ 07446
201-818-2871

American Federation of Astrologers (A.F.A.)
P.O. Box 22040
Tempe, AZ 85382

A.F.A.N.
(Networking, Legal Issues.)
8306 Wilshire Blvd.
Berkeley Hills, CA 90211

ARC Directory
(Listing of astrologers worldwide)
2920 E. Monte Vista
Tucson, AZ 85716
602-321-1114

Computer Programs

Matrix Software
(Programs for IBM Compatibles, at the student and professional level.)
315 Marion Avenue
Big Rapids, MI 49307
(1-800-PLANETS)

Astro Communications Services
(Programs for IBM compatibles and MAC, variety of computer charts, Telephone Consultations.)
Dept. AF693, PO Box 34487
San Diego, CA 92163-4487
(1-800-888-9983)

Astrolabe
(Variety of programs for all computers, beginner to professional level, wide selection of computer readings.)
Box 1750—R
Brewster, MA 02631
1-800-843-6682

A.R.T. Software
(Programs for the Mac.)
P.O. Box 191
Cumberland Center, ME 04021

Microcycles
PO Box 78219
Los Angeles, CA 90016-0219
(1-800-CYCLES)

Air Software
115 Caya Avenue
West Hartford, CT 06110
(1-800-659-1AIR)

Time Cycles Research
(Programs for the Macintosh.)
27 Dimmock Road
Waterford, CT 06385

Astro-Cartography
(Charts for location changes.)
Astro-Numeric Service
Box 336-AD
Ashland, OR 97520
1-800-MAPPING

Conference and Workshop Tapes

Pegasus Tapes
P.O. Box 419
Santa Ysabel, CA 92070

National Council for Geocosmic Research
(Conference tapes.)
NCGR Headquarters
105 Snyder Avenue
Ramsey, NJ 07446
201-818-2871

International Society for Astrological Research (ISAR)
(Lectures, workshops, seminars.)
P.O. Box 38613
Los Angeles, CA 90038

ISIS Institute
P.O. Box 21222
El Sobrante, CA 94820-1222

Astro Analytics Productions
P.O. Box 16927
Encino, CA 914116-6927
818-997-8684

Astrology Schools

New York School of Astrology
(Intensive curriculum, seminars, bookstore, conferences, public events.)
545 Eighth Avenue-10th Floor
New York, NY 10018-4307
212-947-3609

Astrology Magazines

American Astrology
475 Park Avenue South
New York, NY 10016

Dell Horoscope
P.O. Box 53352
Boulder, CO 80321-3342

Aspects
Aquarius Workshops
P.O. Box 260556
Encino, CA 91426

Planet Earth
The Great Bear
P.O. Box 5164
Eugene, OR 97405

The Mountain Astrologer
P.O. Box 11292
Berkeley, CA 94701

CHAPTER 13

Your Year-Round Calendar for Creating a Healthier Lifestyle

Of the big changes in the past few years, those involving our health care may have the greatest effect on our future well-being. At this writing, as Pluto, the planet of transformation, is winding up its trip through Scorpio, the sign that rules insurance and life-or-death matters, we are scheduled for sweeping health-care reforms. It should be no surprise that the one who designed and launched the transformation in American health care should be an intense and dedicated Scorpio, Hillary Rodham Clinton.

At the same time, Saturn is moving through Pisces, which rules hospitals. This planet calls attention to what isn't working, and while in Pisces, it calls for devotion to helping others. Over this year, many health-care institutions are sure to be reexamined and restructured. With monumental changes shaking up our health-care system, we'll be asked to take on more responsibility for our own health, beginning with adopting a healthier lifestyle.

Astrology can help you sort out your health priorities and put your life on a healthier course by getting in step with these times of reform. Since astrology began, different parts of the body, and their potential illnesses, have been associated with specific signs of the zodiac. Today's astrologers still work with these ancient associations, using them not only to locate potential health problems, but also to help clients harmonize their activities with those favored by each sign.

Using the stars as a guide, you can create your own master plan for a healthier lifestyle by focusing on the part of your body that is ruled by each sign, during that sun-sign period. For example, during Pisces, the sign that rules the feet, you might evaluate your shoes for fit and comfort or start a walking program. You could step up to an aerobics class or regular tennis games during Mars-ruled Aries, a high-energy sign. During nature-oriented Taurus, you should switch to more outdoor exercise, like hiking. This approach varies your workout routine to harmonize with the astrological atmosphere. And you'll be more likely to sustain your fitness program if there is enough variety to keep you from getting bored. If you follow this sign by sign pathway, by the end of the year you'll have improved your health from head to toe.

The following guide should help you select activities which harmonize with each sun-sign period.

Capricorn—a great time to get started!
(December 22–January 19)

You couldn't pick a better time to start off on a new health and fitness regime than discipline-oriented Capricorn. Maybe that's why this is the busiest time of the year for gyms and health spas. Why not give yourself a Christmas present of a membership in a local gym or YMCA? Under Capricorn, which favors structure and organization of all kinds, you'll be motivated to start off the new year by getting into an exercise routine. However, it's important to find a plan you can stick with, so consider first consulting with a coach or a personal trainer who'll design a routine that's best for you.

Capricorn rules the skeletal structure, which makes this a great time to look at the state of your posture, your bones and joints. It's never too early to counteract osteoporosis by adding weight-bearing exercise to your routine. If your knees or joints are showing early signs of arthritis, you may need to add calcium supplements to your diet. Check your posture, which affects your looks and your health. Remember to protect your knees when you work, perhaps adding exercises to strengthen this area.

Capricorn, the sign of Father Time, brings up the subject of aging. If sags and wrinkles are keeping you from looking as young as you feel, you may want to investigate plastic surgery. Many foods have antiaging qualities and might be worth adding to your diet. Teeth are also ruled by this sign—a reminder to have regular cleanings and dental checkups.

Capricorn is also the sign of the workaholic, so be sure not to overdo in your quest for health. Keep a steady, even pace for lasting results. Remember to include pleasurable activities in your self-care program. Grim determination can be counterproductive if you're also trying to relieve tension. Take up a sport for pure enjoyment, not necessarily to become a champion.

Your Capricorn-time stress-busters: Check your office environment for hidden health saboteurs, like air quality, lighting, and comfort. Get a back-support cushion if your chair is uncomfortable. If you work at a computer, check your keyboard and the height of the computer screen for ergonomic comfort.

Aquarius—individualize! (January 20–February 18th)

Aquarius, the sign of high-tech gadgets and new ideas, should inspire you with new ways to get fit and healthy. You don't have to follow the crowd to keep fit. There are many ways to adapt your exercise routine to your personal needs. If your schedule makes it difficult to get to the gym or take regular exercise classes, look over the vast selection of exercise videos available and take class anytime you want. Or set up a gym at home with portable home exercise equipment.

New Age health treatments are favored by Aquarius, which makes this an ideal month to consider alternative approaches to health and fitness. Since Aquarius rules the circulatory system, you might benefit from a therapeutic massage, a relaxing whirlpool, or one of the new electronic massage machines.

Calves and ankles are also Aquarius territory and should be emphasized in your exercise program. Be sure your ankles are well supported, and be careful of sprains.

This is also a good time to consider the air quality around you. Aquarians are often vulnerable to airborn allergies and are highly sensitive to air pollution. Do some air quality control on your environment with an air purifier, ionizer, or humidifier. Since this is flu season, read up on ways to strengthen your immune system.

Aquarius is a sign of reaching out to others, a cue to

make your health regime more social—doing your exercises with friends could make staying fit more fun.

Pisces—feet first! (February 19–March 20)

Perhaps it's no accident that we often do spring cleaning during Pisces. The last sign of the zodiac, which rules the lymphatic system, is super-sensitive to toxins. This is the ideal time to detox your system with a liquid diet or supervised fast. This may also help you get rid of water retention, a common Pisces problem.

Feet are Pisces territory. Consider how often you take your feet for granted and how miserable life can be when your feet hurt. Since our feet reflect and affect the health of the entire body, devote some time this month to pampering them. Check your walking shoes or buy some shoes tailored for your kind of exercise. Investigate orthotics, especially if you walk or run a lot. These custom-molded inserts could make a big difference in your comfort and performance.

The soles of our feet connect with all other parts of our body, just as the sign of Pisces embodies all the previous signs. This is the theory behind reflexology, a therapeutic foot massage which treats all areas of the body via the nerve endings on the soles of the feet. For the sake of your feet, as well as your entire body, consider treating yourself to a session with a local practitioner of this technique.

Pisces is the ideal time to start walking outdoors again, enjoying the first signs of spring. Try doing local errands on foot, as much as possible.

Aries—energize! (March 21–April 19)

This Mars-ruled sign is a high-energy time of year. It's time to step up the intensity of your workouts, so you'll be in great shape for summer. Aerobics, competitive sports, activities that burn calories are all favored. Try a new sport that has plenty of action and challenge, like soccer or bike racing. Be sure you have the proper headgear, since Aries rules the head.

Healthwise, if you've been burning the candle at both ends or repressing anger, this may show up as headaches. The way to work off steam under Aries is to schedule extra time at the gym, take up a racket sport or ping pong, anything that lets you hit an object hard! Go into spring training with your local baseball team!

Taurus—back to nature! (April 20–May 20)

Spring is in full bloom, and what better time to awaken your senses to the beauty of nature? Planting a garden can be a wonderful, relaxing antidote to a stressful job. Long walks in the woods, listening to the sounds of returning birds, and smelling the spring flowers help you slow down and enjoy the pleasures of the Earth.

This is a month to enjoy all your senses: Add more beautiful music to your library, try some new recipes, take up a musical instrument, learn the art of massage. This pleasure-loving time can be one of the most sensual in your love life, so plan a weekend getaway to somewhere special with the one you love.

This is also a time to go to local farmers' markets and to add more fresh vegetables to your diet. While we're on the subject of food, you may be tempted to overindulge during the Taurus period, so be sure there are plenty of low-calorie treats available. If you are feeling too lethargic, your thyroid might be sluggish. Taurus rules the neck and throat area, which includes the thyroid glands and vocal cords.

Since we often hold tension in our neck area, pause several times during the day for a few stretches and head rolls. If you wake up with a stiff neck, you may be using the wrong kind of pillow.

Gemini—stay in touch! (May 21–June 20)

One of the most social signs, Gemini rules the nerves, our body's lines of communication. doing things with others is therapeutic now. Include friends in your exercise routines. Join a friendly exercise class or jogging group. Gemini-type sports require good timing and manual dexterity as well as communication with others, like tennis or golf.

If your nerves are on edge, you may need more fun and laughter in your life. Getting together with friends, going to parties, doing things in groups brings more perspective into your life.

Since Gemini also rules the lungs, this is an ideal time to quit smoking. Investigate natural ways to relieve tension, such as yoga or meditation. Doing things with your hands—playing the piano, typing, doing craftwork—is also helpful.

Those of you who jog may want to try hand weights during the Gemini months, or add upper-body exercises to your daily routine.

Cancer—create a healthy home! (June 21–July 22)

Good health begins at home, and Cancer is the perfect time to do some healthy housekeeping. Evaluate your home for potential toxins in the water or building material. Could you benefit from air and water purifiers, undyed sheets and towels, biodegradable cleaners? How about safer cooking utensils of stainless steel or glass?

This is also a good month for nurturing others and yourself, airing problems and providing the emotional support that should make your home a happier, more harmonious place to live.

Cancer rules digestive difficulties, especially gastric ulcers. Emotionally caused digestive problems—those stomach-knotting insecurities—can crop up under Cancer. Baby yourself with some extra pampering if you're feeling blue.

Boating and all water sports are ideal Cancer-time activities. Sometimes, just a walk by your local pond or sitting for a few moments by a fountain can do wonders to relieve stress and tension.

If you've been feeling emotionally insecure, these feelings may be sensitized now, especially near the full moon. Being with loved ones, old friends, and family could give the support you need. Plan some special family activities that bring everyone close together.

The breast area is ruled by Cancer, a reminder to have regular checkups, according to your age and family history.

Leo—heart and spine time! (July 23–August 22)

We're now in the heart of summer, the time when you need to consider your relationship to Leo's ruler, the sun. Tans look great, but in recent years we've all been cautioned about the permanent damage the sun can do. So don't leave home without a big hat or umbrella, and some sunblock formulated for your skin type.

If you've been faithful to your exercise program, you probably look great in your swimsuit. If not, now's the time to contemplate some spot-reducing exercises to zero in on problem areas. This is prime time for outdoor activity—biking, swimming, team sports—that can supplement your routine. Leos like Arnold Schwartzenegger and Madonna have profited immensely from weight training. Since this is a time to glorify the body beautiful, why not consider what a body-building regime could do for you?

Leo rules the upper back and heart, so consider your cardiovascular fitness and make your diet healthier for your heart. Are you getting enough aerobic exercise? Also, step up exercises that strengthen the Leo-ruled upper back, like swimming.

If you have planned a vacation for this month, make it a healthy one, a complete change of pace. Spend time playing with children, expressing the child within yourself. The Leo time is great for creative activities, doing whatever you enjoy most.

Virgo—analyze! (August 23–September 22)

Virgo rules the care and maintenance of the body in general, and the abdomen, digestion, lower liver and intestines in particular. This is a troubleshooting sign, the perfect time to check your progress. Schedule medical exams and diagnostic tests, and generally evaluate your health. If you need a change of diet, supplements, or special care, consult the appropriate advisers.

It's also a good time to make your life run more efficiently. It's a great comfort to know that you've got a smooth organization backing you up. Go through your files and closets to eliminate clutter; edit your drawers and toss out whatever is no longer relevant to your life.

In this back-to-school time, many of us are taking self-improvement courses. Consider a course to improve your health—nutrition, macrobiotic cooking, or massage, for example.

Libra—balance your life! (September 23–October 22)

Are your personal scales in balance? If you're overdoing in any area of your life, Libra is an excellent time to address the problem. If you have been working too hard or taking life too seriously, what you may need is a dose of culture, art, music, or perhaps some social activity.

If your body is off balance, consider yoga, spinal adjustments, or a detoxification program. Libra rules the kidneys and lower back, which respond to relaxation and tension-relieving exercises. Make time to entertain friends. Be romantic with the one you love. Harmonize your body with chiropractic work. Cleanse your kidneys with plenty of liquids.

Since this is the sign of relationships, you may enjoy working out with a partner or with loved ones. Make morning walks and weekend hikes family affairs. Take a romantic bicycle tour and picnic in the autumn countryside. Put more beauty in all areas of your life.

Libra is also the sign of grace, and what's more graceful than the dance! If ballet is not your thing, why not swing to a Latin or African beat? Dancing combines art, music, romance, relaxation, graceful movement, social contact, and exercise—what more can you ask?

Scorpio—transformation! (October 23–November 21)

If you have been keeping up an exercise program all year, you should see a real difference now, if not a total transformation. Scorpio is the sign to transform yourself—try a new hair color, get a makeover, change your style. Eliminate what's been holding you back, including self-distructive habits—Scorpio is a sign of willpower and determination.

This sign rules the regenerative and eliminative organs, so it's a great time to turn over a new leaf. Sexual activity comes under Scorpio, so this can be a passionate time for love. It's also a good time to examine your attitudes toward sex and to put safe sexual practices into your life.

It's no accident that this passionate time is football season, which reminds us that sports are a very healthy way to diffuse emotions. If you enjoy winter sports, why not start preparing for the ski slopes or ice skating? Scorpio loves intense life-or-death competition, so be sure your muscles are warmed up before going all out.

Sagittarius—set goals! (November 22–December 21)

Sagittarius, ruled by jovial Jupiter, is holiday time, a time to kick back, socialize with friends, and enjoy a whirl of parties and get-togethers. High-calorie temptations abound, so you may want to add an extra workout or two after hitting the buffet table. Or better yet, head for the dance floor instead of the hors d'oeuvres. Most people tend to loosen up on resolve around this time of year; there's just too much fun to be had.

If you can, combine socializing with athletic activities. Local football games, bike riding, hikes, and long walks with your dog in tow are just as much fun in cooler weather. Let others know that you'd like a health-promoting gift—sports equipment, a gym membership, or an exercise video—for Christmas. Plan your holiday buffet to lessen temptation with plenty of low-calorie choices.

In your workouts, concentrate on Sagittarius-ruled areas with exercises for the hips, legs, and thighs. This is a sports-loving sign, ideal for downhill or cross-country skiing, ice skating or roller blading, and basketball.

You may find the more spiritual kinds of exercise, such as yoga or taï chi, which work on the mind as well as the body, more appealing now. Once learned, these exercises can be done anywhere. Yoga exercises are especially useful for those who travel, especially those designed to release tension in the neck and back. Isometrics-type exercises, which work one muscle group against another, can be done in a car or plane seat. If you travel often, investigate equipment that fits easily in your suitcase, such as water-filled weights, jump ropes, elastic exercise bands, and home-gym devices.

This sign of expansiveness is the ideal opportunity to set your goals for next year. Ask yourself what worked best for you this year and where you want to be at the end of 1996. Most important, in holiday-loving Sagittarius, go for the health-promoting sports and activities you truly enjoy. These are the best for you in the long run, for they're the ones you'll keep doing with pleasure.

CHAPTER 14

Your Aquarius Personal Life—Including Your Decision Maker

The Aquarius Man: Mr. Charisma

You're a charismatic heartthrob who is always tantalizingly out of reach. But this contradiction makes you even more fascinating. Your magnetic attractiveness, contrasted with your air of distance and detachment, seems to invite others to project their fantasies upon you (and makes you an excellent candidate for public life). Hollywood has had a stable of Aquarian stars who embodied the American ideal of virility—Clark Gable (The King), Paul Newman, Burt Reynolds, Tom Selleck, and John Forsythe, to name a few. Because you manage to be simultaneously remote and accessible, no one really knows the real you. The embodiment of this mysterious Aquarian persona is former President Ronald Reagan, an actor who reached the highest office in the land, fulfilling our public image of a President, yet few who worked with him felt truly close to him. You're the man we vote for, even though we are not quite sure what you stand for or what you are really like.

Often you use your position in the spotlight to accomplish humanitarian goals. It is the rare Aquarian celebrity who does not have a charity or worthy cause that he promotes. Sometimes you combine self-promotion with altruistic motives, another interesting Aquarian contradiction, where you gain much personal publicity by identifying with a cause. A perfect example is Paul Newman's successful line of salad dressing, popcorn, and lemonade—with his picture on the label and the proceeds awarded to a charity. Your ideas are sometimes so far ahead of their time that others may call them crazy—but they're crazy like a fox. You have the knack of extending whatever you do to reach the broadest audience, so listen to those flashes of inspiration and take them to the limit for fame and fortune.

In a Relationship

Free-thinking Mr. Aquarius is downright old-fashioned about marriage. Aquarian former Vice President Dan Quayle waved the banner for family values in the face of women's liberation. You'll guard your private life carefully and usually will not wander, unless your wife is the domineering or manipulative type who severely restricts your freedom. In that case, you will leave her on the doorstep, like Rhett Butler left Scarlett O'Hara, and distance yourself emotionally.

You need a woman who is "one of the great broads," as Paul Newman described his wife, which can be a very tall order to fill with a contradictory Aquarius. She'll have to be a combination of saint, sister, and seductress! An Aquarian's wife must be your best friend; she must be unpossessive enough to grant you plenty of space, and never succumb to moods. She should have interests of her own, yet be supportive of you, share your causes, and, of course, be loyal and faithful. However, she must also be able to tolerate sharing life with a slew of your buddies and with your consuming outside interests. You can fully accept, and even prefer, a woman with a life of her own. But her career should relate to, or complement, yours or you'll never see each other.

The Aquarius Woman: The Independent Romantic

Never underestimate the Aquarius woman! Though you may seem like a fluffy blonde bombshell like Zsa Zsa Gabor, a wistful waif like Mia Farrow, or a fragile romantic like Jane Seymour, there's a serious mind underneath. You'll soon prove there's far more to your charisma than the way you look. As an air sign, you are basically idea oriented and a great communicator. But as an Aquarius, you'll want to put your ideas to use, making a better world for everyone.

The Aquarius woman is a fascinating challenge! You appear friendly, open, flirtatious, and sometimes a bit wild. But if anyone tries to dominate or confine you, you'll quickly flash your sharp wit, insightful mind, and powerful will. You can be unsinkable, not caring a bit for public opinion when you are standing up for what you believe in, and trying to create a better world for everyone. In fact, no matter how you present yourself, as a conservative corporate type or a flamboyant eccentric, you need to feel that you are championing something greater than your personal goals.

You are always, in some way, an original. Aquarians can be as outrageous and avante garde as Yoko Ono or Princess Stephanie of Monaco, as zany as Zsa Zsa Gabor, or as forthright and sisterly as Oprah Winfrey, but they are unique and unpredictable. In the extreme, you love surprise for its own sake and deliberately enjoy shocking your audience out of its fixed ideas.

Sometimes you become so involved with your cause that you neglect personal relationships, but usually you find a way to include friends and family in your many outside activities. Many Aquarian mothers think nothing of bringing their children into their workplace. Sometimes this works out very well, since exposure to different situations can broaden the mind of everyone involved. But there is a down side as well: Sometimes your whole life is lived in public, surrounded by people, leaving no time for intimate moments with those who want to be close to you (some Aquarians actually fear being left alone).

The Aquarian woman's singlemindedness is a two-edged sword. When you feel you know what is best for everyone, you push ahead, not hearing the word "can't." However, you are often at your best when you're most detached, remaining open to opposing ideas and providing much-needed insight and perspective, finding innovative ways to bend the rules to benefit everyone. Because you're so fascinated by what makes people tick, many Aquarians make wonderful psychologists and social workers. Regardless of your field, your primary interest is in influencing others rather than exploiting them.

In a Relationship

An Aquarian usually looks for a liberated liaison and invents her own matrimonial rules. You'll be loyal and faithful, but not always home. Or you'll bring your interests right into the living room, which becomes an office, meeting room, classroom, or film set. Sometimes you focus on outer goals at the expense of your inner life, leaving no time for intimate relationships. Aquarius finds routine of any kind too confining and can invent some ingenious ways of taking care of chores or delegating them. Some Aquarians have large extended families who help share the domestic dilemmas.

Marriage to you is a friendly pact, where a liberated husband does his share of homework. In turn, you'll take over a sizeable slice of the financial burden. The Aquarius woman may sing "diamonds are a girl's best friend," but she doesn't mind buying them for herself! Your ideal husband will be proud of your accomplishments and encourage you to keep your outside interests. You'll return the favor by giving him a life of delightful surprises and steady devotion.

The Aquarius Family

The Aquarius Parent

As a mother, you may feel curtailed by child-rearing duties and by the routine responsibilities of motherhood. But rather than give up your outside activities, you'll cope by finding an enlightened day-care center, calling on your extended family, or developing a support system that will free you to continue your career or outside interests. Aquarians can even include your children in your work atmosphere (it was surely Aquarian mothers who persuaded companies to provide day care for children of employees). Aquarian film stars are known to have trailers on location for their children and find them small roles to play. And it was an Aquarian (Helen Gurley Brown, editor of *Cosmopolitan*) who wrote the book titled *Having It All.* You believe it is good for children to be exposed to a wide range of experiences, developing social consciousness along the way. You may often leave your children in the care of others, but you feel that this develops independence. If a clingy needy child becomes a special challenge to you, you'll find an innovative solution, perhaps an extended-family situation, a joint sharing with other mothers, or sessions with a child psychologist. Since Aquarians especially appreciate the uniqueness of each human being, you are well equipped to help your children develop independence and creativity by allowing them the freedom to experiment and find out what is truly right for them.

The Aquarius Stepparent

Since you enjoy having an extended family and sharing your life with others, you should be a very successful stepparent. Many Aquarian qualities make you well suited to this often-delicate position—your lack of possessiveness toward your mate will allow him or her to spend guilt-free time with his children. And "gregarious Aquarius" will happily open your home to activities that include the whole family. You'll think up some unusual and interesting things to do together. Your objectivity serves you well as a trusted adviser and pal, one who won't shock easily or pass judgment. You'll encourage the youngster who is exceptional or unusual to develop his or her talents. And you'll help the shy, insecure child learn how to get along in groups or express feelings in a creative way.

The Aquarius Grandparent

Aquarians who have always been ahead of the crowd may find the world catching up in their grandparent years, when their unique qualities are finally appreciated. Young of mind as well as heart, you can astonish and turn on the younger generations. You're interested and well informed on all that's new. Perhaps you'll have your own PC and challenge your grandchild with video games. Not one to hang around in a rocking chair, you'll be off to yoga class, you'll teach meditation, or you will have your hand in local politics—or at least have some vociferous opinions about the state of the world. You're the person rebellious youngsters confide in when they want to try something new, something Mother and Dad might not approve of. Shockproof Aquarian grandparents not only offer objective advice, they are living inspiration to grandchildren to invent their own lives.

Your Aquarius Decision Maker!

Astrology can help you with all kinds of decisions, from what kind of clothes to wear to what color to paint your room. Here are some of the ways you can use the stars to find the style that suits you best.

How Should I Furnish My Home?

Aquarians like wide-open spaces with plenty of room for a variety of activities and people coming and going. Home for Aquarius is sure to be much more than a family-oriented space. You may hold meetings at home or pursue an interest that has special requirements, like a computer room or a home laboratory. You might have an experimental greenhouse in your bathroom, or turn the dining room into an Oriental meditation room. Your home will always have a touch of the unconventional; perhaps you will use your rooms in a very unique way, or your choice of colors might be somehow surprising. You might have the latest technological marvel or something as far-out as an isolation tank in your bedroom. One thing is for sure: Your home will be uniquely yours; you'll make your own rules in decorating, as in everything else.

What Music Will Put Me in a Good Mood?

Electronic music, New Age jazz, Roberta Flack, or your birth-sign composers—Mozart, Schubert, and Mendelssohn. Opera as interpreted by Placido Domingo or Leontyne Price. You'll have the latest electronic sound equipment to play them. Or you might record your own music mix for a highly original, customized sound.

Where Should I Go On Vacation?

Your vacations often have a spontaneous, unpredictable quality. You'll value the experience as much as the location. You might find traditional resorts boring, and tend to steer away from status places. Charming country inns might also be the wrong direction—too quiet for you. You'd prefer a relatively undiscovered place or one related to your latest interests, or a health or meditation retreat. Arizona's power vortexes or Indian cultures might draw you. Romantic Quebec or Liechtenstein, or the outdoor life in Sweden or Oregon are other Aquarius-ruled possibilities.

You like to travel on the spur of the moment, taking a spontaneous trip to somewhere that turns you on! You'll pack your bags and be off in a minute, often without a map! Aquarius does well traveling in a group—someone in the crowd is sure to be well organized. If traveling alone, you're sure to make friends wherever you go, since you're not shy and easily attract kindred souls.

What Are My Best Aquarius Colors?

Blue and white patterns, unusual mixes of patterns, bright psychedelic colors, electric blue. You have a flair for using color in a fresh way, breaking the rules of color combinations. A mix of bold colors and patterns that might look outrageous on everyone else will make an interesting statement on you. During the sixties, the Aquarian look took center stage, with a fashion freedom that has never been equalled. Bold color mixes, psychedelic tones, computer graphics, and synthetic outer-space metallics are all part of the Aquarian influence.

What Should I Wear?

Like the other fixed signs, you'll make your own personal fashion statement and stick with it! You can be sensual like Farrah Fawcett, jet-set like the Gabors, high-fashion like Marisa Berenson, or avante-garde like Yoko Ono. You may be "no-fashion" because you're concerned about more important things, but your look will always be interesting and provocative. You'll avoid looking like everyone else. You're a trendsetter rather than a follower—you'll be the one everyone talks about, the one who wears jogging shoes with an evening gown, like Cybill Shepherd once did. Experiment to play up or exaggerate your unusual features rather than distract from them—like Geena Davis, you can carry off unique clothes that would look all wrong on anyone else. Try out unpredictable pattern mixes, psychedelic colors, avante-garde jewelry, and hair that's either very short or waist length. Strike a balance between overplaying your hand with shock tactics or, on the other hand, playing it too safe.

Who Are Aquarius Fashion Designers?

Look to designer Krizia (unusual patterns and carefree knits) and Ungaro (sexy dresses and mixes of bright colored patterns) for inspiration.

Where Should I Go for Dinner?

Aquarius usually decides on the spur of the moment where to go, depending on your mood and the company you're with. The newest, trendiest spots are sure to appeal. However, you may be on a special diet, so keep a list of restaurants that serve macrobiotic or vegetarian fare. The element of surprise and originality is exciting to Aquarius. Try a picnic in an unusual place, or call up some friends you haven't seen recently and have an instant party in an unusual place. Restaurants that are high in the sky or that have a view are especially good for Aquarians, who love the feeling of space.

CHAPTER 15

Getting Together: How Aquarius Pairs Up with Other Signs

Here is a lineup of your sun sign's compatibility with every other sign. Remember that most successful relationships have a balance of harmonious points and challenges, which stimulate you to grow and which keep you from getting bored with each other. So if the forecast for you and your beloved (or business associate) seems like an uphill struggle, take heart! Such legendary lovers as Juan and Eva Peron, President and Mrs. Ronald Reagan, Harry and Bess Truman, Julius Caesar and Cleopatra, The Duke and Duchess of Windsor, Ruth and Billy Graham, George and Martha Washington are among the many born under supposedly incompatible sun signs.

Aquarius–Aries

SMOOTH SAILING. If you both share common goals or work for the same worthy causes, this relationship can be a winner. Aries pushes your ideas, is stimulated by your mind, and loves your surprises! You can have some exciting adventures together, especially when your originality fans their fire!

ROUGH WATERS. Aries needs attention, but you have so many other interests that you can't possibly put them first all the time. Unfortunately, they may not agree that your causes are more worthy than they are. So your detachment could send them looking elsewhere for ego gratification.

Aquarius–Taurus

SMOOTH SAILING. This couple could go far, with your innovative ideas combined with their practical know-how. You inspire Taurus, while they put you on solid ground. You share many of the same enthusiasms for bettering the environment. And you shake them up now and then, which does them a world of good.

ROUGH WATERS. Taurus is predictable; Aquarius is full of surprises. You are not security minded; in fact, you find budgets or any restrictions too limiting. And Taurus possessiveness can really be suffocating. They often think your ideas are crazy and wonder why you need so much independence. Better think this one over first.

Aquarius–Gemini

SMOOTH SAILING. You are two people collectors who never get lost in the crowd. You give each other all the space you both need to explore and experiment. You love Gemini's many-faceted personality, and you inspire them with ideas even they never imagined.

ROUGH WATERS. Gemini finds it hard to commit to one idea or cause, while you carry your banner high and demolish all opposition. Though you are not a possessive type, the idea of two-timing turns you off, especially when it comes to sharing someone you love. There's a certain lack of conviction here. Examine your theory of relativity before you get too involved.

Aquarius–Cancer

SMOOTH SAILING. Success depends on whether Cancer can identify emotionally with your goals. They can complement you very well, providing the intimacy and one-to-one warmth, while you handle the crowds. You can count on their devotion to back you up and their shrewd business sense to make a profit.

ROUGH WATERS. Home-loving Cancers have very strong emotional needs, which may not interest Aquarius.

And their possessiveness can seem smothering to someone who needs a lot of space. You'll have to spend some time at home and do a lot of hand-holding to make this work. It might be helpful if you work at home, or your partner works in the same place with you. That way, you can see each other often yet still pursue your own ideas.

Aquarius–Leo

SMOOTH SAILING. Here are two opposite types, yet both love to be on stage, surrounded by people. Leo's warmth and graciousness complement Aquarian objectivity and concern for mankind. You'll both attract attention—a great costarring team.

ROUGH WATERS. All goes well as long as there's a meeting of minds. But Leo wants wholehearted commitment, which may rub Aquarius the wrong way. And the Lion demands so much continual attention, while you have other things to do. Common interests are what's needed to focus your joint energies. Leo must learn to curb jealous or competitive urges so you'll have the space you need.

Aquarius–Virgo

SMOOTH SAILING. An interesting odd couple. Both are highly intelligent and could stimulate each other mentally. Aquarius is happy to let Virgo organize, while they handle the public. And neither needs constant attention from the other. There is no jealousy here to deflect your affections.

ROUGH WATERS. Aquarius has many interests going at once and Virgo may have to fight for time, never mind top priority. This could take the form of incessant nagging. Virgo seems too practical and earthbound for Aquarius, who hates to bother with details, including the budget. Can you tolerate Virgo reminding you constantly to get organized, or always tidying up after you? Are the compromises going to be worthwhile?

Aquarius–Libra

SMOOTH SAILING. Here's a good mental mate. You are two idealists who love to discuss and debate your cause endlessly. And you both enjoy group activities. You applaud Libra's good judgment, while they uphold your worthy causes. And you both dislike sticky emotional scenes.

ROUGH WATERS. Libra needs to be surrounded by beautiful objects and a harmonious atmosphere. Aquarius likes to shake people up. Your shock tactics can jolt their equilibrium. You may also be too opinionated for them. If your cause is rebellious and your crowd becomes raucous, count on Libra to make a quick exit. You may be too busy with your multiple interests to satisfy their need for reassurance, flattery, and companionship.

Aquarius–Scorpio

SMOOTH SAILING. Scorpio loves your original ideas, while they give you deep experiences and passion you've never even dreamed possible. Scorpio loves being the power behind your throne, letting you please the crowds while they pull the strings. You'll give each other plenty of space to take your power trips, then you'll have a rapturous rendezvous.

ROUGH WATERS. Both of you have strong opinions and a need to control. But Aquarius demands independence, while Scorpio needs to be needed. The problems come when you both feel unsatisfied on a deep level. If you want this one to last, better give Scorpio some powerful reasons.

Aquarius–Sagittarius

SMOOTH SAILING. Sagittarius is as independent as you are. And you're both unpredictable. Sounds like a great match, when your electricity plus Sagittarius fire sparks great ideas. You give each other plenty of space to wander, and then you rendezvous to compare travel notes. You'll never object to each other's outside interests.

ROUGH WATERS. Someone has to tend the home fires if they are to stay aflame, and neither of you is the domestic type. Someone else may have to manage the money, too. You may well ask what you need each other for. Well, you want each other, so that's enough—or is it?

Aquarius–Capricorn

SMOOTH SAILING. When the lone wolf and the maverick get together for a cause, you're a great team. Practical, earthy Capricorn will organize while you raise funds and give speeches. Capricorn respects your idealism and commitment, and you know you can count on them.

ROUGH WATERS. You are both more involved in work and ideas than in personal life. But Capricorn is a traditionalist who likes a solid home environment, while you'd prefer to expend your energies elsewhere. Can a rule maker (Capricorn) and a rule breaker (Aquarius) coexist peacefully? When Capricorn pushes for more structure and you push for more freedom, you'll need some strategy sessions to make this one last.

Aquarius–Aquarius

SMOOTH SAILING. Nothing shocks either of you, so you'll love surprising each other! You know when to give each other space, and when your presence is needed. You both understand the concept of equal partnership and are best friends as well as lovers.

ROUGH WATERS. You may stay best friends without a real romantic spark, or you could float off in other directions. You both look for ways to expand your mind and may not find them in a mirror image. However, shared causes and mutual interests may be enough to hold you together.

Aquarius–Pisces

SMOOTH SAILING. The impersonal Aquarius and the emotional Pisces are next-door neighbors who mean much to each other. Pisces gives you emotional depth and creative fantasies. You give them good friendship and objectivity, and they appreciate your original ideas and electric charisma.

ROUGH WATERS. Pisces needs 24-hour-a-day romance, which could bore you after a while. And their more soggy emotions leave you cold. Better find another outlet where you can help the needy. Or better yet, find one together!

CHAPTER 16

Your Aquarius Career Potential

Where to Look for Your Best Job Opportunities

Since yours is a bright, inventive mind that must find answers, you do best in a forward-looking job, where you can put your innovative ideas to good use. You'll find the scope you need in a nontraditional company, with a younger staff and open-minded management. Or you may want to freelance or start your own business, since you function very well independently. Though your singlemindedness suits you for research, most of you prefer to come before the public or work with groups, improving society in some way. Teaching, politics, social work, or psychology attract Aquarians. The high-tech computer and electronic industry appreciates your inventive genius. Artistic types will gravitate to avante-garde arts, electronic music, and experimental theater. You might make a career of New Age healing arts or astrology, or you may teach meditation or mind-control techniques. Stay away from jobs that are confining, have too many rules, or are steeped in tradition.

Aquarius in Charge

You are a liberated boss who gives your subordinates all the space they need, an open, friendly atmosphere, and ample benefits. Aquarius believes in permissive management—minds given free rein do the best work. You're always open to new ideas and often run your operation in a nontraditional way. You may get impatient when others can't keep up with your quick mind or understand those revolutionary ideas. You're usually miles ahead of everyone else! But your charisma and persuasiveness usually win over more traditional types to a new way of thinking. You function well in a crisis, when your marvelous ability to detach from emotional stress and analyze a problem comes to the rescue. Your focus on the overall well-being of the organization may leave a few threads hanging in your immediate environs, but you're a whiz at delegating those chores to others.

Aquarius Teamwork

Paradoxically, Aquarius expresses individuality through interaction with groups. However, your ideas are so innovative that you stand out in any crowd. You are ambitious, but you are more interested in a high-profile spot where you can reach a wider audience than in money making for its own sake. You work best when given a great deal of freedom; you can't stand to have someone breathing down your neck or telling you what to do. You're a communicator who brings company issues to the outside world or the outside world to your company, with union activities and charity benefits. You're quick to take up a collection for a worthy cause or campaign against management injustice. Routine work never holds you for long, you'll job-hop until you find the place where you can put your ideas to practical use.

To Get Ahead Fast

Look for a permissive company that lets you be yourself and is open to new ideas.

Play up these characteristics:

- Intelligence
- Inventiveness
- Concentration
- Charisma
- Salesmanship
- Intuition

Famous Aquarius Millionaires:

Study these Aquarian tycoons for tips on how to make the most of your best qualities:

Barry Diller of QVC television network
Dr. An Wang of Wang Computers
H. L. Hunt
Akio Morita of Sony
Marvin Davis
Yoko Ono
Norton Simon
Michael Jordan
John McEnroe
Louis Rukeyser of "Wall Street Week"

CHAPTER 17

Aquarius Astro-Outlook for 1995

During 1995, mighty Jupiter will stimulate your friendships dynamically. You are going to get more and more out of close relationships, out of the social side of your job, and out of group activities. Church and club involvements will bring peace of mind and a definite sense of adventure and excitement.

Thanks to the Saturn transit in your horoscope, you will enjoy a more stable year in finances and income. Situations can crystalize in your money matters and there can be gains from consolidation of financial interests.

Early in April, Uranus will enter Aquarius. As you know, Uranus is your planetary ruler and this means that big changes in lifestyle and place of residence can be brewing. Uranus will hover at your front gate up until early June, when it will fall back into Capricorn, where its conjunctions with Saturn and Neptune the past decade have literally changed the world.

Keep alert to what is going on in your roots of living, in the private part of your horoscope over the spring of 1995, for therein is an inkling of what you can expect from this major orb when it really establishes itself in your sun sign next year.

We live in a society where longtime conservatives go liberal and vice-versa. Uranus may be preparing similar changes in the way you think, decide, and approach a problem, and in the way you carry out duties, responsibilities, and obligations.

March offers marvelous opportunities for improving your

personal appearance while Venus is transiting your sun sign.

With Mars erratic in Virgo and Leo over January through March, these are not months to take chances with your marriage or business partnerships. Science assures us that men and women change differently as they grow older. Strong flexibility is required in all alliances over 1995. Hold off buying the big-ticket items for now.

There is a buildup of accident-producing potential in your horoscope over the middle of April, and you can expect pressures in your community, family, home, ownership, and property matters as April closes. Taxes will be rising again.

After May 22, there is favorable stimulation of your love life. The period between June 11 and July 5 is one of your best and, for single members of this solar group, this is an auspicious cycle for meeting your heart's desire.

Uranus and Neptune are never many degrees from conjunction this year, and over the second half of 1995, they can goad you into closing out no-win interests and other matters.

Your motivation for vacation travel is strong after July 21, and what you want out of your activities is illuminated for you on August 10. Another good travel period takes place around September 24.

There will be a total eclipse of the sun on October 24, 1995, at zero degrees Scorpio, when there could be many negative rumors about your career, your product, and where they fit into this dynamically changing society. Your love life is fabulously illuminated for you on and about December 7.

CHAPTER 18

Eighteen Months of Day-by-Day Predictions—July 1994 to December 1995

JULY 1994

Friday, July 1 (Moon in Aries) Go slowly! Cooperation is sluggish and fatigue can be a factor. Financial trends are slow, but power is building up for you behind the scenes and can bring enlightenment in health and work factors. An exciting member of the opposite sex is standing in the shadows. Hot combination numbers: 2 and 4.

Saturday, July 2 (Moon in Aries to Taurus 10:23 a.m.) You can establish closer relationships with people who have seemed standoffish in the past. Accept all invitations, including one that may seem halfheartedly given. Move out from any sidelines you may have been hugging, but watch any tendency to be overly bold and aggressive under the existing aspects. Your color is blue. Lucky lottery numbers: 4, 13, 22, 31, 40, 2.

Sunday, July 3 (Moon in Taurus) Things are looking brighter and love is a strong force in your life. Parent-child relationships are fine. Spontaneity in your entertainments will make them all the better. Creativity, originality, and flexibility will make this a red-letter day. There are plenty of social opportunities now. Your number is 6.

Monday, July 4 (Moon in Taurus to Gemini 11:12 p.m.) Traditions, the status quo, and good financial underpinnings are implied by the day's aspects. Taurus and

Virgo have significant roles. Strongly physical love is beckoning you. Expressions of love won't go unappreciated now. Your color is coral pink; count on the number 1.

Tuesday, July 5 (Moon in Gemini) A romantic atmosphere dominates, with love favorably stimulated, especially love of the creative, social, imaginative, and original kind. There is a strong sense of newness between lovers. Spontaneous partying and entertaining are also favored. Gemini has the power today. Cherry red is your color; your number is 3.

Wednesday, July 6 (Moon in Gemini) The social side of life is stepped up, especially at noontime, on the job, and immediately after work. Improvements in day-to-day relationships are noted. This is a fine day for gathering kindred spirits about you and letting things pop in a glorious and memorable way. Another Aquarius is also on stage. Lucky lottery numbers: 5, 23, 32, 41, 14, 16.

Thursday, July 7 (Moon in Gemini to Cancer 10:17 a.m.) Libra has some questions for you. It's a grand day for enjoying the dramatic panorama of summer. The season offers you many unusual opportunities for relaxation with the right people, and for writing, singing, and dining out in a fun place. Your colors are magenta and yellow. Hot combination numbers: 7 and 8.

Friday, July 8 (Moon in Cancer) The new moon is born in your sixth house and illuminates health, nutrition, and diet matters. It's a fine time to improve and correct your work or the setup of your work area. A Scorpio and a Pisces are in the picture. Your winning colors are earth and ginger; your lucky number is 9.

Saturday, July 9 (Moon in Cancer to Leo 6:43 p.m.) Service is rendered graciously under these aspects. A favor you seek will be granted this morning, for you are on the receiving end of many kindnesses now. Work gets done without any show of jealousy or envy, but you could encounter these two monsters while socializing. It would also be wise to avoid foods that aren't just right this evening. Lucky lottery numbers: 2, 11, 20, 9, 23, 29.

Sunday, July 10 (Moon in Leo) What your beloved has in mind should win acceptance with you. Marriage, sharing, and working in tandem are all well aspected. Wealth production is favored, but it is more intellectual and mental than actual physical effort. Write, begin a summer diary, or read light fiction for best results. Emerald is your color; your best number is 4.

Monday, July 11 (Moon in Leo) Ask a Leo what it's all about. Public relations, legal, and marital interests get first-class lunar stimulation. You have the power to bring people together today, to arrange, rearrange, organize, instigate, and generate. An older person can present a litany of grievances. Rose is your color; play the number 8 to win.

Tuesday, July 12 (Moon in Leo to Virgo 12:48 a.m.) Gray-green is your color. Virgo comes to your assistance. It's a cycle for investing, budgeting, and working on security interests. Do what you can to prevent a divorce among your friends or neighbors. You could get the feeling that others have been taking advantage of you. Hot combination numbers: 1 and 5.

Wednesday, July 13 (Moon in Virgo) Virgo has the important role. This is a good cycle for implementing changes, improving the caliber of your product, and attending conferences and interviews. If your marriage or any other type of close emotional relationships has been going through troubled waters, today marks the turning point. Your color is plum. Lucky lottery numbers: 13, 23, 30, 3, 12, 21.

Thursday, July 14 (Moon in Virgo to Libra 5:15 a.m.) Travel gets green lights. It seems only fair that you get the preference today (or so many people will be thinking). Libra is your best companion. There are strong physical dimensions to your love relationships now. Have you forgotten to buy a birthday or anniversary card? Your color is cerulean blue. Hot combination numbers: 5 and 6.

Friday, July 15 (Moon in Libra) Gemini and another Aquarius are in the know. Reading health and sickness-prevention magazines is no waste of time. Business-pleasure combinations will go well away from home. Improved nutritional and dietary programs are going to produce good results for you. Your color is apricot; your number is 7.

Saturday, July 16 (Moon in Libra to Scorpio 8:35 a.m.) Moving about, seeing the sights, touring from one place of historic interest to another are possible in today's scenario. You see far ahead and can make plans for the closing months of 1994. Dine on or near the water tonight, preferably in an elevated area. Lucky lottery numbers: 16, 9, 29, 45, 36, 27.

Sunday, July 17 (Moon in Scorpio) Your career considerations, problems, and achievements can intrude on this day of rest. It's a wonderful day for talks with empathetic coworkers. Scorpio and Pisces are helpful. It's a fine day for walking around your own community, watching a waterfall, spending time in a park. Titian red is your color; play the number 2 to win.

Monday, July 18 (Moon in Scorpio to Sagittarius 11:09 a.m.) Check things out with a sun-in-Cancer woman. You are taking it all in today and postponing a decision until later, for you excel in mulling things over in your own mind. In lovemaking, there is more passion and much demonstrative affection. Those hurt by war, poverty, and illness are more close to your heart than ever before. Your color is lilac; the number 6 is lucky.

Tuesday, July 19 (Moon in Sagittarius) Deep within you is a feeling that wonderful days are coming. You love this month and the beauty it displays along the highways and byways of life. Sagittarius makes a good companion. Drive into a rural or mountainous area and enjoy all the fabulous shades of green. Hot combination numbers: 8 and 3.

Wednesday, July 20 (Moon in Sagittarius to Capricorn 1:30 p.m.) Nobody is going to want to be cooped up today. Take shut-ins out for a drive. A family picnic would go well. Beach and water activities are beckoning you and the yen to travel was never greater. Aries and Leo come front and center. Your colors are cherry and peach. Lucky lottery numbers: 1, 20, 10, 19, 28, 37.

Thursday, July 21 (Moon in Capricorn) Capricorn would like you to make a decision and close out that project. Relationships with your own children and other young people may leave you with the conviction that the generation gap is widening. The more cheerful you are today, the better for you and those around you. Your color is pumpkin. Hot combination numbers: 3 and 4.

Friday, July 22 (Moon in Capricorn to Aquarius 4:38 p.m.) Today's full moon illuminates what is rooted in the past. There is enlightenment on getting along with corporations and their faceless commands. There can be much aggravation over the antics of big business, banks, investment houses. Does your diet require changes at this time? Magenta is your color; your number is 5.

Saturday, July 23 (Moon in Aquarius) It's all yours—the ball is in your court, and it's your duty and responsibility, your gains and profits. Hold the initiative, set the pace, redirect your life plans if this is your pleasure. You can have things the way you want them in your lunar high cycle. Another Aquarius says it all. Lucky lottery numbers: 7, 23, 43, 34, 16, 25.

Sunday, July 24 (Moon in Aquarius to Pisces 9:56 p.m.) Push your highly personalized interests, aspirations for the future, and things of an intimate and private nature. You are in the driver's seat and in many ways you can get what you want. Speak up, not letting others take advantage of you. New beginnings will go well. Your color is snow white; your lucky number is 9.

Monday, July 25 (Moon in Pisces) Pisces and Virgo cooperate well. You can make more money today than you originally believed, as a new source of capital presents itself. Today is fine for special sales, garage and patio sales, bargain hunting, and bartering things you no longer need. Your color is ruby; your lucky number is 4.

Tuesday, July 26 (Moon in Pisces) The desire to be loved gently but totally is strong under today's aspects. You are fascinated with all the mysterious ways of loving. Logic, determination, and practicality have small roles to play in this maze. The day, the time, and the place require real turning on. Your color is yellow. Hot combination numbers: 6 and 3.

Wednesday, July 27 (Moon in Pisces to Aries 6:31 a.m.) Aries makes a grand appearance. You gain much where you go after the winnable and the possible, leaving the impossible dreams to the singers. The desire to make loved ones happier is a strong trend. Educational matters, your learning processes, studies, and hobbies are strongly stimulated. Saffron yellow is your color. Lucky lottery numbers: 8, 44, 35, 26, 17, 27.

Thursday, July 28 (Moon in Aries) There are trends of daring, boldness, and even of aggression represented. Young men expcct too much and their demands can stir up resentment. Give your best to those you love today and don't become upset if a youngster speaks the raw and unvarnished truth. There are gains from being where the action is. Your lucky number is 1.

Friday, July 29 (Moon in Aries to Taurus 6:13 p.m.) Things are settling down in your immediate area and you sense that you have a strong control over these. Local, here-and-now, and pressing matters are all well aspected. Your learning processes are powerfully activated. Listen, read, study, and do some research. Aries has questions for you. Your colors are turquoise and rich blue. Hot combination numbers: 3 and 5.

Saturday, July 30 (Moon in Taurus) You are superconscious of what you own and what you may soon possess under prevailing aspects. Domestic, residential, real estate, ownership, and property matters are receiving first-rate stimulation. Taurus will cooperate with you. Your winning colors are magenta and ecru. Lucky lottery numbers: 30, 43, 14, 5, 23, 32.

Sunday, July 31 (Moon in Taurus) Gather as many members of your family as you can around your dinner table, or throw a cookout or picnic. It will be a lot of work but the emotional gains will be worthwhile. You want to be a part of the larger family, an active member of the clan, grateful to your ancestors. Your number is 7.

AUGUST 1994

Monday, August 1 (Moon in Taurus to Gemini 7:05 a.m.) You begin this month in the catbird's seat, giving off strong approval, appreciation, and inner satisfaction with your life. You love and are loved, and you are bringing smiles of pleasure from airy types such as Gemini, Libra, and Aquarius. Smile often, be positive and affirmative. It's a day for pastels. Your lucky number is 8.

Tuesday, August 2 (Moon in Gemini) You continue in an optimistic frame of mind and your personality assets are inviting, courting, and attracting love and respect. It's an excellent day for relationships with parents and offspring. Fine trends exist for spur-of-the-moment parties and entertainments. You feel one with the season. Hot combination numbers: 1 and 4.

Wednesday, August 3 (Moon in Gemini to Cancer 6:22 p.m.) Make love. Let your adored one know what you are thinking by airing your aspirations during pillow talk. You can be yourself today with those you love and who love and admire you in return. You are compulsive in your drive for a closer communion with your beloved. Your colors are fuchsia and russet. Lucky lottery numbers: 3, 12, 21, 30, 39, 48.

Thursday, August 4 (Moon in Cancer) Schedule any surgery an offspring may need well before the end of vacation. The day favors health and work improvements, as well as serious talks with supervisors and coworkers. The evening is fine for getting fellow employees together at a cafeteria or restaurant. A Cancer or Virgo will prove helpful. The number 5 is best.

Friday, August 5 (Moon in Cancer) Let a Pisces and a Cancer have some say in your plans and the programming of events. This is a fine day for talks with your dentist or doctor and for beginning a new exercise program in line with your health needs. You are generous in your evaluation of others and they want to be in your company. Your winning colors are marigold and azure blue. Hot combination numbers: 7 and 2.

Saturday, August 6 (Moon in Cancer to Leo 2:31 p.m.) Marriage, public relations, and legal involvements offer the light at the end of a tunnel. Leo and Sagittarius have key roles. You do well in sharing today, in carrying your part of the load. There is criticism where work is shifted to the shoulders of another. Red is your color. Lucky lottery numbers: 9, 6, 27, 18, 36, 45.

Sunday, August 7 (Moon in Leo) Today's new moon illuminates adventures you are planning, ushering in dramatic potential in love, money, partnerships, contracts, and agreements. This is a fine day for letting your hair down with the right person. If you're at home, open your doors to unusual types who spread sunshine wherever they go. Your best number is 2.

Monday, August 8 (Moon in Leo to Virgo 7:42 a.m.) Special meetings, conferences, and talks with executives can make this a day to remember. Virgo and Libra come front and center. Today is fine for talks with a banker and broker, and good trends exist in budgeting, investing, and financial improvements. All security matters are favored. Yellows are in vogue; the number 6 is a winner.

Tuesday, August 9 (Moon in Virgo) Today favors banking, investing, budgeting, and studying financial trends. Be sure you look your best this morning, for you could meet a particularly discerning person who sees and tells all. New starts in new directions are indicated. Awareness is strong and your ability to transform can make this a fascinating day. Virgo and Capricorn have key roles. Your color is aquamarine; your number is 8.

Wednesday, August 10 (Moon in Virgo to Libra 11:07 a.m.) Taurus will make a contribution to the day's progress. Security and service matters are in focus. It's a good day for opening a new checking or charge account.

Information, research, and the improvement of the grounds of your home are indicated. Your sex appeal and accompanying magical wizardry can win admiration. Your color is cerulean blue. Lucky lottery numbers: 1, 10, 21, 28, 37, 46.

Thursday, August 11 (Moon in Libra) Travel, beginning a summer vacation, and getting away to new scenes are favored. Long-range interests can be served well, too. It's a fine day for seeing old friends who have moved away, and for dining out, especially high up in an airy setting. Libra and another Aquarius can make your day. The number 3 is lucky.

Friday, August 12 (Moon in Libra to Scorpio 1:56 a.m.) Open your ears to Gemini's voice. Pursue the search for additional capital by reading the right magazines and talking to the right people. Advertising, publicity, and public relations get new starts. Don't dwell on what you don't have, but consider all the gifts of the spirit that are yours. Pick five: 5, 15, 25, 32, 40.

Saturday, August 13 (Moon in Scorpio) Scorpio entertains. You have the power on your own ground, with people you understand and with those who are intellectual enough to speak truths and avoid quibbling. You can make strong impressions on neighbors, on those who share your political opinions, and on those who work in the same profession or vocation. You are moving toward self-realization. Lucky lottery numbers: 13, 27, 34, 7, 16, 43.

Sunday, August 14 (Moon in Scorpio to Sagittarius 4:53 p.m.) Luck is with you in familiar, usual, and traditional matters. Your career needs can spill over into your private life. Check things out with a Cancer and a Pisces. An oriental chicken recipe would suit you and your beloved this evening. You could hear about some genuine buys in real estate. Your lucky number is 9.

Monday, August 15 (Moon in Sagittarius) Sagittarius will make an announcement. Phone or write letters, keeping in close touch. You can achieve much through the social side of your job, in group activities, and in genuine friendship. Church and club participation matters are favored.

Outdoor activities beckon you. Vermilion red is your color; your number is 4.

Tuesday, August 16 (Moon in Sagittarius to Capricorn 8:18 p.m.) Be diplomatic and avoid anything that smacks of tactlessness, for protocol is critical. Be courteous and look your best for good results under these aspects. Moving about in an exotic area would do the trick for you today. Speak up to let the world know how you feel. Kelly green is your color; your lucky number is 6.

Wednesday, August 17 (Moon in Capricorn) You yearn to be more involved with the future than with the present or the past. Let Capricorn have some say in things. You are making major decisions in a nice, quiet way. This is a good cycle for completions, finishing up, dealing with large organizations, and helping your mate with work you don't ordinarily do. Your color is canary. Lucky lottery numbers: 17, 28, 35, 8, 26, 44.

Thursday, August 18 (Moon in Capricorn) Financial interests are speeded up. You have much vitality and get more done than those surrounding you. You do well in warding off pleasant distractions. Know when a change isn't necessarily an improvement or a correction. Newer technologies appeal to you as you leap forward in your career. Your color is ecru. Hot combination numbers: 1 and 5.

Friday, August 19 (Moon in Capricorn to Aquarius 12:34 a.m.) Go for it! It's your day. In this lunar-cycle high, you set the pace, take the lead, hold the initiative, and benefit from the amount of self-confidence and self-reliance you can muster. Introduce new time-, labor-, and money-saving devices and methodologies. Your color is bronze; your number is 3.

Saturday, August 20 (Moon in Aquarius) Stir up some social invitations today. Your suggestions are accepted as royal commands, and people want to shine in your reflected glory. There are big payoffs where you sport your stuff and do your best. Sports, games, and grand entertaining are all doing well. Lucky lottery numbers: 20, 34, 41, 5, 14, 23.

Sunday, August 21 (Moon in Aquarius to Pisces 6:28 a.m.) The full moon enlightens you in highly personalized matters. This is your day to shine in large groups. Dress up to the hilt, look rich and royal. You invite, beckon, attract, and court the best that there is. There is illumination of all your virtues and assets. Aqua is your color; your number is 7.

Monday, August 22 (Moon in Pisces) This is a good earning-power and income day. Matters related to career, status, and prestige are favored. Luck attends you in savings, investments, budgeting, and bargain hunting. It's one of those days when you view life as a long-distance journey and you aim to travel in style. Your color is ecru; your number is 2.

Tuesday, August 23 (Moon in Pisces to Aries 2:55 p.m.) Virgo and Pisces come front and center. This is a wonderful day for counting your blessings and facing all financial tests with self-confidence. You could throw your hat in the ring for an increase in salary. New income can be derived from a serious discussion you hold today with your banker or broker. Hot combination numbers: 4 and 7.

Wednesday, August 24 (Moon in Aries) Check things out with Aries. You can get a better view of the future now. What is immediate and present can be accomplished early in the morning. You have the King Midas touch and make everything come up roses. Volunteer, doing your charitable work with pleasure. Lucky lottery numbers: 24, 35, 42, 6, 15, 33.

Thursday, August 25 (Moon in Aries) You have unbeatable motivation and energy today and can get more than your usual quota of work done. You are at your best when you are in charge of situations and when you invest your time and energy wisely in pursuit of highly visible goals. Shop for items that make you more awake and alert. Aries is a good adviser. Hot combination numbers: 8 and 9.

Friday, August 26 (Moon in Aries to Taurus 2:13 a.m.) Taurus and Virgo have key roles. Domestic, residential, and property matters are favored. Today's trends are ready made for your advancement and enjoyment of everything that is unique to your gender. You do well by becoming involved right away. Mocha is your color. Hot combination numbers: 1 and 4.

Saturday, August 27 (Moon in Taurus) An appearance of success and of being well loved will invite achievement and approval. Your domestic scene knows its ups and downs—there is laughter but there also are quarrels and disagreements. Some will say that you are wearing your heart on your sleeve. Purple is your color. Lucky lottery numbers: 27, 41, 12, 3, 21, 30.

Sunday, August 28 (Moon in Taurus to Gemini 3:08 p.m.) Fine trends exist for entertaining within your own home. You can charm the birds out of the trees today. You are rather possessive of loved ones, however, and there can bc somc resentment growing because of this. Throughout the day, communications will produce results. Canary and white are your colors; your lucky number is 5.

Monday, August 29 (Moon in Gemini) As the month began with much approval, appreciation, and love in your life, so it will end. Gemini and another Aquarius have key roles today. You are warming to the season even more and can do well in spontaneous, outdoor entertainments and parties. Cherry red is your color; the number 9 is best.

Tuesday, August 30 (Moon in Gemini) Fine trends exist for a heart-to-heart talk with youngsters returning to school. Let your offspring know what you expect from them. A discussion of television viewing certainly is in order—when it should be on and when it must be turned off in the interest of schoolwork. Hot combination numbers: 2 and 7.

Wednesday, August 31 (Moon in Gemini to Cancer 3:00 a.m.) As thc month ends, you have favorable situations for catching up on any work that may have been neglected. Today is fine for scheduling fall housecleaning work and any maintenance and restoration work that must be done on your home and your property. A Cancer and a Capricorn will give good advice. Lucky lottery numbers: 31, 39, 6, 4, 40, 22.

Thursday, September 1 (Moon in Cancer) Pesky jobs around your house can be performed prior to noon and again after eight o'clock. Persistence is appreciated under the existing aspects. A Cancer and a Virgo are full of service, advice, and genuine help. Your colors are the brownish reds. It's a good day for improving your diet. Hot combination numbers: 3 and 5.

Friday, September 2 (Moon in Cancer to Leo 11:37 a.m.) You can get plenty of work done today and thereby please your supervisors, mate, and others. Your willingness to do more than your share holds you in good stead over the rest of the month. Domestic situations can be improved by you and the responsibility you demonstrate. Hot combination numbers: 5 and 1.

Saturday, September 3 (Moon in Leo) Leo makes dramatic entrances and exits. It's a fine day for dressing up and being noticed. In little, minor ways you can please your beloved more than you may realize. The better organized you are this morning, the better your day will go. Your colors are gold, ocher, and canary. Lucky lottery numbers: 7, 16, 25, 34, 43, 18.

Sunday, September 4 (Moon in Leo to Virgo 3:33 p.m.) The yen for travel is strong and it wouldn't be a bad idea to take another glimpse of the seashore. Bargains in travel and resorts are in focus. In finding the sun, you can depend on a Sagittarius and an Aries. You might even be able to borrow a good friend's house near the water. Your color is azure blue; your number is 9.

Monday, September 5 (Moon in Virgo) Today favors new approaches toward money matters. Social and financial prestige are linked together. The trends call for attention to duty and for showing responsible attitudes in everything. The new moon enlightens you in overall security gains. You can give good advice to loved ones. Virgo takes charge. Your colors are turquoise and silver; your lucky number is 4.

Tuesday, September 6 (Moon in Virgo to Libra 6:57 p.m.) Check developments out with Taurus and Capricorn. You can reach good compromises with partners, executives, and coworkers under these trends. You can be exposed to lots of begging under these rays, however, and only a certain percentage of it is honest and acceptable. Russet is your color. Pick five: 6, 12, 18, 24, 30.

Wednesday, September 7 (Moon in Libra) Your mind is encompassing much that is at a distance and in the long-range category. You can spread yourself a little thin today and get away with it. Wherever you look, there are opportunities and people anxious to know you better. Libra and another Aquarius are on stage. Lucky lottery numbers: 8, 17, 26, 35, 44, 7.

Thursday, September 8 (Moon in Libra to Scorpio 8:26 p.m.) Passion increases as Venus moves in Scorpio. The physical is not taking any backseat to the intellectual. Lovers travel together now. There can be increased interest in an affair involving dear friends. You can hear some dramatic news from a distance. Research can be stepped up. Count on the number 1.

Friday, September 9 (Moon in Scorpio) A Scorpio will influence your thinking. Career gains are evident, so you can cash in on your earned reputation today. You use authority wisely. There are special sales that can net you a little extra. There are times when you have to object to the burdens others try to put on you. Your colors are bronze and forest green; your number is 3.

Saturday, September 10 (Moon in Scorpio to Sagittarius 10:25 a.m.) Check things out with a Pisces and a Cancer. Swimming, other beach activities, and relaxing in the sunshine are favored. A post-vacation getaway where the post-season prices are in force would be a wonderful idea. You can rid yourself of a self-destructive habit under these aspects. Lay in a supply of items you can use in your career. Lucky lottery numbers: 5, 10, 14, 23, 32, 41.

Sunday, September 11 (Moon in Sagittarius) Sagittarius enters the picture. It's a warmhearted, friendly day when friendship takes every opportunity to develop. There are illusions, pretensions, and glamorous situations represented. While you can successfully overwhelm others, there is some danger of misleading yourself. Deep pink is your color; your number is 7.

Monday, September 12 (Moon in Sagittarius) You could encounter much arrogance today. You may be rather surprised at the requests that come your way. Still, your high self-confidence opens new doors for you. You can find eager assistance for the work that must be completed over the next few days. Coffee is your color; your number is 2.

Tuesday, September 13 (Moon in Sagittarius to Capricorn 1:44 a.m.) Capricorn is standing tall on important issues. It's a fine time to deal with large organizations and attend to work that your mate ordinarily would perform. Put all your ducks in a row before making any long-lasting decision. Know the ins and outs of the appliances you are buying. Summer won't let you forget it. Forest and okra greens are your colors. Pick five: 4, 13, 22, 31, 40.

Wednesday, September 14 (Moon in Capricorn) Clear the decks for an upcoming surge of work. What hasn't been showing anything much can be discarded today. Old doors can be closed so that new ones can be opened. Virgo and Taurus are in the picture. It's a day for attending to your own knitting and making sure you are not disappointing your boss and employer. Lucky lottery numbers: 6, 15, 24, 33, 42, 14.

Thursday, September 15 (Moon in Capricorn to Aquarius 6:42 a.m.) Now in your lunar-cycle high, you can get your own way by demonstrating enormous self-confidence and self-reliance. Take the lead, hold the initiative, speak your mind, and keep at it. Another Aquarius will understand your complicated feelings. Gold is your color. Hot combination numbers: 8 and 4.

Friday, September 16 (Moon in Aquarius) It's your day to do what you will. The opposition is without teeth. Accept all challenges and show how well you can get the job done in your own imaginative and creative way. You dislike repetition and you can demonstrate now that it is not necessary, since all the different paths are open to you. Look out for the number 1.

Saturday, September 17 (Moon in Aquarius to Pisces 1:31 p.m.) You can gather your wits about you this morning and surprise others by the amount of work you get done, for things can come easily to you today. You're friendly and cooperative and you know what you want. A Gemini and a Libra come front and center. Open things up, invite, court, and acquire. Rich blue is your color. Lucky lottery numbers: 3, 12, 30, 17, 21, 39.

Sunday, September 18 (Moon in Pisces) The spiritual and the material are in evident opposition under today's aspects. There's money to be made and wonderful financial ideas floating about, but there is also an accompanying sense that wealth does not bring joy. You may turn your back on material things and do some effective meditation today. Antique white is your color; your number is 5.

Monday, September 19 (Moon in Pisces to Aries 10:30 p.m.) Today's full moon will enlighten you in wealth production, in possible sources of new capital, and in the maintenance of the valuables you own. There is illumination of what you want out of life. Pisces should be consulted. What is transpiring behind the scenes may count for more than what is evident. Ecru is your color; your number is 9.

Tuesday, September 20 (Moon in Aries) Go for the prizes today, for competition is your oyster. The peace of soul and of mind that you have constructed will hold you in good stead today so that you know when, where, and how to proceed. Organizational matters may bore you as the day advances, and in the evening you want quiet entertainment. Your number is 2.

Wednesday, September 21 (Moon in Aries) Let Aries in on your secret. Azure is your color. Romance can be helped along by exotic spices. Somewhere in your community, there is a merchant who has the knack of brightening your corner. Boudoir activities will be helped along this evening by earlier living-room activities. Lucky lottery numbers: 13, 4, 40, 31, 22, 21.

Thursday, September 22 (Moon in Aries to Taurus 9:47 a.m.) Narrow your sights and zero in on advantages and opportunities that are announcing themselves. Speed can be the most helpful ingredient. You excel in getting out of any crisis or predicament. Leo has the answers. Barley can become a main course when cooked with onion, garlic, parsley, tomatoes, and sesame seed oil. You can make do with what you have on hand instead of shopping. Hot combination numbers: 6 and 5.

Friday, September 23 (Moon in Taurus) Taurus and Libra are in the bigger picture. Residential, community, household, and family matters can be served well under the prevailing aspects. Real estate interests should not be neglected just because they bore you. You dislike clichés today and the people who push them constantly. Hot combination numbers: 8 and 2.

Saturday, September 24 (Moon in Taurus to Gemini 10:41 p.m.) Don't let any family discussion get out of hand. Rather, work for speedy agreements. You can beautify your home today and clear away summer's debris on the lawn and in the backyard. You yearn to create the proper surroundings for Indian summer. Lucky lottery numbers: 1, 24, 10, 19, 28, 37.

Sunday, September 25 (Moon in Gemini) Gemini comes calling and the plot thickens. You can give the impression that you are in love with love today. You're more imaginative and creative than others want you to be, for you will set a fast pace in going after the prizes. You may find yourself bored with so-called solid citizens. Old rose is your color; the number 7 is a winner.

Monday, September 26 (Moon in Gemini) Libra will demand fairness where decisions are being made. It's a day for putting any possible limitations behind you as you step lively and air your ambitions. Travel, what you have perking for yourself at a distance, and all long-range interests have the green lights. Carmine is your color; your best number is 2.

Tuesday, September 27 (Moon in Gemini to Cancer 11:12 a.m.) Career, professional, and authority matters are speeded up. Talk is far from cheap on the job today and too much can be said. Don't be too daring in the way you propel innovative ways into the picture. Others want nothing that might slow the project down. Scarlet and white are your winning colors. Pick five: 4, 40, 22, 27, 19.

Wednesday, September 28 (Moon in Cancer) A Cancer-born woman and a Pisces-born man are in the picture. Intuition will play a major role in what you decide now. Hard work will prove therapeutic. The fast-paced scenario is to your liking. Creativity is the key to success. Assure younger loved ones that you love them. Lucky lottery numbers: 6, 15, 24, 33, 42, 28.

Thursday, September 29 (Moon in Cancer to Leo 8:55 p.m.) Fine trends exist for catching up on work that should have been finished earlier. Service is improving and you will notice this at once. Family togetherness can make this a happy day, and fine trends also exist for giving health, diet, and nutrition their due. Keep busy and invite good feelings. Your number is 5.

Friday, September 30 (Moon in Leo) Long-range and long-distance interests are favored, so keep in touch with people at a distance. If you feel it's time for a brief respite with your mate, then this evening could prove special. Stick to promises and agreements for the best results. Know your own feelings before analyzing another. Number 7 is your best bet.

OCTOBER 1994

Saturday, October 1 (Moon in Leo) Partnerships, contracts, agreements, and working in tandem are part of this progressively good scene. Marriage gets good grades and green lights for deeper commitments. You do well where you happily share the duties, responsibilities and obligations. Consult Leo. Lucky lottery numbers: 1, 6, 15, 24, 33, 42.

Sunday, October 2 (Moon in Leo to Virgo 2:39 a.m.) Virgo and Capricorn have significant roles. There are good trends in savings, investments, budgets, and financial improvements and corrections. You have the "go" signals to get on with changes you have been considering since the end of summer. An improved kitchen budget is in order. Your number is 8.

Monday, October 3 (Moon in Virgo) Take care of pesky jobs that have been hanging fire too long. Remember what you owe others in deeds, actions, approval, and appreciation. Don't let the sun go down on any ridiculous misunderstanding. Where love and money are concerned, you may have to dig deeply for the answers. Gray is your color; the number 4 is your best bet.

Tuesday, October 4 (Moon in Virgo to Libra 4:56 a.m.) Make plans for taking care of the birds over the upcoming months. Appreciate October's bright blue weather with a deeper sense of unity with Mother Nature. The day accents kindness, gentility, and fairness. Libra and another Aquarius are watching. Your color is russet; stick with the number 6.

Wednesday, October 5 (Moon in Libra) Today's new moon illuminates what you have done for yourself at a distance. Long-range and long-distance matters are favored over what is immediate. There is enlightenment in philosophical and theological matters. You can feel that this will be an exciting month, with much learning. Libra rules the roost. Your lucky color is coral. Lucky lottery numbers: 5, 7, 25, 34, 43, 16.

Thursday, October 6 (Moon in Libra to Scorpio 5:22 a.m.) You relate well to successful types, the big achievers, and the ambitious. If you ask questions, you may be surprised at the answers you receive. There are fabulous opportunities for gaining support, assistance, and advice, and for taking a giant step forward in your career. Scorpio is helpful. Hot combination numbers: 9 and 3.

Friday, October 7 (Moon in Scorpio) Your popularity is more than just a bubble—much can be built upon it. The full potential of October's bright blue weather is with you. There is a sense of excitement in the air and you want to involve yourself in the antics of others. Today is fine for planning festivals, hayrides, and masquerade parties. Push the number 2.

Saturday, October 8 (Moon in Scorpio to Sagittarius 5:47 a.m.) Sagittarius comes aboard. Parties, entertainments, special reunions, and other types of get-togethers are indicated. Large groups are in the picture, and church and club membership and participation get strong support. You decorate, color, and paint with joy and beauty. Lucky lottery number: 4, 13, 40, 22, 31, 8.

Sunday, October 9 (Moon in Sagittarius) You can claim higher economic and social prestige and status under the existing trends. You will enjoy a walk around your own neighborhood today, preferably with a good conversationalist, perhaps a Sagittarius or a Gemini. You are open to suggestions, compliments, favors, and greater responsibility. Your number is 6.

Monday, October 10 (Moon in Sagittarius to Capricorn 7:44 a.m.) Career matters are sluggish. People are absent, tardy, and too unconcerned. You may feel that assistants are not pulling their weight. Even so, socializing gets good grades. Friendships of long standing are making their contribution. An Aries has something to say that you should listen to. Your number is 1.

Tuesday, October 11 (Moon in Capricorn) Things are not as you may think they are. There is much that is hidden. It would be difficult to predicate today's trends on those of yesterday. Today is fine for finishing up, inviting unusual people to your dinner table, and working to help an older loved one. Capricorn and Virgo signify. Your winning colors are peach and auburn. Hot combination numbers: 3 and 7.

Wednesday, October 12 (Moon in Capricorn to Aquarius 12:09 p.m.) Today is excellent for making do with what you have on hand, and for conclusions, ridding yourself of no-win projects, and ordering things by mail. A Taurus can prove helpful. Plan new approaches and new attitudes. Don't hesitate to spend a little money on your personal appearance. Lucky lottery numbers: 5, 12, 14, 41, 23, 32.

Thursday, October 13 (Moon in Aquarius) You will sense a lot of bounce in your personality and in what you are achieving now that you are in your lunar-cycle high. Pounce on highly personalized matters and you may be surprised at how well you handle them. You're sure of yourself today, anxious to make your mark. Be sure you act with top-flight self-confidence. Your color is blue; your lucky number is 7.

Friday, October 14 (Moon in Aquarius to Pisces 7:19 p.m.) Speak up, airing your aspirations and your grievances, for you will be heard today. Brilliant ideas will flash through your mind, helping you to organize a rather exciting day. Healthy self-esteem can come into view when you are told the good news about your recent efforts. Orchid is your color. Hot combination numbers: 9 and 1.

Saturday, October 15 (Moon in Pisces) This is a good money-making day. You may be surprised to find some special money earmarked for you. Work you did long ago can now pay off. Good news can come via the phone or the mails. A Gemini may have some good pointers for you, but you are going to have to overcome an initial resentment first. Your color is amber. Lucky lottery numbers: 2, 15, 11, 20, 29, 38.

Sunday, October 16 (Moon in Pisces) Pisces has the answers you need and the sooner you get them this morning, the better. Loving attention will prove to be health giving. There can be too much anxiety over rising prices and the cost of living generally. There are lots of rumors about community corruption. Hit with number 4.

Monday, October 17 (Moon in Pisces to Aries 4:56 a.m.) Move about your local area today. Aries is in the driver's seat. A sense of adventure can give you the intuitive feeling that something unusual and different is about to happen. You will not be disappointed! Creative thinking will help you solve all problems. Your color is prune; your lucky number is 9.

Tuesday, October 18 (Moon in Aries) Discuss an improved nutritional and dietary program with an expert. There are strong and thrilling physical dimensions to your love relationships today. You can suddenly become aware of the way others recycle lovemaking memories. The atmosphere in which you work can be improved. Pistachio is your color. Hot combination numbers: 2 and 4.

Wednesday, October 19 (Moon in Aries to Taurus 4:34 p.m.) Today's full moon enlightens you in local matters, communications, and transportation costs. You can breeze ahead in your studies and hobbies under these aspects, with a Leo and a Sagittarius on your side. Mischief making is in the air where neighborhood kids gather. Raspberry is your color. Lucky lottery numbers: 13, 4, 19, 22, 31, 40.

Thursday, October 20 (Moon in Taurus) Let Taurus tell you all about it. Domestic issues can dominate this morning. Be cautious about wearing your heart on your sleeve. Luck is with you in family conferences, making your home more comfortable, and doing your part in a charitable community program. Ivory is your color; your number is 6.

Friday, October 21 (Moon in Taurus) What goes on in your home today is going to impact your future. Guard against saying too much to a loved one who has been ill. A new source of income may be trying to announce its existence to you. Studies and hobbies will show remarkable progress. Red beans, long-grain rice, and spicy sausage go with this evening. Virgo is present. Hot combination numbers: 8 and 9.

Saturday, October 22 (Moon in Taurus to Gemini 5:28 a.m.) Gemini will add light, color, talk, and excitement to this day. Reddish-purple is your winning color when it comes to wardrobe accessories. The spotlight is on your love life, your yen to get along better with people, and ways to please your mate. Passion mounts this evening. Lucky lottery numbers: 1, 10, 19, 28, 37, 46.

Sunday, October 23 (Moon in Gemini) Conversation, communications, and transportation matters have the lead. You can take on some new responsibilities under these aspects and make your mark in a new way. Siblings agree with you but not with each other. What used to seem simple suddenly has become complex. Flame is your color; your lucky number is 3.

Monday, October 24 (Moon in Gemini to Cancer 6:15 p.m.) Scorpio makes an entrance. You yearn to be at peace with those about you. You welcome any show of originality and imagination, preferring those who are flexible within a disorganized, unreliable system. Think big and you may be surprised at your gains. Play the number 7 to win.

Tuesday, October 25 (Moon in Cancer) A Cancer and a Pisces are on stage. Be sure you are dressed appropriately today. In planning upcoming meals, go all out to impress others with variety and your own ability to try out new recipes. Brisket of beef with tiny parsley potatoes are on your preferred menu this evening. Your color is magenta; your number is 8.

Wednesday, October 26 (Moon in Cancer) Wonderful rays exist for celebrating some occasion that probably fell on another day this month. Situations are fluid. You will have little difficulty in bringing about corrections, improvements, and change. Reorganization of work may make everything go better over the rest of the month. Indigo is your color. Lucky lottery numbers: 1, 26, 10, 19, 28, 37.

Thursday, October 27 (Moon in Cancer to Leo 5:05 a.m.) Leo and another Aquarius make good partners. You may sense some conflict between a mercenary approach and a humanitarian one, but say as little as possible rather than stir up a hornet's nest of resentment from both quarters. Turquoise is your winning color. The complexities of the day bring rewards. Hot combination numbers: 3 and 5.

Friday, October 28 (Moon in Leo) The day is full of chatter and you may notice how self-centered some grown-ups can be. What you can accept in children you find hard to accept in adults, so there can be some desire to cut bait and flee. An Aries may want to join you and for the time, it's places and events more than people. Play the number 5 to win.

Saturday, October 29 (Moon in Leo to Virgo 12:21 p.m.) Check decisions out with your mate or business partner. Acting alone in anything important may be a little risky under these aspects. You will enjoy highly personal relationships. You can improve communication with in-laws and with friends of your beloved. Ginger is your color; your lucky number is 8.

Sunday, October 30 (Moon in Virgo) Excellent aspects exist for reviewing and possibly making budgets more stringent. Today is also wonderful for harvest festivals and hayrides, and for enjoying Indian summer and early fall. Virgo and Capricorn are in charge. You do well in talks with your banker and broker under these financial aspects. Your color is chartreuse; your numbers are 3 and 4.

Monday, October 31 (Daylight Saving Time ends) (Moon in Virgo to Libra 2:47 p.m.) Good aspects exist for parties and celebrations, and for improving the appearance of your home, special room, front porch, and lawn. This is a fine day for making changes that you have been contemplating for some time—the accent is on boudoir, closets, and dressing room. Taurus smiles at you. Pick five: 6, 15, 33, 24, 42.

NOVEMBER 1994

Tuesday, November 1 (Moon in Libra) Batten down the hatches in everything connected with career, authority, professional, and vocational commitments. Libra and Gemini have key roles. Don't give in to the yen to move too far from home and job today. Keep the communications channels open. Your color is wheat; your number is 3.

Wednesday, November 2 (Moon in Libra to Scorpio 4:19 p.m.) Act upon any information that comes to you right away. Long-range and long-distance matters are favored over the local, usual, here-and-now, and pressing. Pull in at the economic seams after sunset and hug the sidelines in career matters as the eclipse patterns form. Don't make any late-evening changes. Lucky lottery numbers: 5, 14, 23, 32, 41, 2.

Thursday, November 3 (Moon in Scorpio) A total solar eclipse occurs in early Scorpio, which can impinge upon your career, reputation, authority, and professional matters. Stay out of the limelight as far as possible. Control anger on the job. If your authority is questioned or wounded, just bide your time. Make no changes today, nor should you force change on others. Hot combination numbers: 7 and 8.

Friday, November 4 (Moon in Scorpio to Sagittarius 2:46 p.m.) If possible, postpone business conferences and interviews until later in the month. Don't quit your job or hire or fire anybody. Lean toward the status quo in everything connected with your career. Don't force issues or issue ultimatums. A Cancer and a Pisces are involved. Hot combination numbers: 9 and 4.

Saturday, November 5 (Moon in Sagittarius) It's not a good day for travel; there is a high accident-producing potential in the wake of yesterday's total solar eclipse. It may be difficult to see very far ahead. Plans are shaky and the attitudes of others can't be trusted. People, places, and ideas are all changing. Sagittarius and Gemini have key roles. Your color is sand. Lucky lottery numbers: 2, 5, 11, 20, 29, 38.

Sunday, November 6 (Moon in Sagittarius to Capricorn 3:02 p.m.) Information is coming through, but career and professional interests are pressured. Ask Aries and Leo what it's all about. The great outdoors is beckoning and a walk in a park or wooded area would bring a sense of joy.

You feel much approval and appreciation coming your way. Hot combination numbers: 4 and 1.

Monday, November 7 (Moon in Capricorn) Fine trends exist for dealing with very large organizations and institutions, and for helping your spouse or another partner with work you don't ordinarily like to do. Capricorn and Virgo come front and center. You can finish up no-win projects and close an old door so that a new one can be opened. Play the number 8 to win.

Tuesday, November 8 (Moon in Capricorn to Aquarius 5:48 p.m.) It's a powerful day for stopping in your tracks and reevaluating what you are doing or trying to do. You are good at making important choices and decisions under the prevailing aspects. It's a day for thinking big and for avoiding anything that smacks of the petty or unjust. Hot combination numbers: 1 and 4.

Wednesday, November 9 (Moon in Aquarius) Today is excellent for doing what you want to do, for holding the initiative, taking the lead, standing tall in any crisis, and airing your personal aspirations. Another Aquarius is in the picture. You are quick to sense what is going on behind the scenes and what is about to occur. You can stumble on good luck. Your winning color is sunburst orange. Lucky lottery numbers: 9, 14, 12, 3, 30, 21.

Thursday, November 10 (Moon in Aquarius) Career interests are speeded up. You can make a strong impact on supervisors and other authorities today. Personality assets are working well for you, and there is much inspiration, encouragement, and guidance associated with the day's trends. Throw your hat into any promising ring today. Gemini and Libra have key roles. Your color is deep pink. Hot combination numbers: 5 and 8.

Friday, November 11 (Moon in Aquarius to Pisces 12:04 a.m.) Wealth production is chugging along under the prevailing aspects. Pisces and Taurus have key roles. Today is fine for talks with your banker and broker, and for inspiring others to do the right thing in any business-financial showdown. Your earning power is rising and so is the value of what you own. Hot combination numbers: 7 and 9.

Saturday, November 12 (Moon in Pisces) Check recycled merchandise for genuine bargains. You can find good bargains where you least expect them. Publicity, advertising, and the smooth flow of information are indicated. Don't carelessly toss mail aside today; there may be something inviting and otherwise promising in that envelope. Scorpio and a Cancer are helpful. Lucky lottery numbers: 9, 18, 27, 36, 45, 2.

Sunday, November 13 (Moon in Pisces to Aries 9:44 a.m.) You may find certain money, accounting, and bookkeeping matters sluggish today. You may wonder why another Aquarius seems so disinterested in money. Much good will emanate from a unique exchange of ideas with an older woman. You're at your best today when you work within the season, so to speak. Your color is olive; your number is 2.

Monday, November 14 (Moon in Aries) Aries springs upon the stage of life. If you push immediate and pressing matters hard today, the results will be unusual. Concentration on the possible can pay off. There also are handsome dividends for you in studies, hobbies, and communications, and in moving around your own neighborhood. Lemon is your color; the number 6 is for you.

Tuesday, November 15 (Moon in Aries to Taurus 9:44 p.m.) All around you, people seem to be marching in step. There is a rare understanding about what must be done at this time. A good business discussion can pay off this morning. Special meetings, conferences, seminars, lectures, and interviews are all well aspected. Leo and Sagittarius have key roles. Tan is your color. Hot combination numbers: 8 and 4.

Wednesday, November 16 (Moon in Taurus) Taurus is present. This is a wonderful day for family relationships, bringing the generations together. You are in the right mood for exercising your natural charm and personal assets. You give others a sense of belonging and freedom. It's a friendly day. Lucky lottery numbers: 1, 10, 19, 28, 37, 46.

Thursday, November 17 (Moon in Taurus) Check things out with a Virgo and a Capricorn. The assistance you seek and receive today is first-rate. Never be too proud to request help. Your career, professional, and authority matters may mean less to you today than you wish and it would be well to keep self-criticism to yourself. Members of your family get your preferential treatment. Apricot is your color; the number 3 is best for you.

Friday, November 18 (Moon in Taurus to Gemini 10:42 a.m.) Today's full moon enlightens you in domestic, property, and ownership matters. You will see the wisdom of buying and selling at the same time. Any property on the market for a long time could be removed now, and ultimately you'll be happy that you removed it. Earth is your color. Hot combination numbers: 5 and 6.

Saturday, November 19 (Moon in Gemini) There's a lot of gossip making the rounds today and some of it can be founded on nasty jealousy. Gemini and Sagittarius can be at each other's throats and you might wish they would go away. Be sure to phone older loved ones who might be lonely today. Lucky lottery numbers: 19, 7, 16, 27, 25, 34.

Sunday, November 20 (Moon in Gemini to Cancer 11:21 p.m.) Your love life is strongly stimulated today. The creative side of your lovemaking can extend itself into intense passion. Small and meaningful entertainments of the spontaneous type could make everybody happy. Children are restless, but make good companions. Your number is 9.

Monday, November 21 (Moon in Cancer) Routine duties may be a bore, but should be respected. What the family at large thinks has to be more important than you would like. Stay out of drafts and be sure you abide by usual preventive-medicine routines. There is work that has to be done this evening. Lilac and ivory are your colors; your number is 4.

Tuesday, November 22 (Moon in Cancer) You may have the feeling that others are not carrying their share of the overall burden, but you have a tendency under these aspects to make extra work for yourself. As the day advances, you sense gains in wisdom and are much more tolerant of aggravating types. Old rose is your color. Hot combination numbers: 6 and 7.

Wednesday, November 23 (Moon in Cancer to Leo 10:33 a.m.) Your career picks up steam and you love it as Venus resumes direct movement in Scorpio. You can find the information you have been trying to run down for some time. You may feel that some older person is unfair in his criticism of teens. You will be pleased that you spoke up today. Auburn is your color. Lucky lottery numbers: 8, 23, 44, 35, 26, 17.

Thursday, November 24 (Moon in Leo) Leo speaks of marriage, cooperation, and the search for harmony and happiness. Legal interests are given a celestial push. You will relate well to the ideas of a Sagittarius. You may feel that your possessions are worth much more than you were told, and you could resent increased prices at stores. Your color is buff. On your menu—Scottish scones. Your number is 1.

Friday, November 25 (Moon in Leo) The art of pleasing your beloved is strongly represented under the prevailing aspects. This is a fine time for a second honeymoon, even if you don't go any farther than your boudoir. Intimate and private discussions will accomplish much. You can chalk up gains in legal and public relations matters also. The number 3 is your best bet.

Saturday, November 26 (Moon in Leo to Virgo 7:09 p.m.) Virgo and Taurus come front and center. Fine trends exist for business discussions with a neighbor who is in the economic know. Buy the things you use constantly in bulk and save a little. A trip to your friendly hardware store can save you the trouble of overdoing some simple household maintenance. Your colors are beige and mauve. Lucky lottery numbers: 5, 14, 26, 23, 32, 41.

Sunday, November 27 (Moon in Virgo) Gracious and charming behavior will get you what you want today. Be practical and determined at the same time, but sugar-coat your words when you feel they may meet with resistance.

Parents and grandparents have the information you seek. Children can add to your evening's delight. Sand and wheat are your winning colors; your lucky number is 7.

Monday, November 28 (Moon in Virgo to Libra 12:22 a.m.) You can profit from a talk with your broker or banker today. There may be simple explanations for your worries. Trust Libra to do the right thing now. You may travel a million miles in your memories under these aspects. Deep purple is your color; your protective number is 2.

Tuesday, November 29 (Moon in Libra) Travel postponed at the time of the eclipse can be embarked upon now. Surely an expanded viewpoint may be even better than actual movement to and fro. Reading, listening, and viewing a television documentary are also favored. Libra and another Aquarius are in the scenario. Your color is okra green. Hot combination numbers: 4 and 6.

Wednesday, November 30 (Moon in Libra to Scorpio 2:22 a.m.) Scorpio and a Cancer have key roles. You can make important contributions to your professional future today. A former supervisor may be instrumental to some career gains at this time. The social side of your job can ask a little more from you before paying high dividends. Your color is pistachio. Lucky lottery numbers: 6, 15, 30, 33, 42, 24.

DECEMBER 1994

Thursday, December 1 (Moon in Scorpio) Grasp the full potential of your career before the holiday and social plans may get in the way of important professional decisions and changes. Important news can arrive by phone or mail. Make sure you have input into social decisions that are being made for later in the month. Scorpio is anxious. Your color is peach. Hot combination numbers: 6 and 3.

Friday, December 2 (Moon in Scorpio to Sagittarius 2:13 a.m.) Your personality invites popularity, since you're in a brighter mood. Lunch can be especially pleasant if you invite a Gemini and a Sagittarius to your table. You'll enjoy the way these two hector each other conversationally and provoke amazing statements from each other. Your color is auburn. Hot combination numbers are 8 and 3.

Saturday, December 3 (Moon in Sagittarius) The social side of your job delivers dividends. Group activities, as well as church and club membership and participation matters, are favored. Today is fine for discussing charitable and humanitarian programs connected with the upcoming holidays. Volunteer rather than be dragged into the matters screaming. Lucky lottery numbers: 1, 3, 10, 19, 28, 37.

Sunday, December 4 (Moon in Sagittarius to Capricorn 1:42 a.m.) Today is excellent for addressing your holiday cards and for clearing away furniture that might get in the way of your holiday decorations and lighting. You will have the feeling that everything is being stepped up and that the mad race has begun. Older people are helpful. The number 3 is your best bet.

Monday, December 5 (Moon in Capricorn) Let Capricorn have some say in things today. Confidential meetings and decisions are well aspected. What is transpiring behind the scenes can impact your thinking and conclusions. It's a good day for knowing which side of your bread is buttered and for demonstrating loyalty to that certain one. The number 7 is your best bet.

Tuesday, December 6 (Moon in Capricorn to Aquarius 2:51 a.m.) Now in your lunar high cycle you are going to get your own way. You can take over, hold the initiative, and gain the upper hand. Where you want your plans to take you this month can be decided today. Another Aquarius can be helpful and understanding. Push highly personalized aspirations. Hot combination numbers: 9 and 3.

Wednesday, December 7 (Moon in Aquarius) Good trends exist for beginning your holiday preparations. Put your outdoor lights up today. Include neighbors in some of your entertainment plans. Make choices, decisions, and encourage loved ones to have input into family holiday plans. Get greeting cards traveling very far into the mails. Lucky lottery numbers: 2, 7, 11, 20, 29, 38.

Thursday, December 8 (Moon in Aquarius to Pisces 7:24 a.m.) Today is your oyster and there's a genuine pearl inside your acts, new beginnings, and associations. New starts in new directions carry high potential, as you attract much love, approval, and appreciation. Contact older loved ones, aunts, uncles, and friends of your parents and grandparents. Your winning number is 4.

Friday, December 9 (Moon in Pisces) Get estimates on home improvements that you would like to have done before the holidays. Invite a friend who knows colors and materials to offer suggestions. Pisces and Cancer can prove helpful. There is something you can do this afternoon to protect your future earning power. Mauve is your color; your lucky number is 6.

Saturday, December 10 (Moon in Pisces to Aries 4:03 p.m.) You could feel that you should have anticipated these disappointments. A neighbor, co-worker, or distant relative can surprise you in a negative way. You could feel that a loved one is unrealistic in his or her conclusions. A Scorpio can give you the right steer. Aquamarine is your color. Hot combination numbers: 8, 10, 44, 26, 35, 17.

Sunday, December 11 (Moon in Aries) Tackle little jobs that have to be done around your home. You have the responsibility to make certain a member of the opposite sex understands what you have said. You have to be careful with the promises you make under these aspects. Stalwart young men can prove a problem in any battle of the sexes. Your lucky number is 1.

Monday, December 12 (Moon in Aries) You can sense how youngsters resent restrictions. There is sheer boldness coming from little children who watch too much television. You would like to hold off making a serious commitment, but somebody can be pushing you toward it. There can be a sense of joy in a communication you receive today. Your lucky number is 5.

Tuesday, December 13 (Moon in Aries to Taurus 3:56 a.m.) Taurus and Virgo figure prominently. You can sense the powerful interdependence among members of your family. There may be some cancellations, postponements, and delays today. You tend to be painstaking in your efforts connected with the season. There is some danger of overplanning and overorganizing. Your lucky number is 7.

Wednesday, December 14 (Moon in Taurus) Let Capricorn say his piece. You tend to resent any restrictions that events and things can put on your plans for the day. Excellent trends exist for shopping, especially over the evening hours. Those hard-to-find presents can suddenly show up. Your colors are magenta and earth. Lucky lottery numbers: 9, 14, 27, 36, 18, 45.

Thursday, December 15 (Moon in Taurus to Gemini 5:00 p.m.) The frantic rat race to squeeze many duties, obligations, and responsibilities into the day can find you rather tired earlier than usual. Creative projects you have to tackle this evening will bring another spurt of energy. You feel rather earthy and want your feelings to find favor with your loved ones. Your lucky number is 2.

Friday, December 16 (Moon in Gemini) You are beginning to feel all the love, gratitude, nostalgia, and sentiment connected with this time of year. You are reaching out to parents and offspring for approval and you are generous in all your dealings with people. There are fine trends for entertaining in your own home. Gemini has the word for it. Your colors are angry reds with snow white. Pick five: 4, 22, 31, 13, 16.

Saturday, December 17 (Moon in Gemini) Communications and transportation matters are favored. You do well in hobbies, creativity in your own home, and in humanitarian and charitable work. Siblings are involved in your day. Another Aquarius can be instrumental to your peace of mind. Your color is indigo. Lucky lottery numbers: 17, 26, 33, 6, 15, 24.

Sunday, December 18 (Moon in Gemini to Cancer 5:25 a.m.) The full moon enlightens you in love, approval, and appreciation. It's a fine day for spontaneous entertaining and for having a heart-to-heart talk with a young person. Getting the job done offers wonderful satisfaction. Today's dialogue, prologues, and epilogues are momentous. Gemini and Sagittarius have vital roles. Your winning color is cerulean blue; your lucky number is 8.

Monday, December 19 (Moon in Cancer) A Cancer and a Capricorn can make your day more adventurous and rewarding. Give due attention to your health today. Watch what you eat and the pace you are setting for yourself. Know what the score is with your older relatives and friends. Your colors are wheat and rust. Hot combination numbers: 3 and 4.

Tuesday, December 20 (Moon in Cancer to Leo 4:13 p.m.) There is some work that must be done and it could be the type you dislike. The social tends to push the laborious out of the way. A Scorpio and a Pisces have key roles. You tend to dislike repetition and routines under the existing aspects. Your winning colors are claret red and green. Hot combination numbers: 5 and 1.

Wednesday, December 21 (Moon in Leo) Everything is looking up. What you may have found difficult earlier in the month is a piece of cake today. Your awareness in marriage and other partnerships means peace wherever you are. You have no difficulty compromising and solving improbables to the satisfaction of others. Your color is beige. Lucky lottery numbers: 21, 7, 16, 25, 34, 43.

Thursday, December 22 (Moon in Leo) Leo rules the roost and you find forms of self-completion in many of your relationships. There can be a special closeness to your mate. Your awareness in domestic, property, and ownership matters is first rate. Luck attends you in sharing, working in tandem, and improving partnerships. Your color is azure; count on the number 9.

Friday, December 23 (Moon in Leo to Virgo 1:01 a.m.) Stabilize situations and lean toward the status quo. Last-minute touches to your holiday plans are guaranteed to do right by you and others. You feel very much able to help others, and Aries and Sagittarius are on your side in any social crisis. Crimson is your color; your number is 2.

Saturday, December 24 (Moon in Virgo) Virgo stands ready to advise as the pace for both socializing and loving increases. Don't let any difference of opinion with a friend get out of hand. The relationship between the various generations is excellent. The fires of memory, traditions, and sentiment are keeping everything moving in the right direction. Lucky lottery numbers: 24, 33, 40, 4, 13, 22.

Sunday, December 25 (Moon in Virgo to Libra 7:27 a.m.) There is a special force of the practical, of basic determination on your part, and of a method that will see you through a busy day. You are not thrown by the changes in plans that others impose on you, nor by a few additional people in your home. The Aquarius welcome mat never was lovelier. Oh what a table you can spread today! Red and green are your colors; your number is 6.

Monday, December 26 (Moon in Libra) Excellent bargains can be found in the larger outlet stores. Libra and another Aquarius can make your day splendid. Good trends exist in local travel, in carrying gifts to shut-ins within a 200-mile radius, and in looking forward as well as back to all those amazing yesterdays. People are ultra-important to you and ultramarine is your winning color. Your lucky number is 1.

Tuesday, December 27 (Moon in Libra to Scorpio 11:17 a.m.) Interesting newcomers and strangers are contributing to your happiness. Gemini appreciates your special allure under these aspects. You discover and rediscover. You see ways to advance your own interests, especially down the line a bit. Look ahead for big gains. Pick five: 3, 12, 30, 21, 39.

Wednesday, December 28 (Moon in Scorpio) Career needs may give you a push away from the social and the seasonal to what is necessary and practical. Scorpio is setting the pace. You handle well the jobs that must be finished before the year ends. Both your social and your economic prestige is rising, which can make you feel more at home and happier. Your color is chestnut. Lucky lottery numbers: 5, 28, 14, 34, 23, 32.

Thursday, December 29 (Moon in Scorpio to Sagittarius 12:46 p.m.) A final December push in your career could bear rich fruit. Being there when less-responsible people are absent can make a big difference to your future. Your sex appeal can add variety to the day and improve your chance of success. Scorpio and Taurus have important roles. Your color is sand; your lucky number is 7.

Friday, December 30 (Moon in Sagittarius) A post-holiday party, including gift giving, would go well under these aspects. Sagittarius sounds off and you can profit from the information. Social travel may be involved in the day's aspects, probably within the 200-mile radius. Or visitors may come your way with presents. Wear kelly green and gold; your lucky number is 9.

Saturday, December 31 (Moon in Sagittarius to Capricorn 12:58 p.m.) This Sagittarian moon is exceptionally social for you and can bring you closer to friends and neighbors. A local party can bring good feelings about the new year. Church and club memberships and participation matters are favored. Gemini says it all. Fitting colors are mauve and beige. Lucky lottery numbers: 31, 2, 11, 20, 29, 38.

JANUARY 1995

Sunday, January 1 (Moon in Capricorn) A Capricorn and a Cancer can affect your thinking. Today is fine for clearing away holiday debris, going through closets and drawers, and generally tidying up. Complete, finish, put things away. The new moon in the private parts of your chart illuminates what is taking place behind thc sccncs. Your color is old rose; your number is 8.

Monday, January 2 (Moon in Capricorn to Aquarius 1:39 p.m.) Prepare for your lunar high cycle, which begins tomorrow. Put things in place; deal in prologues and presentations of ideas; secure cooperation. Finish up chores that should have been finished in 1994. A Taurus and a Virgo can be helpful. The value of the work you do can reflect itself in your contentment. Your number is 3.

Tuesday, January 3 (Moon in Aquarius) You may feel that loved ones are not as affectionate as they should be. Even so, you can achieve a great deal independently. Push highly personalized interests. Stand up for your rights. You are favored if you take strong stands. Another Aquarius is in your corner this evening. Hot combination numbers: 5 and 6.

Wednesday, January 4 (Moon in Aquarius to Pisces 4:49 p.m.) Announce, promulgate, activate, stimulate, and keep things moving. Friends who live quite close by would love to get a phone call from you. Your color is maroon. Don't be distracted by any jealousy you run into over the late afternoon. This evening draws attention to obnoxious people. Lucky lottery numbers: 7, 16, 25, 34, 43, 4.

Thursday, January 5 (Moon in Pisces) Money making takes off with a big bang and financial January is under way. Pisces and a Cancer have front seats. Discuss your career future and let your employer know if your standard and cost of living are not being met by your salary. This is a good day for revamping household budgets. Orchid is your color; your number is 7.

Friday, January 6 (Moon in Pisces to Aries 11:56 p.m.) The Twelfth Night calls for a masquerade party, with king, queen and court jester in control. There are people who envy your disposition, poise, and self-assurance. Your health gets a boost as you observe good preventive-medicine routines. Phone calls can bring unusual information. Lucky lottery numbers: 9, 18, 27, 36, 45, 16.

Saturday, January 7 (Moon in Aries) All personal matters are speeded up as Mercury enters Aquarius. Aries can give good directions to your day. Push local, studies, hobbies, communications and short-distance travel interests. On your menu today—brisket of beef with noodles. This evening can bring good news about a relative. Winning colors are olive and earth. Hot combination numbers: 2 and 3.

Sunday, January 8 (Moon in Aries) Some will think you're a human dynamo due to all the pioneering, moving about, and activating of projects that are marking efforts.

Avoid worrying about progress in your career. What is required now is patience and forebearance. Give due attention to your hair and skin. Hot combination numbers: 4 and 8.

Monday, January 9 (Moon in Aries to Taurus 10:58 a.m.) Less television and more reading should be your rule; and children should be held to this dictum. The trends are favorable for improving the lives of youngsters and encouraging them to think and to create. Stir their imagination and show your own flexibility in any time of crisis. Amber is your color; your number is 1.

Tuesday, January 10 (Moon in Taurus) Encourage Taurus. Loved ones are interested in the stands you are taking on relevant legislation. You want your family to stand out for their sense of unity at this time. Select wardrobe accessories that will complement your complexion. Visit a hairstylist. Hot combination numbers: 2 and 5.

Wednesday, January 11 (Moon in Taurus to Gemini 11:57 p.m.) Loved ones will cooperate with your efforts inside and outside the home. Virgo can be relied upon to pick up the pieces. What appeared to be an obstacle can be overcome this afternoon, making the rest of this cycle go more smoothly. Patience and perseverence pay off. Cherry is your color. Lucky lottery numbers: 5, 14, 23, 32, 41, 11.

Thursday, January 12 (Moon in Gemini) Let Gemini in on your plans. This is a marvelous day for parties, entertainments, enjoying spontaneity in social life. Love, romance, courtship, and parent–child understanding are accented. An abundance of energy will stand you in good stead as you socialize. Turquoise is your color. Hot combination numbers: 7 and 6.

Friday, January 13 (Moon in Gemini) You are exposed to forebodings, old wives tales, and also the fact that most superstitions about Friday the 13th are based on historical fact. Libra is in your corner. The romance of places and things is represented. Conversation is fascinating. Cinnamon is your color. Pick five: 13, 4, 31, 9, 18.

Saturday, January 14 (Moon in Gemini to Cancer 12:20 p.m.) Reach out to loved ones. Discuss situations with parents and children. You could receive an important message. There can be complaints from older loved ones, who feel housebound and isolated. Trust the opinions of another Aquarius. Consider those who would be inspired by a phone call from you. Baby blue is your color. Lucky lottery numbers: 14, 21, 29, 2, 11, 20.

Sunday, January 15 (Moon in Cancer) You have strong support in family matters, health improvements, and work that has to be done at this time. You would rather postpone some activities, but they seem to prod you along. As a result, you can know an early fatigue this evening. It's not a day for burning your candle at both ends. Gold is your color; your number is 4.

Monday, January 16 (Moon in Cancer to Leo 10:36 p.m.) The full moon illuminates your health and the work that has to be done over the next few weeks. Today is fine for discussing any possible uncertainty you may experience with a Cancer or Capricorn. A neighbor is looking to you for understanding in a trying situation. Your winning color is magenta; your lucky number is 8.

Tuesday, January 17 (Moon in Leo) Leo shows up. Fine trends exist in marriage, other partnerships, contracts, and agreements. Legal settlements can be pushed at this time. The past is having a strong impact on you and you may find yourself remembering those who no longer are with you. You are ready to make a wise purchase. Hot combination numbers: 1 and 5.

Wednesday, January 18 (Moon in Leo) Conversation can bring spouses closer together. This is a good time for seeing people, being outgoing, and for permitting yourself to enjoy those with whom you tend to disagree. You are a concerned listener. Invite somebody to join you for a stroll in a safe place. Lemon is your color. Lucky lottery numbers: 3, 12, 21, 30, 39, 48.

Thursday, January 19 (Moon in Leo to Virgo 6:39 a.m.) Virgo will prove helpful. Good trends exist in savings, investments, corrections, improvements, and changes. Keep conversation lighthearted; save the gloom and doom for later. There is special enlightenment for you in budgeting, measuring cost of living and standard of living against what you have on hand. Your number is 5.

Friday, January 20 (Moon in Virgo) Taurus wants to know you much better. Talks with your banker and broker will go well today. You can swing over from the old and accepted to the new and not quite acceptable. Aim high. Tell your serious aspirations to a Capricorn. Salmon is your color. Hot combination numbers: 7 and 6.

Saturday, January 21 (Moon in Virgo to Libra 12:54 p.m.) Another Aquarius can help you make a personal decision. You can appear to be rather self-centered in the eyes of loved ones. There is no doubt you are the dominant member of the team and you can lead others to minor victories. Advance own ideas and stake your claims. Amber is your color. Lucky lottery numbers: 9, 18, 27, 36, 45, 21.

Sunday, January 22 (Moon in Libra) Libra and Aries figure prominently. Travel, moving about so that you can see many people, and what you have perking for yourself at a distance are favored. If you take a lackadaisical attitude, nothing will get done. You tend to be a good influence in the lives of your children and other youngsters. Your number is 2.

Monday, January 23 (Moon in Libra to Scorpio 5:32 p.m.) Keep on the go and others will meet you halfway. There's a fine momentum to the day, and you can step up your pace and actually accomplish more than you planned. Strike while the iron is hot. Hold the initiative and push for greater acceptance of your aspirations. Silver is your color; your lucky number is 6.

Tuesday, January 24 (Moon in Scorpio) Scorpio and Pisces figure prominently. You can push career interests, get over obstacles that have stood between you and a promotion, and generally feather your own nest. Others will admit that you are a good influence upon their children.

You can cash in on earned reputation. Your lucky number is 8.

Wednesday, January 25 (Moon in Scorpio to Sagittarius 8:37 p.m.) Executives and supervisors are willing to listen to what you have to say. Fine trends exist for inspiring coworkers and generally improving your position on the job. There is special enlightenment in ways to more fully use your personality and character assets. Lucky lottery numbers: 25, 37, 1, 10, 19, 28.

Thursday, January 26 (Moon in Sagittarius) Personal interests become sluggish as Mercury retrogrades in Aquarius. Sagittarius can get you over some obstacles. Friendships, group activities, and church and club membership and participation interests move along swiftly. Carmine and white are winning colors. Hot combination numbers: 3 and 2.

Friday, January 27 (Moon in Sagittarius to Capricorn 10:26 p.m.) Gemini and Leo have front seats. Parties, entertainments, celebrations are favored. Spend as much time with people who enjoy socializing as possible. What you set in motion today will show marvelous endurance and can be the beginning of major social and financial gains. Hot combination numbers: 5 and 4.

Saturday, January 28 (Moon in Capricorn) Capricorn has good advice for you. Good trends exist for bringing some matters to a close, for operating somewhat behind the scenes. Avoid exposing your hand in any showdown. Matters rooted in the past have a way of coming around again. Accept the truth that the month is ending. Old rose is your color. Lucky lottery numbers: 7, 16, 25, 34, 43, 28.

Sunday, January 29 (Moon in Capricorn) Pounce on those household chores that should be done prior to the end of the month. A savory beef stew should be on your menu today when you are strongly anxious to please loved ones. Capricorn and Virgo may silently have strong opinions and perhaps you should consult them. Sky blue is your color; your number is 9.

Monday, January 30 (Moon in Capricorn to Aquarius 12:03 a.m.) This is your second lunar high cycle this month and it is fine for conclusions, finalizing, presenting your ideas, and standing tall in defense of what you believe. Others will respect you all the more when you take your own part, blowing your own horn a little. Be involved, not too free or detached. Your lucky number is 2.

Tuesday, January 31 (Moon in Aquarius) You can get your own way and win others over to your point of view under the prevailing aspects. If you don't speak out on the controversial issues, others may conclude that you lack awareness and belief in yourself. Another Aquarius is in the picture. Your colors are lime and lemon. Hot combination numbers: 4 and 3.

FEBRUARY 1995

Wednesday, February 1 (Moon in Aquarius to Pisces 3:05 a.m.) The month begins with favorable stimulation of wealth production, earning power, and income. But personal interests are a little sluggish. Another Aquarius and a Pisces are in this picture. Your winning colors are ebony and dark brown. Everyday matters are priorities. Lucky lottery numbers: 6, 15, 24, 33, 42, 19.

Thursday, February 2 (Moon in Pisces) Push monetary interests. Hold business and financial conferences. Check matters out with a Scorpio and a Cancer. On your menu today should be a dish that speaks of love, concern, the old traditions, and a homey togetherness. Your lucky colors are apricot and orange. Don't argue over how money is earned, spent, or lost. Hot combination numbers: 8 and 4.

Friday, February 3 (Moon in Pisces to Aries 9:12 a.m.) Tread the straight and narrow path in regard to family and home interests. Cost of living increases can be centered in your kitchen and car. A bit of background music can add to the essence of this day. Peace of mind is available in your own home. Hot combination numbers: 1 and 7.

Saturday, February 4 (Moon in Aries) Set negative feelings aside. You are empowered to offset the agressive tactics of a relative or friend. You may feel that your own judgment is too harsh to pass on to a youngster, but chances are the kid expects a stiff lecture for infractions of the rule. Lucky lottery numbers: 3, 12, 21, 30, 39, 48.

Sunday, February 5 (Moon in Aries to Taurus 7:09 p.m.) Capricorn and Aries will impact your day. You are in tune with what is transpiring behind the scenes. Organization efforts are not very good, however. The urge to get some no-win projects out of the way can be strong. If you concentrate on the local, immediate, and pressing matters, you'll accomplish more. Ivory is your color; your lucky number is 3.

Monday, February 6 (Moon in Taurus) Taurus will help you complete a project. Family matters are high on your agenda. You become very much aware of changes taking place in your community. Residential maintenance can be in the picture, much to your annoyance. Coffee and bronze are winning colors. Hot combination numbers: 5 and 9.

Tuesday, February 7 (Moon in Taurus) Domestic, real estate, ownership, and property matters get green lights. In social relationships, you can chalk up victories and successes. Fine trends exist for buying a plant, sending flowers to an older loved one, and having jewelry cleaned or repaired. Apricot is your color. Hot combination numbers: 7 and 6.

Wednesday, February 8 (Moon in Taurus to Gemini 7:44 a.m.) Work on improving kitchen budgets. Your menu calls for an item that expresses love, something one's heart can hunger for, making your dinner table all the more festive. Memories can be constructed that will hold loved ones in good stead years from now. Wear angry reds. Lucky lottery numbers: 9, 18, 27, 36, 45, 8.

Thursday, February 9 (Moon in Gemini) Gemini and another Aquarius have key roles. Home and heart are at the center of your personal solar system. Excellent trends exist in lovemaking; pleasing members of your family; and enjoying a romance, party, or entertainment. Don't forget to write and to phone. Deep pink is your color; your lucky number is 5.

Friday, February 10 (Moon in Gemini to Cancer 8:17 p.m.) You see the beauty rather than the blight. You remain positive even in the company of negativism. People like you, approving of and appreciating you. So the day is one that is full of rewards. The proper dining atmosphere will help your digestion and tickle your palate. Winning combination numbers: 7 and 6.

Saturday, February 11 (Moon in Cancer) A Cancer and a Pisces are in your corner. You could come across some good hints and suggestions related to preventive medicine today. Also, this is the day to work in your garage, attic, or basement or to clear away debris on your land. You'll have no trouble inviting and winning cooperation. Pastels will banish gloom. Lucky lottery numbers: 9, 18, 27, 36, 45, 20.

Sunday, February 12 (Moon in Cancer) Scorpio rules the roost. You could experience a sudden attraction for somebody who never has looked this good to you before. Contact lenses? Improved wardrobe? New hairstyle? You may be a little disconcerted over this. Read in order to improve your basic security. Strawberry is your color; your number is 2.

Monday, February 13 (Moon in Cancer to Leo 6:31 a.m.) You could find your spouse or partner edgy and irritable, but is this merely your own conclusion? Marriage, legal, public relations, and interests allied to all of these are under minor pressures. Leo and Aries have key roles. Aim for light, color, and comfort in any decorating or movement of furniture. Your number is 6.

Tuesday, February 14 (Moon in Leo) Contact one of your old Valentines. There is a bubbling, champagne-popping, and effervescent environment surrounding you. Things are bright and beautiful, and marriage gets strong lunar support. Sagittarius is friendly. Hope encircles you all day. Blue and beige are your colors. Hot combination numbers: 8 and 7.

Wednesday, February 15 (Moon in Leo to Virgo 1:52 p.m.) Sharing, working in tandem, cooperating, and conciliating are strong trends. You could have the feeling that you need others more than they need you. It may be difficult for you to take the lead, however. Luck is with you if you go along with the wishes of your partner. White is your color. Lucky lottery numbers: 1, 10, 19, 28, 37, 46.

Thursday, February 16 (Moon in Virgo) All highly personalized interests pick up steam as Mercury resumes direct movement in Aquarius. Virgo shows up early and is willing. You get along well with people involved in security matters—banker, broker, insurance people. Luck is with you when you handle your own finances. Your lucky numbers are 3 and 4.

Friday, February 17 (Moon in Virgo to Libra 7:00 p.m.) Push for more money, another source of income, and greater return on your investments. Keep good tax records this year and you will be able to deduct more expenses than anticipated. It will be easy to get along with an older woman and receive good advice from her. Taurus will impact your day. Hot combination numbers: 5, 14, 23, 32, 41, 17.

Saturday, February 18 (Moon in Libra) Libra shows up. Don't make decisions until you have all the facts. Travel, long-range matters, and matters of the higher mind are indicated. There are misleading rumors and plenty of idle gossip making the rounds. Protect all flanks from con artists. Mauve is your color. Lucky lottery numbers: 7, 16, 25, 34, 43, 18.

Sunday, February 19 (Moon in Libra to Scorpio 10:55 p.m.) You gain much economically and socially by keeping on the go. Information is flowing freely now, so it would be wise to use the telephone. Make at least one long-distance call. An aunt and uncle are ready to help you in important ways. An older man is in your corner. Your lucky colors are aqua and peach; your number is 9.

Monday, February 20 (Moon in Scorpio) Scorpio is ready to explain it all to you. Push important career advantages. Strike up a conversation with a shy person who knows the inner-office story. Luck is with you today, if you are in the company of a very sexy, adventurous, and talkative type. Lilac is your color; your lucky numbers are 4 and 5.

Tuesday, February 21 (Moon in Scorpio) Take advantage of all the special sales and end-of-season bargains. What you save today can make next month go easier. Dark red is your lucky color. People notice you now, including some who would like to know you better. But be on guard, for somebody's intentions may be dishonorable. Your lucky number is 6.

Wednesday, February 22 (Moon in Scorpio to Sagittarius 2:13 a.m.) Sagittarius is present. Friendship pays off and you may be amazed at how well some of these close relationships have weathered many a storm. You will enjoy being part of a vibrant group. The parents of a friend can be especially instrumental in some good fortune coming your way. Maroon is your color. Lucky lottery numbers: 8, 17, 26, 35, 44, 22.

Thursday, February 23 (Moon in Sagittarius) Today is fine for joint investments of time, energy, and money. Friends of your friends want to spend some time with you. Don't shortchange friendship. Do what church and club involvements expect you to do, but be on guard against those who tend to misquote and misinterpret. Rust is your color. Hot combination numbers: 1 and 2.

Friday, February 24 (Moon in Sagittarius to Capricorn 5:11 a.m.) Complete outstanding work that others are waiting for. You can build upon a high reputation earned in the past. What's going on behind the scenes can rebound in your favor. Trust the decisions and advice emanating from Capricorn and Cancer. Get to the root causes of problems. Your color is flame; your number is 3.

Saturday, February 25 (Moon in Capricorn) Your winning colors are primrose and gray. This is a good cycle for putting the pieces together, for mending, maintaining, and fixing. People around you may be disturbed by some tidbits of gossip making the circuit. Luck is with you in completions, in finishing up old tasks. Lucky lottery numbers: 25, 33, 41, 5, 14, 23.

Sunday, February 26 (Moon in Capricorn to Aquarius 8:14 a.m.) The day can change suddenly from an accent on endings to a stress on new beginnings. Over the evening you can feel very much in the driver's seat, able to make your own decisions and to win others over to your point of view. You can feel that at long last you are getting that break. Your lucky number is 7.

Monday, February 27 (Moon in Aquarius) Now fully into your lunar high cycle, you can write your own ticket. Others stand aside, support your aspirations, realize that you mean business. Dress to the hilt, attract attention, speak up in your own behalf. Self-confidence will get you what you want. Russet is your color; your lucky number is 2.

Tuesday, February 28 (Moon in Aquarius to Pisces 12:16 p.m.) Invite, court, and sell, for you are going to win big under the prevailing aspects. Approve and appreciate and show courtesy and good manners, which still carries more weight than one can believe in this era of selfishness. You can win the support of former critics. Hot combination numbers: 4 and 8.

MARCH 1995

Wednesday, March 1 (Moon in Pisces) The new moon in Pisces illuminates your financial situation. There is enlightenment in the formation of new and more useful budgets. It's a good day for airing your aspirations, both moneywise and socially. Searching the darker corners of your mind for explanations of your anger will pay off tonight. Melon is your color. Lucky lottery numbers: 7, 16, 25, 34, 43, 18.

Thursday, March 2 (Moon in Pisces to Aries 6:30 p.m.) A Scorpio and a Cancer have front seats. A chat with your supervisor can rid the air of dangerous questions.

Keep harmony in your own home by doing something about recent disagreements. You can't take too much responsibility here. You are effective when you give yourself a little time alone. Your number is 9.

Friday, March 3 (Moon in Aries) Aries and Sagittarius have key roles. Be assured that others feel considerable guilt that so much of their good lives stem from your sense of duty and obligation. Local, usual, and familiar situations are favored; so are communications, studies, hobbies, and local travel. Eggshell is your color; your number is 2.

Saturday, March 4 (Moon in Aries) You can rise to challenging responsibilities in the interest of your beloved. What you have been preparing or nurturing in the pickling process can now be brought to fruition. Your learning processes are first rate and you take in all that you see, hear, and touch. Lucky lottery numbers: 4, 13, 22, 31, 40, 17.

Sunday, March 5 (Moon in Aries to Taurus 3:50 a.m.) Taurus and Virgo are in this picture. Your family has the dominant role in your life today. Community, real estate, property, and ownership matters are also favored. Your winning colors are cream and dark green. Don't permit the doom and gloom types to pass their depressing feelings on to you. Try the numbers 5 and 1.

Monday, March 6 (Moon in Taurus) Capricorn will tell what's wrong with the work. Refuse to be thrown by the unexpected spending of a younger loved one. You can improve a chicken by marinating it in skim milk for one hour. Be especially cautious while moving about in unfamiliar places. Family meals can be pleasant. Mauve is your color; your number is 9.

Tuesday, March 7 (Moon in Taurus to Gemini 3:55 p.m.) You are in an earthy cycle, where determination and method have leading roles. Some physical deterioration in the construction of your house can reveal itself under existing aspects. You can make progress on work that tends to be boring and full of complicated details. Earthy brown is your color. Hot combination numbers: 2 and 3.

Wednesday, March 8 (Moon in Gemini) Gemini comes calling. There are some aggravating situations and Gemini can teach you the trick of shrugging a shoulder and picking up more interesting topics of conversation. This is a fine love period, perfect for entertaining the friends of your beloved, giving a party, figuring out love's conundrums. Lucky lottery numbers: 4, 13, 22, 31, 40, 5.

Thursday, March 9 (Moon in Gemini) Be especially cautious while driving close to home, near schools, and where youngsters play. Fine trends exist for signing papers, contracts, and agreements, and for showing self-confidence in the face of much gloom and doom. Know what and where your goals are and then march directly toward them. Your number is 6.

Friday, March 10 (Moon in Gemini to Cancer 4:40 a.m.) There can be some deception in the picture. People refrain from telling the unvarnished truth for fear of unwanted involvements. Envy and jealousy are making the rounds. Avoid anything that smacks of mental depression. Don't overburden yourself with work that is contrary to your tastes or principles. Hot combination numbers: 8 and 7.

Saturday, March 11 (Moon in Cancer) A Pisces and a Cancer will impact the day. Take care of your health; dress appropriately when taking a stroll. Don't expect your assistants to be first rate, mostly because coworkers can feel a little envious of your knowledge. Neighbors can seem meddlesome. Beige is your color. Lucky lottery numbers: 1, 10, 19, 28, 37, 46.

Sunday, March 12 (Moon in Cancer to Leo 3:28 p.m.) Take advantage of this day of rest and just relax. A good mystery novel might be your cup of tea under these aspects. The financial pages of your newspaper will help you get a feel for the economic future. Iron out any possible impasse with your beloved. Snow white is your color; your lucky number is 3.

Monday, March 13 (Moon in Leo) Leo requires time and authority. Sharing and cooperative ventures are favored. Marriage and other partnerships, and legal and public relations interests can be served. Your color is turquoise. Luck is with you where you heed what you are being told. Watch what you eat tonight. A good number for you is 7.

Tuesday, March 14 (Moon in Leo to Virgo 10:54 p.m.) You can have the feeling that your partner has too many irons in the fire. You are at your best today when you look the part you are playing. There is some trickiness coming at you from a coworker or business colleague. It may be wise to explain to young people how vitally important one's reputation is. Try the number 9.

Wednesday, March 15 (Moon in Virgo) Pisces and Virgo are in the picture. Wealth production is stepped up and you can realize more of a profit now than you anticipated. Ask questions rather than running the risk of misinterpreting information. You can make a decision now to sell what you no longer need. Lucky lottery numbers: 2, 11, 20, 29, 38, 47.

Thursday, March 16 (Moon in Virgo) You feel loved, settled, respected, and appreciated; what more could you ask? You are at your best when you are inaugurating or implementing changes, corrections, and improvements. You want the day to produce something solid but it is a day of intangibles. White and black are winning colors; your number is 4.

Friday, March 17 (Moon in Virgo to Libra 3:18 a.m.) The full moon in your eighth house illuminates security matters, changes, improvements, and corrections. There is news about budgetary changes, improved investments, and how to sidestep waste. Crimson and violet are winning colors. Cousins can make excellent companions. Hot combination numbers: 6 and 5.

Saturday, March 18 (Moon in Libra) Libra gives you the green light in travel, accomplishing long-range and long-distance requirements. Yellow is your color. You do well today where you ward off distractions and engage in serious effort. Friends at a distance have your welfare at heart. Sky blue is your lucky color. Lucky lottery numbers: 8, 17, 26, 35, 44, 18.

Sunday, March 19 (Moon in Libra to Scorpio 5:52 a.m.) You may be called upon to help somebody who is hard pressed for ready cash. Even if this is a relative, you must get the loan and some method of payment down on paper. Do what you can to retain the esteem of difficult teenagers. Is somebody being unreasonably cool to you? Wear violet accessories. Your number is 1.

Monday, March 20 (Moon in Scorpio) Consider the many resources you have at hand for achieving inner peace and satisfaction. Look around and decide which maintenance work in your home should top your agenda. There are many mental activities open to you and they will provide a good balance to your day. Apple green is your color; your number is 5.

Tuesday, March 21 (Moon in Scorpio to Sagittarius 7:57 a.m.) Aries and Scorpio will impact your day as spring and the new astrological year begin. You can make excellent headway in your career and put your reputation on the line today. The world is very much your oyster as new inspiration and encouragement are born in your horoscope. Teal blue is your color; your lucky numbers are 7 and 6.

Wednesday, March 22 (Moon in Sagittarius) Sagittarius is being diplomatic and tactful, and courtesy will open doors for you. Friendships, group activities, and church and club membership and participation get top billing. Your required chores of shopping and food preparation can help you achieve a healthy body. Lucky lottery numbers: 9, 18, 27, 36, 45, 22.

Thursday, March 23 (Moon in Sagittarius to Capricorn 10:31 a.m.) Leo has the answers as well as the self-confidence. A friendly attitude can move mountains on a day when anger could bring retaliation. Where possible, walk more, reduce lifting to manageable amounts, and alternate vigorous activity with periods of rest and relaxation. Cherry is your color. Lucky combination is 2 and 3.

Friday, March 24 (Moon in Capricorn) Capricorn will help you complete March's dominant project. Today is fine for running down elusive information. You could encounter annoying, evasive tactics from younger relatives. There is some outmoded thinking getting in the way of true understanding. Questions may have to be asked. Hot combination numbers: 4 and 7.

Saturday, March 25 (Moon in Capricorn to Aquarius 2:10 p.m.) Mental activity is just as important as physical on a day like this. You can solve some problems in the privacy of your own mind. People will be dropping by and, as the day advances, you can feel a need to be with a group. Fine rays exist for writing meaningful letters over the evening. Marigold is your color. Lucky lottery numbers: 15, 6, 24, 33, 42, 20.

Sunday, March 26 (Moon in Aquarius) Now in your lunar high cycle, you have the upper hand. Your decisions will be respected and honored. Let the world see you at your best. Stake your claims, making your point with self-confidence and self-reliance. Another Aquarius and a Leo can be in the picture. Sort and sift the gold from the dross. Your number is 8.

Monday, March 27 (Moon in Aquarius to Pisces 7:18 p.m.) You can pick and choose successfully today. Open new doors in business and financial matters. In romance, you can gain the upper hand and win approval from your beloved for some of your far-out Aquarian ideas. Renew old energies this evening. Ultramarine is your color; your number is 3.

Tuesday, March 28 (Moon in Pisces) This is a wonderful day for pushing hard in business. You can up your earning power and income and also find new sources of income. Fine rays exist for selling, buying, and exchanging. What you own is increasing in value. Pisces and a Cancer come front and center. Strawberry is your color; your number is 5.

Wednesday, March 29 (Moon in Pisces) Pisces and Virgo come aboard. If you give unadulterated attention to money matters today, you are bound to achieve good results. The season is egging you on and you can find real pleasure in planting and growing things. Others may make excuses that leave you cold. Wear off-white and emerald. Lucky lottery numbers: 7, 16, 25, 34, 43, 17.

Thursday, March 30 (Moon in Pisces to Aries 2:26 a.m.) Aries and Leo will impact your day. Narrow your sights and pounce on emerging opportunities to take charge. Local, immediate, and pressing matters top your agenda. You get ideas across well today. Push for acceptance of work that might be a bit controversial. Melon is your color; your number is 9.

Friday, March 31 (Moon in Aries) The new moon spotlights work that must be finished now. Your learning processes are good and your self-discipline was never better. Fine trends exist for catching up and breezing ahead in important tasks. Sagittarius has a key role. Your winning colors are mauve and beige. Hot combination numbers: 2 and 8.

APRIL 1995

Saturday, April 1 (Moon in Aries to Taurus 11:59 a.m.) Young males can impact your day. There is considerable boasting and bragging that doesn't seem honest or deserving. Sales, bargain hunting, and spending quality time with loved ones are favored. There is helpful assistance from Leo and Libra. Amber is your color. Lucky lottery numbers: 1, 10, 19, 28, 27, 46.

Sunday, April 2 (Moon in Taurus; Daylight Saving Time begins) Spring cleaning programs can be organized and begun. Domestic improvements are high on your agenda. Talks with members of your family who want to change their living arrangements will produce. Maintaining an even keel is the big idea under prevailing aspects. Tangerine is your color; your lucky number is 3.

Monday, April 3 (Moon in Taurus) Taurus and Virgo have key roles. Most of all, you appreciate what you are used to and the things you totally understand. You shy away from changes that seem too extreme and cling to the familiar. You are very much a part of the family and the community. Sky blue is your color; your number is 7.

Tuesday, April 4 (Moon in Taurus to Gemini 12:49 a.m. EDT) Gemini comes calling and things are looking up. Your creativity, originality, imagination, and flexibility are all stimulated. Today is fine for making love, giving a spontaneous party, bringing parents and offspring together. Emotions are ticklish, and there is a sense of adventurous urgency. Hot combination numbers: 9 and 8.

Wednesday, April 5 (Moon in Gemini) Gemini and another Aquarius will be on hand. Make love today, be romantic, sentimental, nostalgic, adventurous. Ecstasy is the payoff for passion well spent. You are favored where you are expanding commitments and reassuring those who need it. Aquamarine is your color. Lucky lottery numbers: 2, 11, 20, 29, 38, 47.

Thursday, April 6 (Moon in Gemini to Cancer 1:40 p.m.) Libra can offer wonderful advice. Orange and beige are winning colors. Parties, entertainments, and spontaneity are all represented. Parent–offspring generation gaps can be bridged for the time being. There are some baffling and irritating types coming your way. Wheat is your color; your numbers are 4 and 3.

Friday, April 7 (Moon in Cancer) More truth than poetry is the order of this day; you want to give everybody the benefit of the doubt. Correspondence with a younger relative will be pleasing. A Cancer and a Capricorn are in the picture. Health and work improvements are indicated. Mauve is your color. Hot combination numbers: 6 and 5.

Saturday, April 8 (Moon in Cancer) You will enjoy taking on more responsibility today. There is plenty of work to be done around the grounds of your home, and a visit to the farmer's market is in order. Buy seeds, plants, and seedlings and get them in the ground before sunset. There could be an erratic, unpredictable mentality in your neighborhood. Lucky lottery numbers: 8, 17, 26, 35, 44, 21.

Sunday, April 9 (Moon in Cancer to Leo 1:16 a.m.) Marriage can be given a big boost under the prevailing aspects. Leo and another Aquarius know how to fix emotional upsets. You are an insightful student of human nature under these trends. Much is being added to your cornucopia of plenty, perhaps behind the scenes. Peach and primrose are your colors; your number is 1.

Monday, April 10 (Moon in Leo) Aries is out in front, urging you and others on to victories. The yen to pull up stakes and find an easier life elsewhere can be strong. Your ambitions and aspirations soar beyond the ordinary. Sociability and service are the keynotes of your afternoon. Your color is white; your lucky number is 5.

Tuesday, April 11 (Moon in Leo to Virgo 9:29 a.m.) Restlessness can be a problem over the morning hours. Financial transactions are geared to success and endurance. Public relations, advertising, and legal involvements are favored. Be on guard against misplacement of items. Effective soul searching is taking place. Purple is your color. Hot combination numbers: 7 and 2.

Wednesday, April 12 (Moon in Virgo) Virgo and Taurus can be helpful without any fanfare or complaining. Don't treat lightly anything that should be taken more seriously. Popularity can be courted under existing aspects. Follow through on promises. Avoid censoring a child in front of others. Lucky lottery numbers: 12, 19, 9, 18, 27, 36.

Thursday, April 13 (Moon in Virgo to Libra 2:20 p.m.) Push savings, improve budgets, seek bargains in the larger outlet stores. Investments should be discussed with your broker. Fanciful thinking is giving a boost to romance and your sense of adventure. Taurus has good advice for you on the economic situation. Apricot and off-white are your colors; your lucky number is 2.

Friday, April 14 (Moon in Libra) Libra enters the picture and things are going to settle down and even themselves out. Sexual secrets are given some enlightenment. Someone is showing great sentiment, but is this a ploy for cash? Good fortune is showering goodies upon you. Be patient and persevere. Old rose and ivory are winning colors. Hot combination numbers: 4 and 8.

Saturday, April 15 (Moon in Libra to Scorpio 4:13 p.m.) Spontaneous socializing will become you. Eclipse patterns can pressure travel, long-range, and long-distance involvements. You may find or conclude that partners are edgy and contentious. Don't force changes upon yourself or others at any time under these aspects. Pistachio is your color. Lucky lottery numbers: 6, 15, 24, 33, 42, 35.

Sunday, April 16 (Moon in Scorpio) Travel continues to be a no-no in the wake of yesterday's eclipse. Information may be slow in coming and you could find the day somewhat sluggish. Yet, the unexpected may occur. Accent stability where you can. Lucky colors are magenta and taupe; your lucky number is 8.

Monday, April 17 (Moon in Scorpio to Sagittarius 4:51 p.m.) Career matters can be held up because communications or machinery parts fail to arrive. Scorpio has useful ideas and will pass them on if you request them. The day favors explanations, investigations, and a kind of enforced harmony on the job. Amber is your color; your lucky number is 3.

Tuesday, April 18 (Moon in Sagittarius) You can count on friends in any crisis or emergency and this is one of those days when this truth occurs to you. There are aspects of stability in money matters and also in love. You find a strong sense of security in being close to many people. The neutral feelings of others is hard for you to fathom. Your number is 5.

Wednesday, April 19 (Moon in Sagittarius to Capricorn 5:54 p.m.) Aries and Leo have good suggestions. Sagittarius is the interpreter of friendship and the lines dividing it from love. The words of a good friend can seem rather extreme, even amazing to you under these aspects. Jumping to conclusions is not a good idea. Flame and ruby are your colors. Lucky lottery numbers: 7, 16, 25, 34, 43, 19.

Thursday, April 20 (Moon in Capricorn) Now you can conclude what the month has been about. You can complete work that has been neglected too long. You may feel that you are changing faster than your associates; you are growing more, increasing your scope and perspective more. Capricorn is a born adviser; listen! Burgundy is your color; your number is 9.

Friday, April 21 (Moon in Capricorn to Aquarius 8:38 p.m.) Taurus sees dollar bills where others don't. You can encounter someone who has suffered a sharp disappointment lately. There is a suspicion that you may withdraw from one group in order to have time to join another. Narrow your sights and go after what is available. Eggshell brown is your color; your number is 2.

Saturday, April 22 (Moon in Aquarius) You are aware of the value of confidentiality today. There are things taking place behind the scenes that can only be suspected. You are strongly bent on protecting the secrets of a loved one. Short distance travel, communications, your learning processes are well aspected. Ecru is your color. Lucky lottery numbers: 4, 13, 22, 31, 40, 16.

Sunday, April 23 (Moon in Aquarius) Stand tall, speak out in your own behalf, let the world know that you are present and want your piece of the pie. You can program your day without fear of interference. Others know that you mean business now, that you are zealous for preferment and profit. Russet and wheat are winning colors; your lucky number is 6.

Monday, April 24 (Moon in Aquarius to Pisces 1:51 a.m.) Push for more money, a bigger share of the profits. Cost of licenses and other fees will be rising. Pisces and a Cancer are concerned about increases in the cost of living and the pricing of luxuries from the market. Do comparative shopping before committing yourself to a purchase. Your lucky number is 1.

Tuesday, April 25 (Moon in Pisces) You continue to have luck in earning power and income. There can be some special money earmarked for you and/or your family. Good strategy can mean more money. Special sales, advertising results, and collecting what is due you are well aspected.

On your menu today—home-baked biscuits. Venetian gold is your color. Hot combination numbers: 3 and 8.

Wednesday, April 26 (Moon in Pisces to Aries 9:41 a.m.) A Scorpio and a Cancer may wish you would participate socially. Luck is with you in all business and financial transactions. On your menu—Italian, Polish, or Cajun sausage sauteed with fresh garlic, mushrooms, green onions, white wine, and spices, served on a bed of Spanish rice. Lucky lottery numbers: 5, 14, 23, 32, 41, 26.

Thursday, April 27 (Moon in Aries) Aries and Leo have a good report for you. The local situation is changing. Families are moving from your community and this can give you a feeling of aloneness. You wish you, who generally welcome change, could enjoy the status quo more. The doomsters are predicting higher prices. Cherry and beige are your colors. Hot combination numbers: 7 and 8.

Friday, April 28 (Moon in Aries to Taurus 7:53 p.m.) Hobbies, studies are favored. You can learn some unusual facts today. You may find yourself taking the opposite point of view during a free-for-all discussion. You can go out of your way due to your marvelous self-reliance. Fine for buying used books and paper products. Emerald is your color; your number is 9.

Saturday, April 29 (Moon in Taurus) Be prepared for some pressure where you are hurrying, overly anxious to please, and in crowded rooms. You could be misquoted and misunderstood under these eclipse patterns. Be on guard against freakish accidents in parking lots. Something could be lost, stolen, misplaced. Cherry is your color. Lucky lottery numbers: 29, 2, 11, 20, 38, 47.

Sunday, April 30 (Moon in Taurus) It would be easy to miss a step under these aspects. Be especially careful while climbing and descending. Don't be so quick to disagree with a loving, but strongly opinionated person. It may be difficult to schedule family get-togethers under existing aspects. Deep pink is your color; your lucky number is 4.

Monday, May 1 (Moon in Taurus to Gemini 7:53 a.m.) Gemini and another Aquarius have important roles. You begin the month in a highly positive mood, loving, anxious to make love, to feel an integral part of the big parade. Anything you can do to encourage and inspire loved ones will be strongly appreciated and bear good fruit. Your lucky number is 6.

Tuesday, May 2 (Moon in Gemini) Consider the sensitive feelings of a loved one before making any startling announcement. Fine trends exist in romance and courtship. Good for coming to grips with any problem in the life of a hyperactive child. There are those who will claim you are wearing rose-colored glasses. Maroon is your color; your number is 8.

Wednesday, May 3 (Moon in Gemini to Cancer 8:45 p.m.) Libra can prove helpful and instrumental to understanding complex matters. You are strongly affectionate and may feel that others are not meeting you half way. You are doubly anxious to keep on the move today. On your menu—corned beef, cabbage, and boiled potatoes. Indigo is your lucky color. Lucky lottery numbers: 1, 10, 19, 28, 37, 46.

Thursday, May 4 (Moon in Cancer) The answers to the questions you ask may surprise you. A Cancer and a Capricorn have key roles. Family values are accented, along with health and work, the people with whom you are in total agreement and those who could be critical of your stands. Rust is your color; your lucky number is 3.

Friday, May 5 (Moon in Cancer) Trust a Pisces and a Cancer, for their advice is wise and accurate. Fine rays exist for health and work improvements. If you're dissatisfied with your figure or weight, start a corrective program. If visiting in a home where everything is neat as a pin, don't upset your hostess by dropping crumbs or ashes. Winning colors are apricot and plum; your lucky number is 5.

Saturday, May 6 (Moon in Cancer to Leo 8:55 a.m.) Scorpio enters the picture. You can get a lot of work done at home and around the grounds of your home today. Secure the cooperation of teenagers and pitch in to clear away debris, fight weeds, and organize a better looking flower and vegetable garden. Copper is your color. Lucky lottery numbers: 7, 16, 25, 34, 43, 23.

Sunday, May 7 (Moon in Leo) Leo makes a dramatic entrance. You have a lot going for yourself in marriage, other partnerships, contracts, agreements, sharing, and cooperation. There can be some minor confusing dimensions to the evening. Mocha is your color. Artistic and cultural pastimes are beckoning to you. Your lucky number is 9.

Monday, May 8 (Moon in Leo to Virgo 6:33 p.m.) Virgo and Taurus can work out better security arrangements for you. Changes tend to make the month move along better. Today is fine for innovations in the way you do your work and in the way you travel to and from the job. Include vitamin-rich citrus fruits, raw cabbage, and sweet potato in your meals. Maroon is your color; your number is 4.

Tuesday, May 9 (Moon in Virgo) Savings, investments, and overall security matters can be improved under these trends. Today is fine for making changes in the way you perform and present your work for approval. Budgets and utility bills may require some attention if you are to have more money at the end of the month. Burgundy is your color; your lucky number is 6.

Wednesday, May 10 (Moon in Virgo) Taurus knows the costs, prices, and several ways to save more. In financial accumulations you can see that proverbial light at the end of the tunnel. On your menu today—saucy haddock with unsweetened pineapple juice, apricot jam, dry mustard, and soy sauce. Add cornstarch to your sauce. Lucky lottery numbers: 8, 17, 26, 35, 44, 10.

Thursday, May 11 (Moon in Virgo to Libra 12:30 a.m.) You have the green light to take off like a big bird. Visit an area where you are about to invest money, time, and possibly energy. Fine rays for running down information about a trip you hope to make over the summer.

Brothers and sisters will help. Pumpkin is your color; your lucky number is 1.

Friday, May 12 (Moon in Libra) Libra is on stage. You have a good view and feeling for the rest of the month. Make plans, program events, reorganize your schedules where this seems advisable. Appreciate your allies and resolve to hold onto them through thick and thin. Diversionary tactics work well. Lime is your color; your lucky number is 3.

Saturday, May 13 (Moon in Libra to Scorpio 2:53 a.m.) Discussions about anything at work that bothers you can be had with neighbors and friends under these aspects. You are able to cash in on earned reputation and employment record, if you are considering a job change. Work around the grounds of your home, and in your garage and basement, will go well. Bronze is your color. Lucky lottery numbers: 5, 14, 23, 32, 41, 13.

Sunday, May 14 (Moon in Scorpio) Scorpio will offer advice that is well within his or her scope. Under prevailing aspects, the accent is on improvements and corrections. A bonanza withheld from you in the past can be shaping up for you now. Be on the alert for errors in judgment that could cost time and money later on. Your lucky number is 7.

Monday, May 15 (Moon in Scorpio to Sagittarius 2:58 a.m.) Sagittarius is your good friend. A good interchange of ideas with an older person may lead to surprising developments. Don't let minor worries undermine your confidence. Stand up for your convictions if you are to keep the respect of important people. Lucky colors are mauve and beige; your lucky number is 2.

Tuesday, May 16 (Moon in Sagittarius) Group activities, the social side of your job, and the friends of your mate are strongly represented. The more you smile and laugh today, the more hearts and doors you can open. Helpful nutritional information is there for you if you want it. Buff is your color. Hot combination numbers: 4 and 3.

Wednesday, May 17 (Moon in Sagittarius to Capricorn 2:36 a.m.) Capricorn demonstrates stability and will help you consolidate tedious tasks. Coral is your color. This is a fine day for completing projects, clearing the deck for future actions, and contacting those with whom you will be working later on in the month. Others hold the business initiative. Lucky lottery numbers: 6, 15, 24, 33, 42, 17.

Thursday, May 18 (Moon in Capricorn) You do well amending the ideas and plans of others. Your flexibility makes you the great compromiser, and feuding factions can use your help today. Sexual desires can be stirred in unusual ways and by peculiar events. Your desire to lead and set the pace is not based on ambition alone but on your wish to do some good in the world. Hot combination numbers: 8 and 7.

Friday, May 19 (Moon in Capricorn to Aquarius 3:39 a.m.) The day can begin slowly, but you are in your lunar high cycle and before noon you are off to the winner's circle. You tend to have the answers that others need. Popularity is more than a bubble. You can set others right, win them over to your point of view, and cash in on personality assets. Your lucky number is 1.

Saturday, May 20 (Moon in Aquarius) Excellent trends exist in meeting the public at large, profiting from a sale, and dealing in plans for the future. You can get others to back some of your money-making ideas under these aspects. Your love of freedom and personal independence is the spur for some genuine achievement. Earth is your color. Lucky lottery numbers: 3, 12, 21, 30, 39, 48.

Sunday, May 21 (Moon in Aquarius to Pisces 8:40 a.m.) Read the financial pages of your newspaper and make plans for a good earning-power cycle ahead. Calmness along with assertiveness will be your twin guides. Gather a group of charitable and humanitarian people about you for a big push in favor of the local homeless people. Apricot is your color; your lucky number is 5.

Monday, May 22 (Moon in Pisces) Gemini may be a little late but, upon arrival, will set the pace and pattern for an enjoyable session. Sharing your feelings will intensify lovemaking under these aspects. There is joy galore and plenty of romance serving your basic needs. You keep things going even when others seem to place obstacles in your path. Lilac and ivory are your colors; your lucky number is 9.

Tuesday, May 23 (Moon in Pisces to Aries 3:13 p.m.) You could be taken to task for your deliberation and caution when a Gemini wants to speed things up. But it's a romantic day, full of sentiment and nostalgia. The past serves the present and memories are a big help in the flight to ecstasy. It's a good earning-power day. Hot combination numbers: 2 and 8.

Wednesday, May 24 (Moon in Aries) Your love life goes sluggish for the time being. Aries will make several important points when there is any discussion of a change of residence and residential area. For now, you could be considered a stick-in-the-mud. As the day advances, change the types of people surrounding you. Kelly green is your color. Lucky lottery numbers: 24, 32, 40, 4, 13, 31.

Thursday, May 25 (Moon in Aries) Concentrate on the possible, the everyday, the acceptable. Avoid going out on tangential limbs and stick to the main road. You will pride yourself on your practicality even though others see you as too extreme in the many causes you support. Immediate and pressing matters demand your attention. Your lucky number is 6.

Friday, May 26 (Moon in Aries to Taurus 1:47 a.m.) Taurus wants to know what you're planning. Domestic interests rate a high place on the day's agenda. Property matters could use a good review. Keep abreast of just what your residence requires during these times of many economic changes. Community programs will appeal to you. Lavender is your color; your lucky number is 8.

Saturday, May 27 (Moon in Taurus) Don't give others the impression that you are too possessive of loved ones. There are some who know the cost of everything and the value of nothing. Avoid discussing your possessions with these types. There is some unfairness in the criticism you hear under these aspects. Lemon is your color. Lucky lottery numbers: 1, 10, 19, 28, 37, 46.

Sunday, May 28 (Moon in Taurus to Gemini 2:07 p.m.) Your motivation and drive in security matters, changes, and improvements is strong. But there can be conflicts between your own children and the children of neighbors that tend to get to you in aggravating ways. There are lazy, slothful types in the picture. Colors for winning are azure and wine; the number 3 is a winner.

Monday, May 29 (Moon in Gemini) It's a perfect day with the moon illuminating your love life. You learn ways to improve relationships with your parents and offspring. As the month winds down, be social, outgoing, entertaining, and humorous. On the spur of the moment, invite people to your home. Ecru is your color; your lucky number is 7.

Tuesday, May 30 (Moon in Gemini) Gemini and Libra are airy, intellectual, and sure of themselves today. There's plenty of scope for your warm-hearted charm. You want approval, appreciation, and understanding under these trends. Socialize with adventurous and romantic types, or take a biography to bed. Hot combination numbers: 9 and 4.

Wednesday, May 31 (Moon in Gemini to Cancer 2:59 a.m.) Cancer and Scorpio come front and center. Watch what you eat at any party, picnic, or questionable restaurant. There are situations where the laws and rules are not being honored. Beautiful scenery can be spoiled by some accident in nature. There are lessons to be learned. Purple is your color. Lucky lottery numbers: 2, 11, 20, 29, 38, 47.

JUNE 1995

Thursday, June 1 (Moon in Cancer) Listen to a Cancer and a Pisces. Good trends exist for catching up on the latest discoveries connected with health and nutrition. Fine for starting new preventive-medicine routines and for finding easier ways of getting your work done on time. No rushing! Your color is azure. Hot combination numbers: 1 and 6.

Friday, June 2 (Moon in Cancer to Leo 3:17 p.m.) The power to draw closer to your beloved is with you. Some of the work that has to be done today can be slightly boring to you. The health of an older loved one can be off-center. You may have to speak sharply to a loved one who is restless. Carmine is your color; your number is 3.

Saturday, June 3 (Moon in Leo) Leo and Gemini have key roles. Marriage and other partnerships, as well as contracts and agreements, are stimulated. Legal involvements are going to be settled soon and new light on them can be cast today. Older folk are on your side in any showdown at this time. Chestnut is your color. Lucky lottery numbers: 5, 14, 23, 32, 41, 3.

Sunday, June 4 (Moon in Leo) Sagittarius and another Aquarius figure prominently. You can improve your image today, not only via the cosmetic trail, but by your attitudes and approaches. You are being observed. Make sure siblings and others don't feel too many burdens are on their shoulders. Your lucky number is 7.

Monday, June 5 (Moon in Leo to Virgo 1:46 a.m.) Virgo will pitch in and help you. Fine rays exist for improving budgets, savings, investments, and overall security interests. Work that prevents waste around your home and the grounds of your home is well aspected. There can be new stability in your private life. Salmon is your color; your lucky number is 2.

Tuesday, June 6 (Moon in Virgo) Aim high—you'll get there under existing aspects. Fine trends exist in accumulating things and in gaining profits by bartering goods for services. What you set in motion now will show good endurance over the rest of June. Dress up this evening and look both rich and royal. Beet and deep red are winning colors; your lucky number is 4.

Wednesday, June 7 (Moon in Virgo to Libra 9:13 a.m.) Taurus and Capricorn are in your corner. You could feel that others are toning down some of your views and making them more acceptable to larger groups. You are a good influence in the lives of your children's friends. Fine trends exist for buying a pet, license, or garden implements. Lucky lottery numbers: 6, 15, 24, 42, 33, 17.

Thursday, June 8 (Moon in Libra) Libra has a key role. It's a fine day for travel, for moving about within the 300-mile radius of your home, and for running down information that can be put to immediate use. Advanced studies, extending your learning processes, and trying to sell what you have created are well aspected. Sky blue is your color. Hot combination numbers: 9 and 7.

Friday, June 9 (Moon in Libra to Scorpio 1:03 p.m.) Another Aquarius will help you settle down and calm your objections about mutual friends and neighbors. What you have going for yourself at a distance benefits from the day's trends. Open your heart to the special needs of youngsters. People may not have the answers to your questions. Your lucky number is 1.

Saturday, June 10 (Moon in Scorpio) Scorpio refuses to close the barn door, even though it's a holiday. You want to spend this Saturday differently than you have spent last Saturday. You want to relax, shift responsibility to the shoulders of others, and capitalize on the seasonal opportunities. Earthy brown is your color. Lucky lottery numbers: 3, 12, 21, 30, 39, 48.

Sunday, June 11 (Moon in Scorpio to Sagittarius 1:50 p.m.) Today is fine for relaxing on or near the water. Beach activities will bring peace of mind. You are good at figuring out what can and can't be done at this time. The social side of your job is well represented. Discuss your career potential with your spouse and other interested relatives. Crimson is your color; your number is 5.

Monday, June 12 (Moon in Sagittarius) Sagittarius comes aboard with a bag of pleasant surprises. It's one of those rare days in June when the changes you bring about are bound to succeed. Church and club membership and participation matters get high grades. Work gets done rather haphazardly. Your color is violet. Try the number 9 today.

Tuesday, June 13 (Moon in Sagittarius to Capricorn 1:05 p.m.) The full moon illuminates social contacts, true friendships, and the social side of your job. There is enlightenment in knowing the marvelous fruits of close emotional ties. Help your beloved with work that you don't ordinarily do. Avoid the prophets of economic gloom and doom. Beige is your color; your number is 2.

Wednesday, June 14 (Moon in Capricorn) Capricorn is a good role model where living up to duties and responsibilities is concerned. Discuss recent changes and ways in which past involvements can help with present situations. Luck attends where you are making your home and place of business crimeproof. Lucky lottery numbers: 4, 13, 22, 31, 40, 14.

Thursday, June 15 (Moon in Capricorn to Aquarius 12:52 p.m.) What is so rare as a day in June (said the poet)—and this is one of those days that you can make quite perfect. The accent is on bridging the generation gap, taking in much wisdom from the written and spoken word, and rejoicing that romance and adventure are in the air. Primrose is your color; your number is 6.

Friday, June 16 (Moon in Aquarius) Now in your lunar-cycle high, you are on top of the heap. Self-confidence becomes you and can take you into situations that compliment old ambitions and aspirations. Obstacles melt away and you can take great leaps forward in life, including your career. Red and tan are your colors. Hot combination numbers: 8 and 7.

Saturday, June 17 (Moon in Aquarius to Pisces 3:13 p.m.) You compete well, accepting challenges as they come your way. Another Aquarius can be helpful. Your self-confidence and enthusiasm for the work you are doing makes you a born winner. This afternoon is for spending time with kindred spirits and for making vacation plans. Plum is your color. Lucky lottery numbers: 17, 29, 37, 1, 10, 28.

Sunday, June 18 (Moon in Pisces) You are exposed to some worthwhile financial cues under the prevailing aspects. Study advertisements and the sales pages of your newspaper. There are bargains to be purchased in the days ahead. The changes you make are bound to succeed. Pisces and Cancer have front seats. Turquoise is your color; your number is 3.

Monday, June 19 (Moon in Pisces to Aries 9:29 p.m.) Today is fine for digging into work that has to be done this week. Be sure you have all the information available before making an important decision. There's more money in the offing if you perform well today and make certain that the hearts of your helpers are in this job. Cherry-and-white is the color; the number is 7.

Tuesday, June 20 (Moon in Aries) Aries and Sagittarius prefer your open-minded approach. Illuminated for you are local situations, studies, hobbies, and the ideas of siblings and neighbors. You are best when you volunteer for additional duties. It's a good day for buying a hat, comb, hairbrush. Tan is your color; your number is 9.

Wednesday, June 21 (Moon in Aries) On this last day of spring, it would be wonderful to get into a rural area where you can observe what nature has been accomplishing. "All's right with the world" is the theme for today. You want to extend your thinking and your feelings. You can feel passionate about scenes. Coffee is your color. Lucky lottery numbers: 38, 2, 11, 20, 29, 47.

Thursday, June 22 (Moon in Aries to Taurus 7:35 a.m.) Taurus and Cancer make an appearance. Share beauty and quietude with loved ones. Excellent trends exist for getting work out of the way. The day and its association with nature and summer proves therapeutic. Spend as much time outdoors as possible. Children are entertaining. Aquamarine is your color. Hot combination numbers: 4 and 3.

Friday, June 23 (Moon in Taurus) There is much charm and charisma surrounding you. The assets of people rather than their liabilities are standing out. Family, home, property, and community are all accented now. In the work you set before yourself, there is a rare enlightenment and understanding. Tomato red is your color; your lucky number is 6.

Saturday, June 24 (Moon in Taurus to Gemini 8:02 p.m.) Fine for preparations, prologues, buying pastel wardrobe accessories, and generally sprucing up your personal appearance. "Fit as a fiddle and ready for love" is an underlying theme today. There is a great deal of creativity, imagination, and originality available to you. Amber is your color. Lucky lottery numbers: 8, 44, 17, 26, 35, 24.

Sunday, June 25 (Moon in Gemini) Today is for loving and being loved. You can enjoy a special sense of closeness with your parents and your children. Invite, attract, court, and enjoy the romantic and adventurous nature of this day. The great outdoors is beckoning to you. Fine rays exist for a picnic. Peppermint-stick pink is your color; your number is 1.

Monday, June 26 (Moon in Gemini) Gemini and Libra have key roles. Give due attention to your beloved. You will get more out of giving love than out of receiving it. Bake, decorate, frame pictures; give curtains, draperies, and carpets a good cleaning. The focus of interest now is emotional harmony. Azure is your color; your lucky number is 5.

Tuesday, June 27 (Moon in Gemini to Cancer 8:56 a.m.) You are going to enjoy an encounter with one of nature's originals. The pot of gold is there for you at the end of the rainbow, and it's a case of making your own rainbow. The spiritual side of your nature is accented. As evening advances, memories take over. Mauve is your color; your lucky number is 7.

Wednesday, June 28 (Moon in Cancer) Make amends if you learn that you have hurt the sensitive feelings of another. Keep in mind that some folk are touchy and see malice where none exists or is intended. You could witness an argument over money. In the privacy of your own mind, you can arrive at the right conclusion. Lucky lottery numbers: 9, 45, 18, 27, 36, 28.

Thursday, June 29 (Moon in Cancer to Leo 9:02 p.m.) Don't overdo in the heat of the afternoon or burn your social candle at both ends this evening. Trust the rules and standards of a Capricorn. Older people may be somewhat critical of you for no definite reasons. Public relations are not working as well as yesterday. Mocha is your color; your number is 2.

Friday, June 30 (Moon in Leo) Leo makes a dramatic entrance and exit. You could feel that you are doing somebody else's work. Marriage and other partnerships are touching an evaluation stage. There is some evidence of popularity, but there are those cheering you on who may not be sincere. Wheat is your color; your lucky number is 4.

JULY 1995

Saturday, July 1 (Moon in Leo) Leo will take you to task for some shortcoming. Marriage, contracts, agreements, sharing, and cooperative effort are accented. Legal and public relations get good grades. A certain amount of obnoxious behavior should be expected under prevailing aspects. Be aware of your mate's special needs. Orchid is your color. Lucky lottery numbers: 4, 13, 22, 31, 40, 30.

Sunday, July 2 (Moon in Leo to Virgo 7:35 a.m.) Virgo will relieve you of burdens. It's a good day for studying economic trends and counting any additional cash you may have on hand but not in a bank. The day helps you to encompass all kinds of wealth. You are at your best when you refuse to be frivolous, even in the face of frivolity. Your number is 6.

Monday, July 3 (Moon in Virgo) Taurus is alert to opportunities. Push savings, investments, and security interests. Fine rays exist for completing one job so that you can give total attention to a new one. You are empowered to stabilize and consolidate. Take the lead in making an important financial decision. Indigo is your color; your number is 1.

Tuesday, July 4 (Moon in Virgo to Libra 3:55 p.m.) The day will prove to be busier than you expected. Crowds don't help matters, for just putting up with them is hard work. The support you didn't receive earlier this year can now materialize in a strange way. Hints and suggestions are coming at you and some of them are quite good. Hot combination numbers: 3 and 2.

Wednesday, July 5 (Moon in Libra) Libra and Aquarius can help you over troubled waters. Good trends exist in savings, budgeting, and investments. There is more financial potential to this day than appears on the surface. Today is fine for raising money in an unusual way—special sales, parting with an heirloom, taking a low-interest loan. Buff is your color. Lucky lottery numbers: 6, 15, 24, 33, 42, 5.

Thursday, July 6 (Moon in Libra to Scorpio 9:19 p.m.) Help a youngster mend his or her ways. Discussions tend to bear good fruit. Avoid impulsive criticism of a contemporary, who has a knack for annoying you. There is some exposure today to false claims. Stall payments that are almost due if you feel summer demands more cash on hand. Hot combination numbers: 8 and 4.

Friday, July 7 (Moon in Scorpio) Scorpio makes a grand appearance. The urge to make tracks is strong. Distant places are calling to you. This is not the day for making the ultimate final decision. If you bide your time, things are going to settle of their own volition. Accounting methods can be improved. Your lucky numbers are 1 and 7.

Saturday, July 8 (Moon in Scorpio to Sagittarius 11:38 p.m.) Travel and long-range actions are favored. If you can spend time on the water today, your mind will be cleared of any possiblc cobwebs. You have the power for winning first place, for increasing your perspective, and for making good impressions on newcomers. Earthy brown is your color. Lucky lottery numbers: 3, 12, 21, 30, 39, 48.

Sunday, July 9 (Moon in Sagittarius) Sagittarius brings laughter and enthusiasm. It's a friendly day, offering you enjoyable group activities and opportunities to bridge the generation gap. The social side of your job certainly serves your career interests at this time. You can set the pace. Magenta is your color; your number is 4.

Monday, July 10 (Moon in Sagittarius to Capricorn 11:44 p.m.) Aries is present. You can gain much from being willing to make changes and to take a chance now and then. Be willing to go that extra mile in order to make a large group of people happy. Church and club involvements offer you special advantages. There is someone waiting for your phone call. Your lucky number is 8.

Tuesday, July 11 (Moon in Capricorn) Capricorn is determined; you might as well consider this offer. You are exposed to the born manager today and there can be some annoyance and boredom resulting. Even so, the day is favorable for kicking any bad habit you may have acquired. Tangerine is your color; your lucky number is 1.

Wednesday, July 12 (Moon in Capricorn to Aquarius 11:21 p.m.) The day calls for defensive measures against gossip, slander, and backbiting. Fine trends exist for completions, epilogues, and for evaluating the month so far. There is some daydreaming that gets in the way of real work and achievement. Luck is with you in joint endeavors. Orange is your color. Lucky lottery numbers: 3, 12, 21, 30, 39, 48.

Thursday, July 13 (Moon in Aquarius) You are in your lunar high cycle and can get your own way. Your enthusiasm for the work that is before you will win you laurels. Actually, you can take a great leap forward in life under prevailing aspects. You can blow your own horn for all it's worth. Taupe is your color; your lucky number is 5.

Friday, July 14 (Moon in Aquarius) The rebel inside you is taking over. What might have been considered extreme opinions several years ago are much more acceptable now. You have your following and they are goading you into action. Be sure that you never permit liberty to become license. Beige is your color; your lucky number is 7.

Saturday, July 15 (Moon in Aquarius to Pisces 12:37 a.m.) This is a good money day. Fine for garage, patio, or yard sales. There's good potential there for you to create a new way of earning cash. There are some chances that loved ones will pile more burdens upon you. Greed and selfishness must be seen as the real enemies. Melon is your color. Lucky lottery numbers: 9, 18, 27, 36, 45, 15.

Sunday, July 16 (Moon in Pisces) Pisces, Scorpio, and a Cancer are considerate and even empathetic under these trends. But still there can be some criticism coming your way by those who feel that your ideas and activities are too high-blown and theoretical. Aunts, uncles, and cousins can be helpful if you would only ask. Your best number is 2.

Monday, July 17 (Moon in Pisces to Aries 5:23 a.m.) Aries means business, and you may show more physical endurance on the local scene, spurring others on to greater effort. But make allowances when others prove to be more conservative in their outlook than you. Your self-confidence in certain theories is bothering your beloved. Silver and pink are your winning colors. Your lucky number is 6.

Tuesday, July 18 (Moon in Aries) There are routines that may have been neglected lately and today can bring a showdown. So pitch in and take care of all immediate and pressing matters. It's a good day for learning, for applying what you have learned, and for digging more deeply into studies and talents. Champagne is your color; your number is 8.

Wednesday, July 19 (Moon in Aries to Taurus 2:20 p.m.) You are empowered to do the right thing in the right way and at the right time. Leo and Sagittarius have banked their fires. Luck is with you where you are taking the family into fuller consideration. You keep on the go and involve youngsters and senior citizens in the sharing. Wheat is your color. Lucky lottery numbers: 1, 10, 19, 28, 37, 46.

Thursday, July 20 (Moon in Taurus) Taurus and Virgo have key roles. Community involvements are favored. Fine trends exist for property upkeep, getting to know some of your newer neighbors, and shunning people who organize for questionable ends. A more spiritual, charismatic love goes out from you toward those experiencing hard times. Your lucky number is 3.

Friday, July 21 (Moon in Taurus) You can freeze up in the presence of someone who is geared toward self-pity. This trait can embarrass you today. Older relatives may point some uncalled-for criticism in your direction. It's a day when those who are upset or unhappy are looking for a scapegoat. The evening brings you closer to young people. Lime and lemon are your winning colors. Hot combination numbers: 5 and 8.

Saturday, July 22 (Moon in Taurus to Gemini 2:23 a.m.) Oh what a wonderful day! There is stimulation of your love department. Love is more passionate and harder bent on ecstasy. But the love of parents and offspring also gets high grades. Fine trends exist for socializing in a rather spontaneous, summerish fashion. Gemini and another Aquarius love each other. Lucky lottery numbers: 7, 16, 25, 34, 43, 22.

Sunday, July 23 (Moon in Gemini) You continue in a strongly loving mood and the whole world is aware of your positive thinking and enthusiasm for living. Spend quality time with children. Bring the generations together. Entertain, party, go to the beach, or climb a hill to get a better view of the beautiful scenery. White is your color; your number is 9.

Monday, July 24 (Moon in Gemini to Cancer 3:16 p.m.) Today is excellent for socializing, visiting, and entertaining visitors in your home. You extend yourself in the interest of those you love. It's a good day for heart-to-heart discussions with your children and other young people. You inject a rare creativity, imagination, and flexibility into the day. The number 4 is a winner.

Tuesday, July 25 (Moon in Cancer) Good trends exist in health improvements. Today is fine for beginning a daily walking program. Work up to five miles a day very gradually, aiming for one mile per day at the beginning. Get to know some of your neighbors by walking in a nearby mall with them early in the morning. Also, do what you can to make daily chores less tiresome. Blue is your color. Lucky lottery numbers: 24, 42, 6, 33, 15, 13.

Wednesday, July 26 (Moon in Cancer) All contracts, agreements, and matters concerned with married life are being speeded up as Mercury enters Leo. Cancer and Scorpio come full center with their questions and other comments. You are taking it all in, but chances are your decision making remains very personal. Cherry and light brown are your colors. Lucky lottery numbers: 8, 17, 26, 35, 44, 12.

Thursday, July 27 (Moon in Cancer to Leo 3:07 a.m.) Today's new moon illuminates ways you can improve marital happiness, change contracts and agreements for the better, and draw closer to your beloved. Sharing and cooperative effort, as well as joint investments, are all singled out for change and improvement. Rid corners of darker rooms and closets of all clutter. Your winning color is burgundy; your lucky number is 1.

Friday, July 28 (Moon in Leo) The day demonstrates your organizational abilities. You can impress your employer with what you achieve now. You have the power in eyeball-to-eyeball situations, but not in behind-the-scenes showdowns. Know where the boss wants you to put the emphasis. Wear a little gold. Your best numbers are 3 and 2.

Saturday, July 29 (Moon in Leo to Virgo 1:12 a.m.) Do nothing to upset the marital applecart or to annoy your spouse at a time when your mate can be irritable. Inspect, investigate, but don't intrude. Luck is with you in joint investments of time, money, and energy. Don't spend too much time in the direct sunlight. Also, watch what you eat this evening. Raspberry is your color. Lucky lottery numbers: 5, 14, 23, 32, 41, 29.

Sunday, July 30 (Moon in Virgo) Virgo has a key role. Accent the security of your family and home. Know where your children are hanging out and with whom. There's nothing wrong in a clannish or tribal approach to family matters. Messages tend to please you. Evening has a more romantic trend. The lighter greens and yellows are in. Your number is 7.

Monday, July 31 (Moon in Virgo to Libra 9:23 p.m.) Fine trends exist in savings, investments, and impressive changes that can result in more cash. Many angles may have to be considered when children ask embarrassing questions. Emphasize the standard of living, rather than the cost of living. You can obtain the best at reduced prices. Canary is your color; your number is 2.

AUGUST 1995

Tuesday, August 1 (Moon in Libra) Libra and Gemini have key roles. What you have perking in your own interest at a distance can be improved under prevailing aspects. Travel, especially for business, will go well. Power is building up for you in highly personalized matters and you can receive some good pointers from distant relatives. Hot combination numbers: 1 and 6.

Wednesday, August 2 (Moon in Libra) Another Aquarius has some answers you require. Express yourself so that you will not be misinterpreted or misquoted. Travel, legal, and public relations interests can be served well. This is a fine day for knowing your own mind and communicating your ideas to those who love you. Emerald is your color. Lucky lottery numbers: 3, 12, 21, 30, 39, 48.

Thursday, August 3 (Moon in Libra to Scorpio 3:29 a.m.) You can serve your career and reputation, and strike out for honors and dignities under these trends. Cash in on past achievements, pushing status and prestige matters. Coworkers and supervisors have good potential for help and understanding. Today is fine for buying items that will help you do your work more efficiently. Burgundy is your color. Hot combination numbers: 5 and 4.

Friday, August 4 (Moon in Scorpio) Scorpio and Taurus figure prominently. The more you please your employer under these aspects, the more secure your job is going to be. You can push personal awareness, intuitive processes, and your ability to recreate situations for the better. Aunts and uncles are in your corner. Your lucky number is 7.

Saturday, August 5 (Moon in Scorpio to Sagittarius 7:14 a.m.) Sagittarius knows where to go. Favors and compliments are represented. Group activities are favored. You can take a great deal of ego food from discussions with kindred spirits. The day is not for work, but rather for pleasure and the pursuit of happiness. Emerald is your color. Lucky lottery numbers: 9, 18, 27, 36, 45, 5.

Sunday, August 6 (Moon in Scorpio) Aries and Leo have key roles. A favor you seek at this time will be granted. Companionship can make this day. You have the knack of knowing the positive good that is in each person. Your unique approach toward individual liberty endears you to all whose freedom has been curtailed. Your lucky number is 2.

Monday, August 7 (Moon in Sagittarius to Capricorn 8:52 a.m.) With some of your social obligations suspended during the summer, you're in good shape for being more charitable and humanitarian minded. Listen to what another is saying about horrendous deprivation not too far from where you live. Siblings and neighbors are interested in what you're thinking. Your number is 6.

Tuesday, August 8 (Moon in Capricorn) Capricorn can give body to your ideas, ideals, aims, and aspirations. Money earned in the past can be put to wonderful use now. Today is fine for cashing in on past experiences. Business and legislation get green lights. Put any possible sleeping talent to use. Decp red is your color. Hot combination numbers: 8 and 5.

Wednesday, August 9 (Moon in Capricorn to Aquarius 9:29 a.m.) Today is fine for preparation, prologues, and prefaces to action. Complete tasks that are hanging fire so you will be free to do your own thing tomorrow when you enter your lunar-cycle high. Sum things up, keep records, file important papers away for now. Face up to any young person who knows few expressions other than "Gimme." Lucky lottery numbers: 1, 10, 19, 28, 37, 46.

Thursday, August 10 (Moon in Aquarius) You're in your lunar high cycle, and major, rare enlightenment is available to you in highly personalized interests. What you want, how to get it, where and when are illuminated for you. Stand tall, stake your claims, hold on to the lead and the initiative. Another Aquarius is helpful. Your lucky number is 3.

Friday, August 11 (Moon in Aquarius to Pisces 10:46 a.m.) Get up early and start your ball rolling, for this is a day when you can take a great leap forward in your career and in your aims and aspirations. Nobody is going to stand in your way under prevailing aspects. Gemini and Libra are very much on your side. Cherry is your color. Hot combination numbers: 5 and 8.

Saturday, August 12 (Moon in Pisces) You can run down some money that is just waiting to be earned. There are financial opportunities forming now that will become more available as the month moves along. Fine trends exist for holding a garage, yard, or patio sale. Advertising and publicity can be transformed into hard cash. Lucky lottery numbers: 7, 16, 25, 34, 43, 12.

Sunday, August 13 (Moon in Pisces to Aries 2:41 p.m.) Today is fine for discussing the economy with a knowledgeable person. You are exposed to a great deal of talk about money, how to earn more, where to move to improve your economic potential, and so on. At the end of the conversation, things can still be baffling. Waste continues to be the real problem. Scarlet and white are winners; your lucky number is 9.

Monday, August 14 (Moon in Aries) Put your faith in an activist, self-confident Aries. Siblings and neighbors bring women complaining and nagging to your home. Avoid phoning a chronic whiner on a day such as this. A lazy person requires assistance; if you decide to pitch in to help, don't criticize. Pink coral is your color; your lucky number is 4.

Tuesday, August 15 (Moon in Aries to Taurus 10:25 p.m.) You will notice that a great deal of work is being done by the extremely self-confident. Church and club membership and participation require part of your free time. All around, you can spot budding romances that experience tells you will go nowhere. Practicality triumphs. Your lucky number is 6.

Wednesday, August 16 (Moon in Taurus) Taurus, familiar routines, everyday schedules, and what is usual, are all on stage. Luck is with you where you are being yourself, easygoing, free, independent, imbued with many ideals. Your convictions can win the approval of a much older person. Family sharing gets top billing. Lemon and lime are winning colors. Lucky lottery numbers: 8, 17, 25, 34, 43, 16.

Thursday, August 17 (Moon in Taurus) Check things out with Virgo or Capricorn. There are new trends in your community that cause discomfort. You could be pushed out of the magnolias of contentment by a slick political type. Iced tea is better for Aquarius than many of the fake fruit drinks. Your color is mint green. Your lucky number is 1.

Friday, August 18 (Moon in Taurus to Gemini 9:40 a.m.) Demonstrate basic personality and character traits—kindness, courtesy, friendliness, and respect for the opinions of others. Charitable and humanitarian concerns should not be suspended until autumn. This evening is perfect for clearing up misunderstandings. Tangerine is your color. Hot combination numbers: 3 and 7.

Saturday, August 19 (Moon in Gemini) Gemini has a lot to say under these aspects. Your love life is stimulated, and passion and ecstasy are good possibilities. Fine trends exist for entertaining people who make you feel good. Today is excellent for directing the energies of children, so that they find happiness on vacation. Lucky lottery numbers: 5, 14, 23, 32, 41, 19.

Sunday, August 20 (Moon in Gemini to Cancer 10:24 p.m.) Entertain, party, dress up so that you look right for the fun and games that go with these aspects. You can attract favorable attention as the moon trines your natal sun. You do well carrying ideas to their natural conclusion. Your learning processes are sharp. Your lucky number is 7.

Monday, August 21 (Moon in Cancer) A Cancer and a Pisces have important roles. You are empowered to improve your health and to rearrange furniture and situations at your place of business so that the days will seem shorter and more satisfying. There are distracting influences that should be isolated as far as possible. Whites and off-whites are right. Your lucky number is 2.

Tuesday, August 22 (Moon in Cancer) Family secrets may require improved protection. There is a tendency for those under 25 to talk about things others don't need or want to know. There is good stimulation of ownership and property matters. There is a lot of vim and vigor serving you. Your colors are beige and prune; your lucky number is 4.

Wednesday, August 23 (Moon in Cancer to Leo 10:13 a.m.) Work may be somewhat neglected and the more it is permitted to pile up, the harder it will be to face later on. Fine rays exist for getting maintenance done before the fall season steps up the commitments of the fixers. Also schedule any minor surgery small children may require before school reopens. Deep pink is your color. Lucky lottery numbers: 6, 15, 24, 33, 42, 23.

Thursday, August 24 (Moon in Leo) Virgo and Leo figure prominently. You and your spouse should get down to the nitty-gritty of budgets, savings, and investments. You are thinking big now, but a bit of financial splurging may be just what you *don't* need at this time. Marriage, contracts, and agreements demand fidelity. Your lucky number is 8.

Friday, August 25 (Moon in Leo to Virgo 7:50 p.m.) Today is fine for a short vacation in a rural area, where cows, sheep, and pigs draw the sun and poultry make noises you well may have forgotten. Villages and small towns have their own attraction and they touch your mind, heart, and soul under prevailing aspects. From the 25th thru the 28th, it would be well to get away from polluted cities. Your lucky number is 1.

Saturday, August 26 (Moon in Virgo) The new moon illuminates where you should go and what you should do, with a strong accent on farms, auctions, rodeos, and visits to the old school and the old church. Former neighbors and friends are very much in the picture. City kids need a taste of the country now and then, and suburban kids need it even more. Black and white are your colors. Lucky lottery numbers: 3, 12, 21, 30, 39, 48.

Sunday, August 27 (Moon in Virgo) Appreciate the sights and the scenery away from home base. Buy items that are hard to find elsewhere. Be assured that you are closing out the summer the right way, letting practical, earthy Virgo, and airy beautiful Libra have some say in what you do. Persuasive tactics improve everything. Your lucky number is 5.

Monday, August 28 (Moon in Virgo to Libra 3:15 a.m.) Your positive thinking, joviality, optimism, and enthusiasm will make this a red-letter day. You love this time of the year. Sharing quality time with your children and mate really can bring all of you closer together. Marriage, sharing, and commitment are the major trends. Your lucky number is 9.

Tuesday, August 29 (Moon in Libra) Close the month with an end-of-summer trek to a resort that is soon to close. Several Libras are in this expanding picture. Your ability to transform ideas into solid achievement was never stronger. Friendships, group activities, and plans for school and for new assignments are in the offing. Cream is your color; your number is 2.

Wednesday, August 30 (Moon in Libra to Scorpio 8:12 p.m.) There's good balance and much fairness linked to the day's aspects. There can be wise decisions and settlements. The day is upbeat, especially where love and friendship are concerned. You can renew any possible waning enchantment in your private life. Step out ahead of the competition. Gold is your color. Lucky lottery numbers: 4, 13, 22, 31, 40, 30.

Thursday, August 31 (Moon in Scorpio) Scorpio enters with a bit of criticism. Push career matters for all they are worth. Whatever effort you put into dressing wisely is being recognized. There is good reason for optimism in your life. Health and work are under favorable stars. Take a leadership role in group activities. Your lucky number is 6.

SEPTEMBER 1995

Friday, September 1 (Moon in Scorpio to Sagittarius 12:57 p.m.) Trust Scorpio. Complete and conclude work that has been neglected and pushed aside. There is good reason for renewed optimism about your career and on-the-job relationships. Your colleagues appreciate your sense of style. Your color is light blue; your number is 5.

Saturday, September 2 (Moon in Sagittarius) You will want to relax today and to see kindred spirits who understand you. Church and club membership and participation get a high spot on your social agenda. The group prevents your becoming too involved or annoyed with any individual. Your winning color is deep pink. Lucky lottery numbers: 7, 16, 25, 34, 43, 20.

Sunday, September 3 (Moon in Sagittarius to Capricorn 3:45 p.m.) Take it easy; see only those who help you relax and feel good about yourself. Friendships that have withstood the test of time are accented. You want to keep things in proportion and balance and it would be wise to avoid the complainers and the naggers. Winning colors are blue and yellow. Your lucky number is 9.

Monday, September 4 (Moon in Capricorn) Capricorn has too many irons in the fire. Find time to figure out what is taking place behind the scenes. Avoid giving anyone too clear a look into the secret sensations of your soul. Dress appropriately for the sake of warding off virus-type ailments, including the common cold. Mocha is your color; your number is 4.

Tuesday, September 5 (Moon in Capricorn to Aquarius 5:47 p.m.) Capricorn and Virgo figure prominently. Get what's left of summer well organized. Plan when and how you are going to put up storm windows and doors, when you are going to do your Indian summer canning and preserving. By thinking big, you can invite a lot of goodwill and respect. Tyrian blue is your color; your number is 6.

Wednesday, September 6 (Moon in Aquarius) You have just moved into your lunar high cycle, when fate treats you well. Friendships can be expanded. Less restraint is required as you push for higher income and improved savings. It's a glorious day for considering yourself, what you want, and who can help you get it. Mustard yellow is your color. Lucky lottery numbers: 8, 17, 26, 35, 44, 14.

Thursday, September 7 (Moon in Aquarius to Pisces 8:08 p.m.) Speak freely in your own behalf. Approach the boss for a raise. Be mindful of all your past achievements. Fine trends exist for changing the direction of your dreams and plans. Another Aquarius, a Gemini, and a Libra have key roles. Let the world see you looking your best, anxious to please, with plenty of self-confidence. Hot combination numbers: 1 and 2.

Friday, September 8 (Moon in Pisces) Push money opportunities. Pisces and Scorpio have key roles. Projects can be funded if you show patience and perseverence. If you assert yourself today, you can advance your own career. Affectionate ties with people at a distance merit a phone call. Determine what you no longer need. Your lucky number is 3.

Saturday, September 9 (Moon in Pisces) The full moon illuminates secrets, confidential matters, and what is transpiring behind the scenes and the mysteries of sexual allure. The puzzles can be put together. What appears tempting and sensual today may not seem so tomorrow. Try to keep a good sense of proportion and balance under these strictures. It's a good money day. Lucky lottery numbers: 5, 14, 23, 32, 41, 19.

Sunday, September 10 (Moon in Pisces to Aries 12:14 a.m.) Aries comes front and center. The local, usual, and familiar will demand its say despite what plans you have made for today. Take giant steps toward minor but long-held goals. Luck is with you in the little things of life, and you are at your best when you concentrate and zero in on new opportunities. Your number is 7.

Monday, September 11 (Moon in Aries) Communications, dialogue, and discussions are on stage. Short-distance travel will go well. Study each situation as it comes up. Don't jump ahead of others and then expect them to be going along with you. Benevolent qualities, executive abilities, and a quick mind are yours. Violet is your color; your number is 2.

Tuesday, September 12 (Moon in Aries to Taurus 7:21 a.m.) Your family takes first place on the economic and social calendar. Know when to stop the gossip presses. There can be some tension between children and parents under these aspects. Friendship demands loyalty and devotion to survive some of the assaults made on it. Hot combination numbers: 4 and 7.

Wednesday, September 13 (Moon in Taurus) Taurus and Virgo have front seats. You can take work matters into your own hands and change things for the better. Luck is with you in friendships, the company you keep, and group activities. Domestic, property, and ownership matters are strongly supported by the stellar scene in your chart. Lucky lottery numbers: 6, 15, 24, 33, 42, 11.

Thursday, September 14 (Moon in Taurus to Gemini 5:48 p.m.) Let Capricorn have some say on an annoying matter. Real estate prices are fluctuating more than you anticipated. The cost of maintaining your home is on the increase and this can anger you today. Travel is fine now, but will run into obstacles around the 22nd. Crimson is your color; your number is 8.

Friday, September 15 (Moon in Gemini) This is a fine cycle for making love, for drawing closer to your beloved, for enjoying children, and giving spontaneous get-togethers. Too much formality detracts from enjoyment now. You do well where you join with loved ones to carry out some family responsibilities. Scarlet is your color; your number is 1.

Saturday, September 16 (Moon in Gemini) Gemini and Libra have key roles. A message arrives and pleases you. You are on the receiving end of many kindnesses today. The yen to buy property, whose price has been lowered, can bug you. The evening has a super-romantic trend and is fine for dressing up and dining out. Black and white are the colors. Lucky lottery numbers: 3, 12, 21, 30, 39, 48.

Sunday, September 17 (Moon in Gemini to Cancer 6:16 a.m.) Prove your mettle by doing something kind for those in trouble. The accent is on health and work improvements. You are at your best when handling family, ownership, and property matters. Adapt, adjust, show flexibility for best results. You are particularly discerning today. Green is your color; your number is 5.

Monday, September 18 (Moon in Cancer) Work routines get high grades and you can please your employer by keeping your nose to the grindstone. You could be subjected to a long lecture about health by someone who has recently had surgery. Another person wants to bore the life out of you with talk about diets. Aquamarine is your color; your number is 9.

Tuesday, September 19 (Moon in Cancer to Leo 6:19 p.m.) People are emotional and tend to wear their hearts on their sleeves. There will be times when you will want to change the conversation to something more edifying. Others may surprisingly see a characteristic in you that you normally hide—the ease with which self-centeredness bores you. Hot combination numbers: 2 and 3.

Wednesday, September 20 (Moon in Leo) Leo takes command. Mate, business partners, contracts, legal involvements, and publicity are in the picture. Up for grabs is some money connected with spontaneity. Courtship, romantic interludes, and overtures are featured. Teamwork is great. Magenta is your color. Lucky lottery numbers: 4, 13, 22, 31, 40, 20.

Thursday, September 21 (Moon in Leo) Teamwork, the sharing of obligations, and an ability to improve relationships with in-laws and the long-term friends of your mate are getting powerful stimulation in your chart. It's a day for reaching out. Go forward with entertainment plans. Sagittarius will help you. Your lucky number is 6.

Friday, September 22 (Moon in Leo to Virgo 4:01 a.m.) Things have a way of catching up with you under prevailing aspects. Mercury retrogrades in Libra and the moon accents the sign Virgo. As a result, you can push savings, minor changes, investments, and work on making your car and house more secure from crime. Olive is your color; your number is 8.

Saturday, September 23 (Moon in Virgo) If you shop carefully and in several places you can save a little money. Where you find a genuine sale, consider some Christmas purchases even though that holiday seems miles away. Advertising and public relations are means to a good end. Pursue various searches for more capital. Earth brown is your color. Lucky lottery numbers: 1, 10, 19, 28, 37, 46.

Sunday, September 24 (Moon in Virgo to Libra 10:50 a.m.) The new moon in your ninth house illuminates travel plans and matters of a long-range and long-distance nature. Libra and another Aquarius excel in teamwork. It's an airy day, Indian summer at its best—you are thrilled as nature unfolds. Read travel folders. Your color is earthy brown; your lucky number is 5.

Monday, September 25 (Moon in Libra) Travel gets good grades. You are clinging to summer and can enjoy a budget retreat to a resort that is yet to close for the winter. What you have going for yourself at a distance is intensely favorable now. Old classmates and former neighbors are very much in the picture. Chocolate and white are winning colors; your lucky number is 7.

Tuesday, September 26 (Moon in Libra to Scorpio 3:20 p.m.) Know what you can and can't do on a day such as this. Success is strongly dependent upon your Aquarius personality assets and special creative talents and skills. Another Aquarius is watching. Planning major business moves should be postponed for the time being, although a partner can be insistent. All the colors of the rainbow are yours. Hot combination numbers: 9 and 5.

Wednesday, September 27 (Moon in Scorpio) Scorpio and Taurus may be competing even while sharing. Your career can make stronger demands on your time and patience. Even so, you can move forward, impressing those in power by your persistence and dependability in times of crisis. Still, you would do it all differently if it were left to you. Canary and lemon are your colors. Lucky lottery numbers: 27, 39, 47, 11, 2, 20.

Thursday, September 28 (Moon in Scorpio to Sagittarius 6:30 p.m.) Give due attention to your career, professional matters, and maintenance of prestige and status. Dress rather formally, kicking blue jeans aside, and favor real shoes instead of sneakers. The day carries great respect for the traditions and for the opinions of the older generation. Beige is your color; your number is 4.

Friday, September 29 (Moon in Sagittarius) The day favors friendships, special companionship, and all links with groups, tribes, and clan. You will want to get to the nitty-gritty of a close emotional involvement. There is brightness, much positive thinking, and lots of enthusiasm for people, places, and programs. Goldenrod is your color; your lucky number is 6.

Saturday, September 30 (Moon in Sagittarius to Capricorn 9:10 p.m.) Sagittarius and Aries are on deck. This is a fine cycle for traveling to see good friends within a 300-mile radius. The generations mix and move about well today. You step out ahead when you show ingenuity as well as your ability to stick to a social plan. Coral is your color. Lucky lottery numbers: 8, 17, 26, 35, 44, 30.

OCTOBER 1995

Sunday, October 1 (Moon in Capricorn) Capricorn and Taurus will impact your day. Find that special item that will liven up your wardrobe. Go out of your way to avoid anything that smacks of mental depression. This is a fine time for completing what should have been kicked out of the way. Your winning color is purple; your lucky number is 8.

Monday, October 2 (Moon in Capricorn to Aquarius 11:59 p.m.) Present work that should have been presented last month. Be sure that your work area is orderly for this is a day when items can be replaced, broken, and cause mischief. This afternoon will be well spent programming upcoming work and social involvements. A favor you did for a friend will be returned now. Your lucky number is 3.

Tuesday, October 3 (Moon in Aquarius) Now in your lunar high cycle, you can pretty much write your own ticket. Push highly personalized interests. Stand tall, let the world know that you are present. Push long-held aspirations. Talk to those who are in a position to make your dreams come true. Another Aquarius has a key role. Hot combination numbers: 5 and 4.

Wednesday, October 4 (Moon in Aquarius) Strive, strut, lead, show self-confidence and self-reliance. Where you are enthusiastic, others will become approving and appreciative. There are some budding opportunities to bring about an impressive change, correction, or improvement in your life. Your health gets a good boost. Lucky lottery numbers: 7, 16, 25, 34, 43, 14.

Thursday, October 5 (Moon in Aquarius to Pisces 3:35 a.m.) Consult Pisces on the economy, on wealth production as it affects you, and on methods of increasing your earning power. Fine trends exist for encouraging a dear friend to try harder. Despite suggestions from others, do not put a friendship to any kind of test. Sand and chestnut are your winning colors. Hot combination numbers: 9 and 4.

Friday, October 6 (Moon in Pisces) Buttonhole supervisors and others in power to get the lay of the land. You can have the feeling that much is transpiring behind the scenes which seems to be evading you. Chances are it concerns new assignments, money shortages, and the impossibility of funding some projects. Violet is your color. Hot combination numbers: 2 and 3.

Saturday, October 7 (Moon in Pisces to Aries 8:41 a.m.) A Scorpio and a Cancer will show both due and undue concern over secrets, confidential matters, and high finance that seems to be thwarted by behind-the-scenes events. Russet and earthy brown are your colors. The evening calls for dressing to the hilt, dancing, and dining out. Lucky lottery numbers: 4, 13, 22, 31, 40, 27.

Sunday, October 8 (Moon in Aries) The full moon forms in Aries and illuminates everyday matters for you. There is new enlightenment through learning, studying, and working on your basic talents. It may be time for making a change, going in a different direction, especially where a hobby is concerned. Coral is your color; your number is 6.

Monday, October 9 (Moon in Aries to Taurus 4:05 p.m.) Aries and Leo are making the rounds. Concentrate on the possible, the usual, the familiar, the everyday and expected matters, and the day will produce plenty for you. You excel at finishing up old chores that others have started. You can tap what is transpiring behind the scenes. Jet black is your color; your number is 1.

Tuesday, October 10 (Moon in Taurus) Taurus and Virgo are in the picture. You tend to be rather possessive of your children and other relatives. This is a good day for arranging flowers, buying jewelry, and discussing matters with your banker or broker. You are more in the know, so to speak, than others may realize. Purple is your color; your lucky number is 3.

Wednesday, October 11 (Moon in Taurus) Capricorn has a commanding lead in any showdown or showoff. Fine rays for advancing basic aims and moving closer to long-held goals. Your family may not quite approve of what you intend to purchase. Others tend to overlook some chores which by default come to you. Ecru and earth are your colors. Lucky lottery numbers: 5, 14, 23, 32, 40, 11.

Thursday, October 12 (Moon in Taurus to Gemini 2:10 a.m.) Gemini can seem a little verbose, or is it inner resentment on your part against what Gemini is saying? You may spot some festering situations in friendships but not want to become involved in this negative way. You may be earning your reputation as a square shooter today. Sky blue is your color; your number is 7.

Friday, October 13 (Moon in Gemini) You are in a good cycle for love. Singles can meet their heart's desire in a fine autumnal setting. Harvest festivals, hayrides, jogs into a rural area are all favored. It's the air elementals (Gemini, Libra, and Aquarius) that impact your day. Your lucky number is 9.

Saturday, October 14 (Moon in Gemini to Cancer 2:20 p.m.) Intellectual pursuits are high on your day's agenda. You could be surprised at something a child says. Shortcuts are favored so that you get your work done on time. You are identifying with Mother Nature as you move about and watch the advance of fall. Mocha is your color. Lucky lottery numbers: 2, 11, 20, 29, 38, 47.

Sunday, October 15 (Moon in Cancer) A Cancer and a Pisces figure prominently. Fine rays exist for improving health and for acquiring information that will help you get your work done more efficiently. The pursuit of accuracy is strongly represented. Searches, investigations, and questions are in tune with the day's major trends. Your number is 4.

Monday, October 16 (Moon in Cancer) No rushing, jumping, or tripping up or downstairs. A shoe or rug could be the cause of a fall or accident. The Mars–Uranus sextile is favorable for taking charge of some change or new development in economic and/or social matters. Amber is your color; your number is 8.

Tuesday, October 17 (Moon in Cancer to Leo 2:46 a.m.) Don't attempt to go it alone today. It's a cycle for sharing, working in tandem, consulting partners, taking a vote. It's a good day for public relations, publicity, improving a contract and an agreement, and it's fine for compromises and for discussing new beginnings. Leo is with you. Purple is your color; your number is 1.

Wednesday, October 18 (Moon in Leo) Share equally. Listen to what your spouse is saying about future plans. There are members of the family who can pit themselves against cooperative programs. Work for better understanding among relatives. Impatient attitudes tend to be barriers. Your color is lavender. Lucky lottery numbers: 3, 12, 21, 30, 39, 48.

Thursday, October 19 (Moon in Leo to Virgo 11:11 a.m.) Aries and Sagittarius have key roles. Today is fine for business conferences, executive board meetings, and for planning an annual meeting around Thanksgiving. It's time to pull in at the seams where there has been talk of expansion. Come in off any financial or business tangents before the 22nd. Pick five: 19, 5, 32, 41, and 1.

Friday, October 20 (Moon in Virgo) Virgo has the tools, machinery, and equipment. You can make your home more secure. Check locks on doors and windows. Is your car safely in the garage? Do you leave your keys in your car when you run into a building to perform some speedy errand? Know where you stand in security matters. Indigo is your color. Hot combination numbers: 7 and 2.

Saturday, October 21 (Moon in Virgo to Libra 8:15 p.m.) You gain scope and perspective and increase your social drive as Mars enters Sagittarius. Taurus comes through as hard to figure out under the day's aspects. There can be some deterioration in law, shrubbery, and trees surrounding your home. Reddish-brown is your color. Lucky lottery numbers: 21, 9, 18, 27, 36, 45.

Sunday, October 22 (Moon in Libra) This is not the time to make changes in the way you do business, save and invest money, and account for expenses. Eclipse patterns are forming and they tend to mist your view of career, professional, technical, status, and prestige matters. Evening comes early. Your color is russet; your number is 2.

Monday, October 23 (Moon in Libra) It's not a good day for travel even though you may have a yen to change your scene. Libra can come through to you as overly silent. There can be sexual disappointments under these strictures. On your menu today—clam chowder with a dash of tarragon and broiled salmon with a dash of mint. Put a bit of roux in your salad dressing. Your number is 6.

Tuesday, October 24 (Moon in Libra to Scorpio 12:07 a.m.) A total eclipse of the sun falls on the Libra–Scorpio cusp. The day is unfavorable for travel, with a buildup of freakish accident-producing potential. Avoid arguments with people close to you. Don't expect much understanding in career, status, and prestige matters. Competition is rife. No forcing changes upon yourself or others. Your lucky number is 8.

Wednesday, October 25 (Moon in Scorpio) There is an increase in accident-producing potential in the wake of this eclipse. Cooperation is low. Your sense of unity can be pressured. A certain aloofness can impede sexual delight. Stick to what is noncontroversial, to what is more spiritual than physical or material. Wear neutral colors. Lucky lottery numbers: 25, 29, 37, 1, 10, 26.

Thursday, October 26 (Moon in Scorpio to Sagittarius 1:56 a.m.) Sagittarius will help you clear the atmosphere of recriminations and uncertainties. Friends are very much in the picture. Is there anything better than good companions? Lean toward kindred spirits who share many of your ideas. Arguments or disagreements you can do without. Flesh is your color; your lucky numbers are 3 and 2.

Friday, October 27 (Moon in Sagittarius) Parties, entertainments, hayrides, and masquerades are all favored. You will want to genuinely relax and laugh a lot under these aspects. Work gets done better where there is cooperation among people who like each other. Order by phone or mail. Hot combination numbers: 5 and 9.

Saturday, October 28 (Moon in Sagittarius to Capricorn 3:15 a.m.) Capricorn will help you complete tasks, chores, and work that has been around too long. The organizational abilities of Capricorn can amaze you under prevailing aspects and you will feel grateful. Evening is favorable for enjoying old fall traditions. Reddish browns are your colors. Lucky lottery numbers: 7, 16, 25, 34, 43, 28.

Sunday, October 29 (Moon in Capricorn; Daylight Saving Time ends) Finish up household chores. Be cautious while dealing with sneaky mischief makers, who can be out in full array. Communications of meaningful type are well aspected and these could be with a Capricorn, Virgo, or Taurus. Find out all you can about a place you plan on visiting. Your lucky numbers are 9 and 2.

Monday, October 30 (Moon in Capricorn to Aquarius 4:23 a.m.) You move into your lunar high cycle and show amazing self-confidence as you make your bid for visible progress in career and other departments of your life. Speak out now in your own behalf. Don't let anybody put you down or push you out of the way. The more you are yourself, the better off you will be. Your number is 4.

Tuesday, October 31 (Moon in Aquarius) Freedom and independence are your guiding sentinels. You are sociable today and desire the friendship of others, including some who have not been well disposed toward you in the past. The emphasis is on sharing experiences with those who seem to be interested in what you have to say. Ruby is your color; your lucky number is 6.

NOVEMBER 1995

Wednesday, November 1 (Moon in Aquarius to Pisces 8:17 a.m.) Today completes your lunar-cycle high and you can gain from pushing for more freedom in your personal life. You can bring both balance and serenity into your life under prevailing aspects. Avoid all conflicts and confrontations, especially over the afternoon and early evening. Lucky lottery numbers: 5, 14, 23, 32, 41, 45.

Thursday, November 2 (Moon in Pisces) Pisces and a Cancer have front seats. Push for higher wealth production, increased earning power, and more income. You may find a secondary job or special way of earning extra money under these aspects. What you own is increasing in value. Your lucky number is 7.

Friday, November 3 (Moon in Pisces to Aries 2:21 p.m.) Scorpio takes a bow. You continue to be in a good earning-power period. There is special money earmarked for you. Money has a connection with the water and with what sails on the water and exists under the water.

Give others the benefit of every doubt. Lime green is your color; your lucky number is 9.

Saturday, November 4 (Moon in Aries) Aries and Leo have key roles. You will be quick to spot opportunities in your own locality. Handle immediate and pressing problems with aplomb. You are more conscious of the advantages you have inherited or received as a gift. Keeping a cheerful outlook can encourage others. Lucky lottery numbers: 2, 11, 20, 29, 38, 47.

Sunday, November 5 (Moon in Aries to Taurus 10:35 p.m.) Aries and Sagittarius figure prominently. Narrow your sights, reduce things to their lowest common denominator, get to the heart of matters. Everyday routines can seem somewhat boring to your younger loved ones. There is accent on the familiar, the usual, always with the underlying theme of developing and almost unseen changes. Auburn is your color; your lucky number is 4.

Monday, November 6 (Moon in Taurus) Consult Leo about an emotional matter. People may be asking favors of you. The help someone seeks from you tends to irritate you. You can decide now that some doors have to be closed before new doors can be opened. Steller forces invite your best effort and you are not one to disappoint fate. Your lucky number is 8.

Tuesday, November 7 (Moon in Taurus) The full moon illuminates your family, home, and community trends. There is new enlightenment as to the best way to present a suspicion to the family at large. Many little tasks can be gotten out of the way as long as you are not dependent on helpers. Taurus is waiting. Your color is pumpkin; your number is 1.

Wednesday, November 8 (Moon in Taurus to Gemini 8:55 a.m.) Virgo and Capricorn are more practical than you, but they still want to have the benefit of your theories and ideals. Information is flowing freely and as a result you can arrive at conclusions and decisions. A sense of adventure is building up in your horoscope. Lucky lottery numbers: 3, 12, 21, 30, 39, 48.

Thursday, November 9 (Moon in Gemini) Gemini shows up when needed. It's a good day for making love, letting the romance of the season get to you, and bringing a courtship closer to a commitment. This is a wonderful cycle for pre-Christmas parties, organization affairs, and annual meetings. Dress so that your basic personality is reflected by what you wear. Hot combination numbers: 5 and 9.

Friday, November 10 (Moon in Gemini to Cancer 8:57 p.m.) This is a day full of positive and optimistic feelings. Parties, entertainments in your own home, and bringing feuding generations together are all possibilities. A friend of your father may volunteer some important information or you may actually solicit these facts from him. Reds and browns are winning colors. Hot combination numbers: 7 and 6.

Saturday, November 11 (Moon in Cancer) Armistice Day finds the fragmented Balkans much as they were on the eve of World War I. It's a time for looking back with a Cancer and Capricorn. Luck is with you today in preventive-medicine routines and where you are giving assistance. Blue is your color. Lucky lottery numbers: 11, 9, 18, 27, 36, 45.

Sunday, November 12 (Moon in Cancer) Be cautious while climbing ladders, washing windows, hanging pictures, and stringing electric lights in and out of doors. Reassure a child who is getting overly excited about the upcoming holidays. There are tidbits of gossip making the rounds which contain mischievous errors. Your lucky number is 2.

Monday, November 13 (Moon in Cancer to Leo 9:37 a.m.) Cancer and Scorpio have key roles. Guard against exposure to drafts and the spread of virus-type ailments. You could find your work going sluggishly. Youngsters are obnoxious in their opinions and demands. Others may be edgy and imply that too much is being asked of them. Carmine is your color; your number is 6.

Tuesday, November 14 (Moon in Leo) Leo's opinions aren't always going to jive with yours. Marriage, old contracts, agreements, legal and public relations interests are accented. The power for drawing closer to your beloved is here, but not if old disagreements are being warmed over even in a quasi-humorous way. Hot combination numbers: 8 and 2.

Wednesday, November 15 (Moon in Leo to Virgo 9:02 p.m.) When push comes to shove, youngsters find it difficult to take instantaneous directions from two parental masters. It's important that you and your mate discuss your children's problems while alone. It's possible to insult the dignity of the very young and inexperienced without realizing it. Mauve is your color. Lucky lottery numbers: 1, 10, 19, 28, 37, 46.

Thursday, November 16 (Moon in Virgo) Virgo will help you work the bugs out of the system. Push savings and investments, collect what is due you, pay bills, and budget carefully so that you will have a little extra cash on hand by the end of the month. Household cleaning chores go well under these aspects. Beige is your color; your number is 3.

Friday, November 17 (Moon in Virgo) Those who love you are noticing the positive qualities of which you can boast. There are some practical decisions to be made today and a Capricorn can prove helpful. You may consider more recycling of trash, and/or switching to a different gas station. You are ultra-conscious of costs and services. Yellowish-browns do well; your lucky number is 5.

Saturday, November 18 (Moon in Virgo to Libra 5:18 a.m.) Today, tomorrow, and the next day are fine for changing your scene temporarily, for getting away from the grind, visiting people who have the knack of cheering you up, and generally dropping the work you have been doing. Libra will make a marvelous companion. Darker country clothing is right. Lucky lottery numbers: 7, 16, 25, 34, 43, 18.

Sunday, November 19 (Moon in Libra) Get closer to Mother Nature. Take walks in the woods, check the advance of late fall, breathe in the marvelous scents of the great outdoors. Evening around a warm fire and the smell of frost just beyond the door are reminding you that life is good. Sensible clothing in browns and blues are right; try the number 9.

Monday, November 20 (Moon in Libra to Scorpio 9:40 a.m.) Aries and another Aquarius assure you that you look well, feel great, and just might consider picking up the pieces of routine and schedule. You're cheerful—this communicates itself to others who feel good just having you around. Career needs are coming over the horizon. Try the number 4.

Tuesday, November 21 (Moon in Scorpio) You will take great leaps forward in your career, professional, and authority matters, with Scorpio egging you on. Talks about your career potential, and possible special school courses you might pursue to better your future, are good ideas. The romance of work and of life permeates your day. Try the number 6.

Wednesday, November 22 (Moon in Scorpio to Sagittarius 10:56 a.m.) The new moon illuminates how you should handle your career at this time. There is enlightenment in the various approaches and attitudes toward power. You can feel important today and you're conscious of hard-earned achievements. A dignified manner works well for you. Champagne is your color. Lucky lottery numbers: 8, 17, 26, 35, 44, 22.

Thursday, November 23 (Moon in Sagittarius) It's Sagittarius wherever you look and listen today. Positive attitudes toward friendship become you and please your loved ones. Parties, entertainments, and enjoyable exchanges of confidences are all to your liking now. Celebrations, good winter foods, and cooking make the day splendid. Try the number 1.

Friday, November 24 (Moon in Sagittarius to Capricorn 10:48 a.m.) It's a day when your environment takes on more character. Even if you live in a big city condo, your thoughts will be of the changing scene far away, of the approach of winter and how it could be felt, sensed, viewed, heard, and scented. Today is fine for a quiet walk with a good friend. Hot combination numbers: 3 and 4.

Saturday, November 25 (Moon in Capricorn) Capricorn offers good assistance as you complete November's deadline work. Both gains and problems experienced today are rooted in the past. Sagittarius continues to offer you devotion and loyalty in friendship as well as unbeatable drive that will improve joint projects. Lucky lottery numbers: 5, 14, 23, 32, 41, 25.

Sunday, November 26 (Moon in Capricorn to Aquarius 11:15 a.m.) Complete, finish up, file away, clear your deck for more personalized action. Taurus and Virgo make an entrance. You may have a growing inkling of what is transpiring behind the scenes. Positive and optimistic feelings are permeating your love department. Bronze is your color; your number is 7.

Monday, November 27 (Moon in Aquarius) How fortunate can you be! As one of your favorite months draws to a close, you move into your lunar high cycle, where you personally can recreate, revamp, and reclaim what was so pleasant in other late Novembers. You can make accurate appraisals and fine decisions. Chartreuse is your color; your number is 2.

Tuesday, November 28 (Moon in Aquarius to Pisces 1:59 p.m.) Stand tall, take giant leaps in your career and other departments of your life. Speak up rather than letting others take credit for work you have done. Go all out in your own interest. It's a day when you can change liabilities into assets. The world becomes your oyster. Watermelon green is your color. Hot combination numbers: 4 and 5.

Wednesday, November 29 (Moon in Pisces) Pisces and Virgo want to share responsibilities. You are in a good position now to get a raise. But you must be more serious in what you say and in the way you approach a supervisor. You feel in good control of what is taking place in your immediate environment. Crimson is your color. Lucky lottery numbers: 6, 15, 24, 33, 42, 29.

Thursday, November 30 (Moon in Pisces to Aries 7:51 p.m.) Collect what is owed to you. You may have to speak harshly to someone who is wasteful or a spendthrift. Watch calories this evening. This is a good cycle for innovations, for showing leadership, and for winning former critics over to your point of view. Ecru and indigo are your colors; your number is 8.

DECEMBER 1995

Friday, December 1 (Moon in Aries) It's going to be a busy month and it would be wise to start making lists of what you have to do and with whom you must communicate, and trying to keep some responsibilities from conflicting with other obligations. Aries and Leo have prominent roles. The family has to be considered more than anything else. Your number is 8.

Saturday, December 2 (Moon in Aries) Sagittarius has a question for you. Keep on the go, moving about in your own neighborhood, seeing people with whom you will be working later on in the month. Contact those who will share committee positions with you and also charitable and humanitarian work that has to be done. Light brown is your color. Lucky lottery numbers: 1, 10, 19, 28, 37, 46.

Sunday, December 3 (Moon in Aries to Taurus 4:40 a.m.) Taurus and Virgo have key roles. Spending quality time with youngsters would be a good idea. What pre-holiday maintenance work you want done should be sized up successfully today. Younger people are looking to you for direction as well as guidance and encouragement. Sky blue is your color; your lucky number is 3.

Monday, December 4 (Moon in Taurus) Shopping for gifts intended for the family at large will do well under these aspects. The chance to get a little shopping done will go better if you do it before the dinner hour. Encourage young people to read and to use their library cards. Your lucky number is 7.

Tuesday, December 5 (Moon in Taurus to Gemini 3:35 p.m.) Taurus will help you decorate your home and grounds for the holidays. You are more able to relate to other generations than may normally be the case. You are especially quick to pick up hints from the elderly. Evening demands genuine relaxation with kindred spirits. Hot combination numbers: 9 and 8.

Wednesday, December 6 (Moon in Gemini) Virgo will add the sensible touch to events. Luck is with you if you are willing to splurge a little for the upcoming holidays. Buy something you want but feel you can't afford at this time. You are at your best today when you show personal determination. Apricot and gold are winning colors. Lucky lottery numbers: 2, 11, 20, 29, 38, 47.

Thursday, December 7 (Moon in Gemini) The full moon illuminates your love life, a romance that is in the development stage, improved ways to reach complex children, and other ways to keep parental criticism of your generation within bounds. Your social agenda may be barren, but you excel in spur of the moment entertaining. Hot combination numbers: 4 and 8.

Friday, December 8 (Moon in Gemini to Cancer 3:44 a.m.) A Cancer and a Capricorn will bring balance to the day. If you feel fatigue, take it easy, curbing your shopping ventures, picking and choosing the family and social events you will attend this month. Amber is your color; your lucky numbers are 6 and 5.

Saturday, December 9 (Moon in Cancer) Stellar forces prepare the way to attack household chores that don't get done very often. You are quick to fathom what someone is implying and suggesting. You could become annoyed with a coworker who is cheating the work or the boss in some nasty way. Turquoise is your color. Lucky lottery numbers: 8, 17, 26, 35, 44, 15.

Sunday, December 10 (Moon in Cancer to Leo 4:24 p.m.) Luck is with you in the good attention you give to your personal and family health. Organize the rest of the month so that each day will not demand more expense of energy than the others. If you feel your dining or living rooms could use a little sprucing up, study the crystal imports from Eastern Europe. Your number is 1.

Monday, December 11 (Moon in Leo) Leo is bouncing with unbeatable energy and stamina. You can cash in on your marital love today and on what you have going for yourself in contracts, agreements, favors, and promises. You can have the feeling that you are not alone in your uncertainties. Help is always at your elbow. Your lucky number is 5.

Tuesday, December 12 (Moon in Leo) Mercury makes its Capricorn ingress and you make short shrift of pesky tasks around the porch, on the patio, or in the breezeway. There are some much-ado-about-nothing incidents marring the day. Coworkers are letting the holiday spirit detract from their work. Apricot is right. Hot combination numbers: 7 and 3.

Wednesday, December 13 (Moon in Leo to Virgo 4:26 a.m.) Consult Virgo on the best way to get a complex job done. You can bind your beloved to you in new and enduring ways under the prevailing aspects. Romantic trends permeate the day and you want to endure, offset, and survive the difficulties you are experiencing from a difficult and rude opponent, perhaps an in-law. Canary and brown are winners. Lucky lottery numbers: 9, 18, 27, 36, 45, 13.

Thursday, December 14 (Moon in Virgo) Your public relations are working well for you and there is evidence of popularity, acceptance, approval, and appreciation. Fine trends exist in pushing improvements, not only upon yourself but also on children and teenagers. Changes, savings, and investments are all favored. Mocha and white are winners; try the number 2.

Friday, December 15 (Moon in Virgo to Libra 2:09 p.m.) The day gives you strong support in the chores that the holiday season calls for. Work where you use screws, bolts, screwdrivers, hammers, and thumbtacks is favored. Today is fine for buying books, other reading and learning materials, and paper products. Shopping along the highway will pay off. Hot combination numbers: 4 and 5.

Saturday, December 16 (Moon in Libra) Libra makes an ideal traveling companion. If holiday gifts are to be delivered, this is a good day to drive Santa Claus to beloved destinations. Fine trends for buying crystal, glass, and picture frames. Older people will be on your side in any family or friendship showdown. Lucky lottery numbers: 6, 15, 24, 33, 42, 16.

Sunday, December 17 (Moon in Libra to Scorpio 8:07 p.m.) What happens today gives you more faith in the fairness of life. Don't stay in any one place longer than you have to, as the moon transits your ninth house. Mars is stimulating the old late-December traditions. You do well to stabilize your spending. Your color is bright blue; your lucky number is 8.

Monday, December 18 (Moon in Scorpio) Scorpio will figure prominently. There is a pinch-hitting role that falls to you as coworkers and others are called away. Take advantage of a situation where someone needs more time for late shopping. Your career gets a shot in the arm and you get more stamina and energy. Wear brown and blue; try the number 3.

Tuesday, December 19 (Moon in Scorpio to Sagittarius 10:13 p.m.) Organizational matters take precedence. Assistants may be neglecting the more boring tasks. The more you stick to plans and programs today, the more you will be able to meet all schedules well. Good trends where you are purchasing underwear and slacks, both for yourself and for loved ones. Hot combination numbers: 5 and 9.

Wednesday, December 20 (Moon in Sagittarius) Sagittarius is your ideal companion and you can share a pleasant pre-holiday commitment. Charitable and humanitarian tasks and fund-raising operations are favored. You may run into people you have known a long time, but rarely see. This evening favors must-attend affairs. Lucky lottery numbers: 7, 16, 25, 34, 43, 30.

Thursday, December 21 (Moon in Sagittarius to Capricorn 9:46 p.m.) Today is a cheerful, friendly day with group activities encouraged by favorable aspects. Aries and Leo have key roles. It's excellent for office parties, exchanging gifts with coworkers. Everything will go well if the talk remains mundane. Reddish browns are your colors; try the number 9.

Friday, December 22 (Moon in Capricorn) The new moon in Sagittarius illuminates the social side of your job and your happy ventures into public life. Church and club membership and participation are high on your agenda. This evening is one of the best December cycles for entertaining in your home. Ivory and off-white are your colors. Hot combination numbers: 2 and 3.

Saturday, December 23 (Moon in Capricorn to Aquarius 8:52 p.m.) Discussions about movies, plays, and television programs are represented. Last-minute touches can be put to holiday tasks. Baking, cooking, and shopping for scarce-item foods, holly, and ivy can surround you with the old traditions. Deceased parents or grandparents are very much in mind. Capricorn's role is important. Lucky lottery numbers: 4, 13, 22, 31, 40, 23.

Sunday, December 24 (Moon in Aquarius) Venus in Aquarius accents loveliness, beauty, graciousness, and courtesy, making this a pleasant period when all seems to be right with your Aquarian world. You spread goodwill and assure those you love that there is permanence to what is positive and good. Wear some new wardrobe accessories. Your number is 6.

Monday, December 25 (Moon in Aquarius to Pisces 9:45 p.m.) It's your Christmas, with the moon illuminating all these personal whys and wherefores. Splurge in the interest of loved ones. Be very much on the scene, contributing to the happiness of those with you. You can be the center of attention while expressing the ideals and concerns that are so much a part of your disposition. Red and green are lucky colors. Your fortunate number is 1.

Tuesday, December 26 (Moon in Pisces) You are definitely the one who gains from the day's special sales. Everything that is half price today will be double price next Christmas season. So lay in now what you can use. In every way, it's a wonderful earning power and overall money day. Another Aquarius will accompany you if you ask. Hot combination numbers: 3 and 6.

Wednesday, December 27 (Moon in Pisces) Pisces will explain it to you. People want to understand what you are all about. What is complex, subtle, and sublime marks your approach to this day. There are some mysteries, a lot of extremes, and sophisticated and exotic viewpoints. The angry reds are right for the day. Lucky lottery numbers: 5, 14, 23, 32, 41, 27.

Thursday, December 28 (Moon in Pisces to Aries 2:06 a.m.) Aries will give some new direction to the day, month, and year. Despite the late date, there are good trends for new beginnings, for investigation and research work. Mistakes may creep into the work that is being done. There's still time for securing a good tax shelter. Hot combination numbers: 7 and 1.

Friday, December 29 (Moon in Aries) It's a fine day away from the work scene, doing your own thing, visiting a place you want to return to after many years, and spending time with people who know how to keep you smiling and relaxing. Old military buddies are in the picture. Romance and enchantment are available. Lavender and purple are winning colors. Hot combination numbers: 9 and 5.

Saturday, December 30 (Moon in Aries to Taurus 10:21 a.m.) Aries and Sagittarius come front and center. You are anxious to keep on the go and to accomplish missions close to your heart. You will be wonderful at doing things you never have done before. A motorcycle, ice skates, even roller skates can be linked to some of these aspects. Your color is chocolate. Lucky lottery numbers: 2, 11, 20, 29, 38, 47, 30.

Sunday, December 31 (Moon in Taurus) Taurus comes aboard. A quiet New Year's Eve with members of your family will go well. Stay within your own community on a night when the traffic can be dangerous. Avoid showing anger if things go wrong. Neighbors can do annoying things under these aspects. Stay cool. Coffee is your color; your lucky number is 4.

ABOUT THIS SERIES

This is one of a series
of twelve Day-to-Day Astrological Guides
for the signs of 1995
by Sydney Omarr

ABOUT THE AUTHOR

Born on August 5, 1926, in Philadelphia, Omarr was the only person ever given full-time duty in the U.S. Army as an astrologer. He also is regarded as the most erudite astrologer of our time and the best known, through his syndicated column (300 newspapers) and his radio and television programs (he is Merv Griffin's "resident astrologer"). Omarr has been called the most "knowledgeable astrologer since Evangeline Adams." His forecasts of Nixon's downfall, the end of World War II in mid-August of 1945, the assassination of John F. Kennedy, Roosevelt's election to the fourth term and his death in office . . . these and many others are on record and quoted enough to be considered "legendary."